Handbook on Teacher Evaluation

Assessing and Improving Performance

James H. Stronge
Pamela D. Tucker

EYE ON EDUCATION
6 DEPOT WAY WEST, SUITE 106
LARCHMONT, NY 10538
(914) 833-0551
(914) 833-0761 fax
www.eyeoneducation.com

Library of Congress Cataloging-in-Publication Data

Stronge, James H.
     Handbook on teacher evaluation : assessing and improving performance /
James H. Stronge and Pamela D. Tucker.
        p.   cm.
     Includes bibliographical references.
     ISBN 1-930556-58-6
     1. Teachers—Rating of—United States—Handbooks, manuals, etc. 2. School
personnel management—United States—Handbooks, manuals, etc. I. Tucker,
Pamela D. II. Title.

LB2838.S815 2003
371.14'4—dc21   2003044872

Editorial and production services provided by

299 E. Kelso Rd., Columbus, OH 43202
click@columbus.rr.com

Also available from Eye On Education

HANDBOOK ON EDUCATIONAL SPECIALIST EVALUATION
Assessing and Improving Performance
James H. Stronge and Pamela D. Tucker

HANDBOOK ON TEACHER PORTFOLIOS
for Evaluation and Professional Development
Pamela D. Tucker, James H. Stronge, and Christopher R. Gareis

DEALING WITH DIFFICULT TEACHERS 2/E
Todd Whitaker

101 "ANSWERS" FOR NEW TEACHERS AND THEIR MENTORS
Effective Teaching Tips for Daily Classroom Use
Annette L. Breaux

REAL TEACHERS, REAL CHALLENGES, REAL SOLUTIONS
25 Ways to Handle the Challenges of the Classroom Effectively
Annette L. Breaux and Elizabeth Breaux

MOTIVATING AND INSPIRING TEACHERS:
The Educator's Guide for Building Staff Morale
Todd Whitaker, Beth Whitaker, and Dale Lumpa

ACHIEVEMENT NOW!
How To Assure No Child is Left Behind
Dr. Donald J. Fielder

TEACHER RETENTION
What is Your Weakest Link?
India J. Podsen

COACHING AND MENTORING FIRST-YEAR AND STUDENT TEACHERS
India J. Podsen and Vicki M. Denmark

WHAT GREAT PRINCIPALS DO DIFFERENTLY
Fifteen Things That Matter Most
Todd Whitaker

THE PRINCIPAL AS INSTRUCIOTNAL LEADER
A Handbook for Supervisors
Sally J. Zepeda

DATA ANALYSIS FOR COMPREHENSIVE SCHOOLWIDE IMPROVEMENT
Victoria L. Bernhardt

THE SCHOOL PORTFOLIO TOOLKIT
A Planning, Implementation, and Evaluation Guide for
Continuous School Improvement
Victoria L. Bernhardt

NAVIGATING COMPREHENSIVE SCHOOL CHANGE:
A Guide for the Perplexed
Thomas G. Chenoweth and Robert B. Everhart

BOUNCING BACK!
How Your School Can Succeed in the Face of Adversity
Jerry Patterson, Janice Patterson, & Loucrecia Collins

INSTRUCTIONAL SUPERVISION:
Applying Tools and Concepts
Sally J. Zepeda

SCHOOL COMMUNITY RELATIONS
Douglas J. Fiore

HUMAN RESOURCES ADMINISTRATION:
A School-Based Perspective 2/E
Richard E. Smith

THE EMERGING PRINCIPALSHIP
Linda Skrla, David Erlandson, etc.

MONEY AND SCHOOLS 2/E
David C. Thompson and R. Craig Wood

STAFF DEVELOPMENT:
Practices that Promote Leadership in Learning Communities
Sally J. Zepeda

TEACHING MATTERS:
Motivating & Inspiring Yourself
Todd and Beth Whitaker

FEELING GREAT!
The Educator's Guide for Eating Better,
Exercising Smarter, and Feeling Your Best
Todd Whitaker and Jason Winkle

DEALING WITH DIFFICULT PARENTS
(And With Parents in Difficult Situations)
Todd Whitaker and Douglas J. Fiore

Dedication

To my daughther, Beth,
with love.
James Stronge

To Larry,
who never wavers in his support for me.
Pamela Tucker

and

To the many teachers and administrators,
who have shared their stories with us,
many hopeful and some discouraging,
about the realities of teacher evaluation.

Table of Contents

List of Figures

Preface

Evaluation is not new to the field of education. For varying reasons—sometimes for improvement, sometimes for accountability, often for both—and with varying degrees of success, personnel evaluation has come to be an accepted and expected part of the educational landscape. Teachers and other employees have been evaluated as long as there have been schools. However, in the current era of high standards and high-stakes testing, with their high-stakes connections to personnel accountability, evaluation is more at the forefront of education than ever. In a review of the professional literature of the last 20 years, some discernible trends in school personnel evaluation have emerged. Accountability developed into a prominent national issue in the early 1980s, particularly with the 1983 publication of *A Nation at Risk,* which brought public awareness to numerous deficiencies in public schools and heralded the need for educational reform. More recently, the *No Child Left Behind Act* has emphasized the need for high quality teachers to ensure success for all students.

Teacher evaluation has the potential to support and develop high quality teachers if it is undertaken as a professional endeavor versus a bureaucratic one. It is an opportunity for schools to create processes for examining the most important work that they do, teaching the nation's children. The possibilities for how this can be done have never been greater or richer. In the *Handbook on Teacher Evaluation* we walk you through the steps of developing and implementing a teacher evaluation system that reflects current thinking and best practices in the field.

How is the Handbook on Teacher Evaluation Organized?

The *Handbook* is organized into three separate major sections. Each section is carefully integrated with the others in order to provide a more useful, practical guide for teacher evaluation.

♦ **Part I** presents eight chapters that provide an in-depth exploration of teacher evaluation, the Goals and Roles Evaluation Model, specific standards for the evaluation of teachers, guidelines for using multiple data sources, ways and means for rating performance, and practical suggestions for implementation.

- **A Conceptual Model**
  The *Handbook* provides a conceptual model that integrates theoretical, professional, and field-based frameworks for the evaluation of teachers. Chapter 1, Teacher Evaluation: Getting Started, provides an overview for teacher evaluation; Chapter 2, Teacher Evaluation: Background and Context, offers a historical review of teacher evaluation, along with criteria for designing evaluation systems.

- **A Step-by-Step Evaluation Process**
  A thorough discussion of the Goals and Roles Evaluation Model is presented in Chapter 3. The Goals and Roles Evaluation Model delineates six distinct steps

in the evaluation cycle. Descriptions of the steps and examples of how to implement each step in a school setting are provided in subsequent chapters.

- **Teacher Job Responsibilities**
  An outline of the professional responsibilities of the teacher, with sample performance indicators representing behavioral manifestations of these responsibilities, is provided in Chapter 4, Developing Teacher Performance Standards. The responsibilities serve as a guideline for developing customized evaluation frameworks, tailored to individual settings.

- **Documenting and Analyzing Performance**
  Chapter 5, Using Criteria to Rate Teacher Performance, provides criteria for rating teacher performance. Chapter 6, Documenting Teacher Performance, delineates the many types of data sources for documenting teacher performance and how they can be blended for a more dynamic evaluation system. Chapter 7, Implementing a Teacher Performance Evaluation System, pulls all the ingredients together and discusses the myriad questions about implementation of a teacher evaluation system. Finally, Chapter 8, Where Do We Go From Here, summarizes what we know about best practices in teacher evaluation and what are recommended future directions for the field.

- **Part II** provides eight comprehensive sets of teacher job responsibilities, organized around specified domains, standards, and performance indicators. The teaching positions included in the sets of teacher job responsibilities include:
  - Classroom teachers (two separate sets of performance responsibilities)
  - English second language (ESL) teachers
  - Gifted/talented enrichment teachers
  - Preschool teachers
  - Reading Recovery teachers
  - Reading specialist teachers
  - Special education resource teachers

- **Part III** provides "tools you can use" in designing and implementing teacher evaluation systems. The various tools that can be used to structure a teacher evaluation system are presented. These tools were adapted from materials developed over the last 15 years for use in individual school districts. A CD-ROM offers the opportunity to start customizing forms to meet a particular school or school district's needs. Among the tools included are:
  - Performance Appraisal Rubric
  - Teacher Goal Setting for Improving Student Achievement
  - Teacher Evaluation Records
  - Portfolio Guidelines and Forms
  - Student and Parent Surveys
  - Summative Review Forms
  - Improvement Assistance Plan
  - Teacher Performance Evaluation Feedback Form

The *Handbook on Teacher Evaluation* is the first in a series on the evaluation of four distinct educational groups: teachers, educational specialists, administrators, and classified employees. Each of the handbooks is organized in a similar manner with three major sections. Part I is intentionally similar in all four handbooks to provide a consistent framework for implementing an evaluation system while emphasizing the differences specific to each group. Parts II and III are unique to each handbook and include detailed frameworks of the job responsibilities for the respective groups of educators and various tools to use in the evaluation process. While each handbook has been written to "stand alone" for use with a specific group of educators, the series of handbooks taken together provides a more integrated and holistic approach to personnel evaluation.

It is our sincere hope that you will find the *Handbook on Teacher Evaluation* to be a valuable resource as you seek to improve the quality of your schools and to support and improve teaching and learning in the schools. Moreover, please consider the other handbooks in this series on the evaluation of educational personnel.

Acknowledgments

Our work in personnel evaluation has spanned twenty years and is founded on our belief that evaluation can be done in a meaningful manner for teachers given a conceptually sound framework, thorough training, strong commitment, and trusting collaboration between teachers and administrators. Often the development work on a new evaluation system itself can re-energize educators as they work together to improve what goes on in the classroom. Evaluation in its simplest form is to "judge," "appraise," and "assess," and these functions are at the core of what it means to be a professional. It is important work, not because it is legally mandated in most places, but because it can be an opportunity to assess what we do, how we do it, and why. We have been fortunate to work with many fine professionals over the years who have taken this work seriously and used evaluation as a means to improve education for all who participate in the process.

We would like to extend our sincere appreciation to all of the individuals and organizations who have assisted us in the evolution of the ideas presented in this *Handbook*. In particular, we wish to acknowledge the following school districts in our home state of Virginia for their efforts to improve teacher and specialist practice through performance evaluation and professional growth systems that incorporate many of the components we recommend in this book: Alexandria City Schools, Dinwiddie County Schools, Hampton City Schools, Roanoke City Schools, Virginia Beach City Public Schools, and Williamsburg-James City County Schools. We drew from their practice to highlight selected concepts and, in some instances, to offer illustrations and materials included in appendices. We are grateful to these and the many school systems from across the country that shared their evaluation procedures and instruments with us.

Just as the content of this handbook reflects the efforts of many people, so does its organization, research, and editing. We wish to especially thank Jennifer Hindman for her organizational skills, editing, graphic renderings and research on existing evaluation systems. Catherine Little provided the fresh set of eyes to edit and integrate the disparate pieces of work that make up this *Handbook*. We appreciate the considerable time and effort they both invested in the project.

Finally, we thank the President of Eye on Education, Bob Sickles, for his remarkable business sense and unfailing support and enthusiasm for our work on the evaluation of educational personnel.

James H. Stronge
Pamela D. Tucker

What's on the CD and How to Use it!

The CD-ROM, for Windows and Macintosh, is designed to make this book more practical and easier to use.

Part II, *Roles and Responsibilities*, is on the CD-ROM in its entirety in *Adobe Acrobat®* (pdf) format. You have permission to print out the lists of job responsibilities, which are organized around specified domains, standards, and performance indicators.

The tools and forms in Part III, *Tools You Can Use*, are available as interactive files, enabling you to fill them out, customize them, and save and print them using *Microsoft Word*.

To use the interactive forms in Part III, follow these instructions:

Complete the form by typing in the blanks provided and/or by clicking on the checkboxes. Use the **Tab** key to move from field to field. When you are finished, save the file with a unique name by using the **Save As** function.

Worksheets and forms are "protected"; that is, the instructions on the form and its structure are locked and cannot be changed unless you choose to do so. If you want to make modifications to the language on the form (such as inserting the name of your school or district or otherwise customizing the language on the form) follow these directions:

1. Choose **Unprotect Document** from the **Tools** menu.
2. Type in the password, "Modify" (it must be typed exactly as shown here; it is case sensitive), and click the **OK** button. The form will unlock and become a regular Word document.
3. Save the file to your hard drive with a new name using the **Save As** function.

While a document is unprotected, form functionality is unavailable. To re-enable form functions, choose **Protect Document** from the **Tools** menu. Note that re-enabling a form will remove any data that you previously inserted into the form fields.

Permission is granted to reproduce all the lists, tools, and forms on the CD-ROM. However, this material may not be sold or repackaged without written permission from Eye On Education.

If you have any difficulty with the CD-ROM, please consult with your technology coordinator or network administrator. Eye On Education does not provide technical support.

About the Authors

James H. Stronge is Heritage Professor in the Educational Policy, Planning, and Leadership Area at the College of William and Mary, Williamsburg, Virginia. One of his primary research interests is in educational personnel evaluation. He has worked with numerous school districts and other educational organizations to design and implement evaluation systems for teachers, administrators, and support personnel. He is the author or coauthor of numerous articles, books, and technical reports on teacher, administrator, and support personnel evaluation. Selected authored or edited publications include the books: *Qualities of Effective Teachers* (Association for Supervision and Curriculum Development), *Evaluating Professional Support Personnel in Education* (Sage Publications), *Evaluation Handbook for Professional Support Personnel* (Center for Research on Educational Accountability and Teacher Evaluation), *Evaluating Teaching: A Guide to Current Thinking and Best Practice* (Corwin Press), and *Teacher Evaluation and Student Achievement* (National Education Association). Most recently, he coauthored *Handbook on Teacher Portfolios for Evaluation and Professional Development* (Eye on Education) with Pamela Tucker and Christopher Gareis. Dr. Stronge also served as director of the Evaluating Professional Support Personnel project conducted by the Center for Research on Educational Accountability and Teacher Evaluation (CREATE). Currently he is the Associate Editor of the *Journal of Personnel Evaluation in Education*. His doctorate is in the area of educational administration and planning and was received from the University of Alabama. He has been a teacher, counselor, and district-level administrator.

Pamela D. Tucker is an assistant professor of education in the Curry School of Education at the University of Virginia, Charlottesville, Virginia. She serves as the director of the Principal Internship Program. She has worked with numerous school systems in the development of new evaluation systems and served as one of the facilitators for the development of Virginia's *Guidelines for Uniform Performance Standards and Evaluation Criteria for Teachers, Administrators, and Superintendents*. Her research focuses on the various aspects of personnel evaluation and the nature of the school principalship. Books coauthored with others include *Handbook on Teacher Portfolios for Evaluation and Professional Development* (Eye on Education), *Evaluation Handbook for Professional Support Personnel* (Center for Research on Educational Accountability and Teacher Evaluation), and *Teacher Evaluation and Student Achievement* (National Education Association). Her article publications address topics such as the legal context for teacher evaluation, helping struggling teachers, and guidelines for linking student achievement to teacher evaluation. As a former special education teacher and administrator in a school for learning disabled students, she has worked with a variety of student populations and has a particular concern for students who are most at-risk for school failure. She earned her Ed.D. in Educational Administration from the College of William and Mary.

Part I

Developing and Implementing a Teacher Evaluation System

1

Teacher Evaluation: Getting Started

There is good reason and strong support for linking teaching with good evaluation practices. While teacher evaluation has long been entrenched in educational practice, fundamental questions about this enterprise and its value have often been ignored. Why evaluate? Who benefits from evaluation? Perhaps most importantly, how are teaching and learning improved through evaluation? Seeking answers to these questions deserves our attention if teacher evaluation is to become a more meaningful and productive effort.

Exploring issues related to the above questions is the focus of the *Handbook on Teacher Evaluation*. In this introductory chapter, we specifically address the following:

- ◆ Why do we need quality teacher evaluation?
- ◆ What are the purposes of teacher evaluation?
- ◆ Why has teacher evaluation often failed to be effective?
- ◆ What components are essential for a quality teacher evaluation system?
- ◆ What are guidelines for developing and implementing quality teacher evaluation systems?
- ◆ What is the purpose of the *Handbook*?
- ◆ What does the *Handbook* not provide?

Why Do We Need Quality Teacher Evaluation?

The opening statement in the report, *What Matters Most: Teaching for America's Future*, is as follows:

> *We propose an audacious goal . . . by the year 2006, America will provide all students in the country with what should be their educational birthright: access to competent, caring, and qualified teachers.*[1]

Without capable, high quality teachers in America's classrooms, no educational reform effort can possibly succeed. Without high quality evaluation systems, we cannot know if we have high quality teachers. Thus, a well designed and properly implemented teacher evaluation system is essential in the delivery of effective educational programs and in school improvement.

Regardless of how well a program may be designed, the program is only as effective as the people who implement and support it.[2] Thus, a rational relationship exists between personnel and programs. In a nutshell, *effective teachers and other personnel* are essential for *effective programs*. If school effectiveness and student success are important, and if productive personnel are necessary for effective programs, then a conceptually sound and well implemented personnel evaluation system for teachers is also important.

Despite the fact that proper teacher evaluation is fundamentally important, this part of the personnel process is all too frequently handled in an ineffective manner, primarily due to the implementation of poor evaluation systems and practices.[3] Regardless of the educator's position, fundamental evaluation needs are basic: Evaluation systems should be fair and comprehensive, grounded in both job performance and organizational requirements. Consequently, an evaluation system should be designed to encourage improvement in the teacher as well as in the school or program.

What Are the Purposes of Teacher Evaluation?

Identifying Evaluation Purposes

There are many ways to conceptualize the purposes of teacher evaluation. For example, Wheeler and Scriven identified 15 different purposes, including hiring, salary decisions, assignments, reduction in force, performance evaluation, retirement exemption, pre-tenure retention/termination, licensing, credentialing, tenure, awards/recognition, post-tenure retention/termination, self-assessment, promotion/career ladder, and mentoring appointment.[4] Additionally, the Personnel Evaluation Standards of the Joint Committee on Standards for Educational Evaluation noted ten separate reasons why high quality personnel evaluation is important in education:

1. to evaluate entry-level educators before certifying or licensing them to teach,
2. to identify promising job candidates,

3. to assess candidates' qualifications to carry out particular assignments,
4. to guide hiring decisions,
5. to assess performance of educators for tenure and promotion decisions,
6. to determine recognition and awards for meritorious contributions,
7. to assist faculty and administrators in identifying strengths and needs for improvement,
8. to plan meaningful staff development activities,
9. to develop remediation goals and activities, and, when necessary,
10. to support fair, valid, and legal decisions for termination.[5]

To provide the context for discussing the purposes of teacher evaluation, we offer the following perspective regarding the purposes of public schools:

Human beings derive meaning in life from two general sources: 1) the experience of personal growth and 2) commitment to causes greater than their own self-interest. . . . Emphasizing one to the exclusion of the other may yield citizens who either care little for the welfare of their society or lack the knowledge to contribute to it.[6]

In remarkable similarity to this perspective of balanced purposes in education are the fundamental purposes of teacher evaluation: improving performance and documenting accountability.[7] The *performance improvement purpose* relates to the personal growth dimension identified in the above quote and involves helping teachers learn about, reflect on, and improve their practice. This improvement function generally is considered *formative* in nature and suggests the need for continuous professional growth and development.[8] The accountability purpose, on the other hand, reflects a commitment to the important professional goals of competence and quality performance. This accountability function typically is viewed as *summative* and relates to judging the effectiveness of educational services.[9]

Linking Professional Growth and Accountability in Teacher Evaluation

These two purposes—professional growth and accountability—are often described as mutually exclusive. Throughout the *Handbook on Teacher Evaluation*, however, we suggest that for teacher evaluation to be most beneficial, a concerted effort must be made to establish a logical link between the two purposes. Tom McGreal suggested that multiple purposes of evaluation can be successfully met within a single evaluation system when the system is viewed as one component of a larger mission—furthering the goals of the organization.[10] And, as Michael Fullan noted, "combining individual and institutional development has its tensions, but the message . . . should be abundantly clear. You cannot have one without the other."[11]

How can we make this logical link between performance improvement and accountability as we design teacher evaluation systems that are more meaningful and useful in improving the quality of education? To begin, we must recognize that these "purposes are not competing, but supportive interests—dual interests that are essential for improvement of educational service delivery."[12] Thus, as we conceive of improvement and accountability purposes as compatible rather than competing, we need to emphasize a simple but fundamental equation:

Improved teaching = School improvement

Ideally, professional growth for teachers improves their teaching knowledge and practice, which, in turn, contributes individually or collectively to school-wide improvement. As Barbara Howard and Wendy McColskey noted, "evaluation that leads to professional growth requires teachers to look honestly at their weaknesses and strengths."[13] In practical terms, performance im-

provement can take multiple forms, including growth at the following levels:

♦ improvement in performance of individual teachers,

♦ improvement of programs and services to students, parents, and community, and

♦ improvement of the school's ability to accomplish its mission.

Quality teacher evaluation can facilitate improvement at each of these levels by providing meaningful feedback and appropriate support and resources.

Despite the complexities of addressing both improvement and outcome concerns, such a combination is needed. As John Saphier observed:

There are those who say supervision must be separated from evaluation because it is impossible for teachers to open up and have productive, growth-oriented dialog with one who judges them. In other words, teacher evaluation is incompatible with stimulating teachers' thinking and growth. We reject that notion. The problem is not that evaluators can't supervise, it is that they cannot supervise often enough.[14]

The accountability emphasis in evaluation relates to assessing both the individual teacher's performance and the accomplishment of the school's goals. It is this function of evaluation that is often perceived as detracting from the formative potential of the supervisory process. "Growth often entails trust and risk-taking, factors which may be undermined by concern for accountability."[15] However, unless summative evaluation is seen as "instrumental in the accomplishment of such major school objectives . . . time and resources so critical to high quality assessment are unlikely to be available."[16]

Why Has Teacher Evaluation Often Failed to Be Effective?

As noted above, there are multiple and compelling reasons why we need high quality, useful teacher evaluation systems operating in our schools. Perhaps most fundamentally, evaluation can be an important tool for supporting and improving the quality of teaching. Unfortunately, teacher evaluation too frequently has been viewed not as a vehicle for growth and improvement, but rather as a formality—a superficial function that has lost its meaning. When school principals and other evaluators approach evaluation as a mechanical exercise and teachers view it as an event that must be endured, evaluation becomes little more that a time-consuming charade.

Just as there are multiple reasons why we need quality teacher evaluation, there are multiple reasons why, historically, we have not achieved this worthy goal. The Joint Committee on Standards for Educational Evaluation stated that prominent criticisms of teacher and other types of performance evaluation practices are that they have failed:

♦ to screen out unqualified persons from certification and selection processes,

♦ to provide constructive feedback to individual educators,

♦ to recognize and help reinforce outstanding service,

♦ to provide direction for staff development programs,

♦ to provide evidence that will withstand professional and judicial scrutiny,

♦ to provide evidence efficiently and at reasonable cost,

♦ to aid institutions in terminating incompetent or unproductive personnel, and

♦ to unify, rather than divide, teachers and administrators in their collective efforts to educate students.[17]

Over the years, both researchers and practitioners have been critical of how teacher evaluation has been both designed and implemented. To illustrate some of the prevalent problems with teacher evaluation, consider the following concerns:

♦ "Research and learned opinion strongly support the contention that teacher evaluation has been of little value."[18]

♦ "For administrators, personnel evaluation can be one of the primary means of ensuring a quality educational program for students, and yet many are hesitant to conduct honest and meaningful evaluations with staff for fear of the potential legal ramifications in cases of unsatisfactory performance."[19]

♦ "In the past, teacher evaluation has generally not been a high-stakes activity, in part because improving the quality of teachers has not been seen as critical for improving the quality of education."[20]

♦ "The bureaucratic culture and conflictive atmosphere that currently dominate our schools inevitably breed distrust. Without trust, any evaluation system, no matter how well intended, is doomed."[21]

These concerns must be considered in the development of improved evaluation systems that can, in turn, support improvement in professional performance and achievement of school goals.

What Components Are Essential for a Quality Teacher Evaluation System?

While the goal may be to build high quality teacher evaluation systems, the reality frequently is a far cry from the ideal. Indeed, too many teacher evaluation systems accomplish neither professional growth nor accountability! If worthwhile teacher evaluation is to become common practice, then we need to emphasize constructive climates for the process of teacher evaluation. Key elements of such climates are as follows:

♦ communication,

♦ commitment, and

♦ collaboration.

Together, these three "Cs" support the creation of the synergy that can elevate evaluation to a meaningful dialogue about quality instruction

Figure 1.1
Relationship of the Three "Cs" to Quality
Evaluation

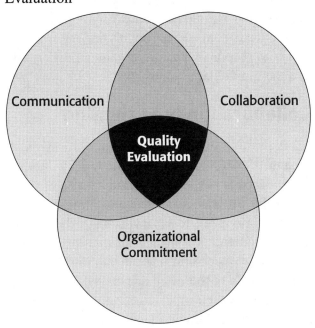

for students, as depicted in Figure 1.1. Each of the three essential elements will be explored in turn.

Communication in Evaluation

"Teacher evaluation systems should reflect the fundamental importance of effective communication in every aspect of the evaluation process. . ."[22] Unless teachers and principals/evaluators communicate early and often about what is learned through evaluation, its value will be minimized and opportunities for growth will be missed. This communication must occur in multiple forms in the evaluation process, including both public and private aspects.

Public communication in teacher evaluation. One key aspect of clear communication in teacher evaluation is related to *public disclosure* of elements about which teachers have a right to be informed. Providing adequate public disclosure can occur by implementing practical steps:

♦ involving teachers and others as key players in designing the evaluation system,

♦ distributing copies of a comprehensive evaluation handbook to every teacher and administrator in the school or school district, and

♦ providing ongoing, systematic training for teachers and evaluators in the proper use of the teacher evaluation system.

These strategies encourage and enhance the common understanding of the evaluation criteria and procedures. For example, in the Williamsburg-James City County Public Schools in Virginia, a plan for dissemination and communication was in place throughout the two-year development of a new teacher evaluation system. The plan included factsheets, "Snack and Chats" at each school, surveys to solicit input from teachers, reports to the School Board, and regular updates to the administrative staff. This process of communication with all constituencies was seen as essential for the understanding and acceptance of the new system.

Private communication in teacher evaluation. A second vital aspect of effective communication in teacher evaluation is its *personal and private* side—ongoing two-way communication between the evaluator and the individual teacher. Perhaps the most important aspect of private communication in teacher evaluation occurs in the form of conferencing between the teacher and the evaluator. In fact, the evaluation conference serves multiple purposes, such as documenting performance for use in decision making, informing teachers about their performance, and motivating teachers to higher levels of performance. Additionally, a good evaluation conference can help with problem solving, strategy development, and goal setting. [23]

Commitment to Evaluation

Organizational commitment to quality teacher evaluation—that is, commitment by the school district leadership and by the teachers themselves—is absolutely essential if the evaluation process is ever to play a vital and valuable role in improving teaching and learning. In fact, we could say that "fundamental to implementing and sustaining a meaningful teacher evaluation program—[is] establishing a culture for teacher evaluation."[24] This kind of commitment involves changing the norms and expectations of the school culture to value and support teacher evaluation as a meaningful and worthwhile enterprise.[25]

Organizational commitment to quality teacher evaluation can be demonstrated in a wide range of activities by the superintendent, administrators, and teachers within the school system. Notably, such activities must include the following:

♦ establishing teaching excellence as a top priority, then

♦ allocating time and attention to the implementation of effective teacher evaluation procedures, and lastly,

♦ devoting available resources, such as professional development funds and legal counsel, to supporting the evaluation process.[26]

"The availability of resources to respond to individual needs serves accountability of the most fundamental kind, accountability rooted in professional norms and values."[27] Time is probably the most precious resource for busy educators and is the most difficult to provide, but by reassigning other duties or giving priority to teacher evaluation, principals and teachers can devote a greater amount of time to this important task. Other useful resources include the following:

♦ the availability of curricular specialists or master teachers to support improvement for all teachers,

♦ remedial assistance for selected teachers when needed,

♦ embedded professional growth that is customized and directly relevant to the individual teachers and individual schools,

♦ funds for professional development opportunities, such as district-wide training opportunities and university courses,

♦ release time for teachers to observe master teachers,

♦ regular review and adjustment of the teacher evaluation system, and

♦ legal counsel to principals in cases of possible dismissal.[28]

As noted by McLaughlin, "teacher evaluation is not an event but a dynamic, evolving process,"[29] which needs continuous support and attention so that it is responsive to the organizational needs and the individual teachers.[30]

Collaboration in Evaluation

Administrator-teacher collaboration is a means of maintaining trust in the evaluation process and is key to developing a sense of ownership by all participants. Both administrators and teachers need to be involved in the design and implementation of new evaluation systems and in their successful implementation. Unfortunately, teachers too often are excluded from the important phases of discussion, development, and decision making in the evaluation cycle. The following quote expresses this concern:

Teachers' involvement is an irreducible requirement. The exclusion of teachers from the process perpetuates a them/us schism between administrators and teachers, which is fatal to teacher evaluation and reinforces a view of teacher evaluation as indifferent to teachers' professional expertise and classroom realities.[31]

What Are Guidelines for Developing and Implementing Quality Teacher Evaluation Systems?[32]

In addition to the importance of the three "Cs"—communication, commitment, and collaboration—noted earlier, the following guidelines can be useful in planning, designing, and implementing a quality teacher evaluation system.

♦ *Relate the overall teacher evaluation system and individual performance roles to goals of the organization.* Planning and designing a quality teacher evaluation system must begin by matching the goals of the school or school system with the needs of students, teachers, administrators, parents, and the larger community.[33] In fact, determining the needs of the organization is a prerequisite for all remaining steps if the teacher evaluation process is to be relevant to the organization's mission and, ultimately, responsive to the public demands for accountability.

♦ *Consider the context of teacher evaluation.* Understanding and accounting for the context of teacher evaluation is another critical factor in developing sound evaluation systems.[34] Some important contextual issues to consider are as follows:

- ♦ the range of subjects taught by the teacher,
- ♦ the size of the class,
- ♦ the make-up of the class (e.g., percentage of low SES students, number of limited-English proficiency students),
- ♦ the condition and quality of the classroom in which teaching occurs,
- ♦ the availability of necessary resources to do the job of teaching (e.g., textbooks, instructional materials, audiovisual supplies, computers and other technology equipment, Internet access), and
- ♦ the resources for staff development and professional growth.

♦ *Base teacher evaluation on clearly defined job duties.* In general, performance evaluation needs to be built upon clear and reasonable duties of the teacher.[35] In other words, "Evaluate teachers on what they were hired to do."

♦ *Use multiple sources of evidence to document teacher performance.* A few guidelines in this regard are as follows:

- ♦ Data collection should be context-specific and based on real job performance.[36]
- ♦ The teacher's evaluation is not a one-shot formal classroom observation, but rather an ongoing, systematic data collection over time.

- ♦ Authentic assessment, such as in performance portfolios, should be considered as part of the teacher's performance record.
- ♦ Student achievement and other measures of student performance should be incorporated in teacher evaluation, where possible.

♦ *Design and use a performance assessment rubric to make fair judgments in teacher evaluation.* Setting standards involves determining appropriate levels of performance (i.e., exceeding expectations, meeting expectations, needing improvement). Procedures for use of performance portfolios must include clearly stated standards to which teachers aspire. It is important that the standards for interpreting data collected from a variety of sources be well understood and consistently implemented in order to ensure fairness and legal defensibility.

♦ *The overall teacher evaluation system should facilitate professional growth and improved performance.* Teacher evaluation with an improvement orientation is intended to provide recognition for noteworthy performance, along with immediate and intermediate feedback for performance improvement and correction where needed. A total teacher evaluation system can ultimately lead to improved performance by the teacher as well as enhanced performance of the teacher's students.

What Is the Purpose of the Handbook?

The purpose of the *Handbook on Teacher Evaluation* is to serve as a resource and practical guide for designing and implementing quality teacher evaluation systems with the features described above. It is based on a specific evaluation model, the Goals and Roles (G&R) Evaluation Model, which reflects current thinking and best practices in evaluation and is designed to address the flaws that often exist in teacher evaluation. The *Handbook* includes a thorough description of the Goals and Roles (G&R) Evaluation Model and the necessary resources with which to implement it. Thus, the *Handbook* is designed to furnish educators with the essential tools for designing a quality teacher evaluation system. Furthermore, the same information offers teachers a blueprint for self-directed continuous improvement.

What Does the Handbook Not Provide?

The *Handbook* is not intended to be a cookbook for evaluation. The Goals and Roles Model assumes that the evaluation process is context specific, inextricably linked to the goals of each school system, each school, and each position. In addition, the *Handbook* does not provide simple answers to the complex undertaking of implementing a sound teacher evaluation system. Rather, it offers guidelines to assist educators with the development of quality evaluation systems that meet local school and individual teacher needs.

Summary

In the final analysis, teacher evaluation is a process for determining how an individual is performing in relation to a given set of circumstances (i.e., mission of the organization, individual objectives, resources available). When the judgments that are made in this process are viewed as endpoints versus the beginning points of an ongoing dialogue between an administrator/supervisor and teacher, evaluation does become irrelevant. Evaluation that is conducted in a superficial manner with little or no resource allocation, using invalid evaluation systems and flawed implementation designs, deprives the school, its teachers, and the public at large of opportunities for improvement and the benefits that professional growth and accountability afford. "All of us, whatever our relationship to the educational enterprise, deserve high quality evaluation. An evaluation system which is built squarely upon individual *and* institutional improvement holds the promise of filling this need."[37] High quality performance evaluation can become a mechanism to promote lifelong learning and instructional effectiveness for teachers. It is to this end that we devote the *Handbook on Teacher Evaluation*. In the following chapters we attempt to fulfill this goal.

Chapter 1 References

[1] National Commission on Teaching and America's Future. (1996). *What matters most: Teaching for America's future.* New York: Author.

[2] Stronge, J. H. (1993). Evaluating teachers and support personnel. In B. S. Billingsley (Ed.), *Program leadership for serving students with disabilities* (pp. 445–464). Richmond, VA: Virginia Department of Education.

[3] Stronge, J. H. (1997). Improving schools through teacher evaluation. In J. H. Stronge (Ed.), *Evaluating teaching: A guide to current thinking and best practice* (pp. 1–23). Thousand Oaks, CA: Corwin Press.

[4] Wheeler, P. H., & Scriven, M. (1997). Building the foundation: Teacher roles and responsibilities. In J. H. Stronge (Ed.), *Evaluating teaching: A guide to current thinking and best practice* (pp. 27–58). Thousand Oaks, CA: Corwin Press.

[5] Joint Committee on Standards for Educational Evaluation. (1988). *The personnel evaluation standards: How to assess systems of evaluating educators.* Newbury Park, CA: Sage, pp. 6–7.

[6] Duke, D. L. (1997). Seeking a centrist position to counter the politics of polarization. *Phi Delta Kappan, 78,* 120–123, p. 121.

[7] Duke, D. L. (1990). Developing teacher evaluation systems that promote professional growth. *Journal of Personnel Evaluation in Education, 4,* 131–144; McLaughlin, M. W., & Pfeiffer, R. S. (1988). *Teacher evaluation: Improvement, accountability, and effective learning.* New York: Teachers College Press; Stronge, J. H. (1997). Improving schools through teacher evaluation. In J. H. Stronge (Ed.), *Evaluating teaching: A guide to current thinking and best practice* (pp. 1–23). Thousand Oaks, CA: Corwin Press.

[8] Iwanicki, E. F. (1990). Teacher evaluation for school improvement. In J. Millman and L. Darling-Hammond (Eds.), *The new handbook of teacher evaluation: Assessing elementary and secondary school teachers* (pp. 158–171). Newbury Park, CA: Sage.

[9] McGahie, W. C. (1991). Professional competence evaluation. *Educational Researcher, 20,* 3–9.

[10] McGreal, T. L. (1988). Evaluation for enhancing instruction: Linking teacher evaluation and staff development. In S. J. Stanley & W. J. Popham (Eds.), *Teacher evaluation: Six prescriptions for success* (pp. 1–29). Alexandria, VA: Association for Supervision and Curriculum Development.

[11] Fullan, M. (1991). *The new meaning of educational change.* New York: Teachers College Press, p. 349.

[12] Stronge, J. H. (1995). Balancing individual and institutional goals in educational personnel evaluation: A conceptual framework. *Studies in Educational Evaluation 21*, 131–151, p. 131.

[13] Howard, B. B., & McColskey, W. H. (2001). Evaluating experienced teachers. *Educational Leadership, 58*(5), 48–51, p. 49.

[14] Saphier, J. (n. d.). *How to make supervision and evaluation really work: Supervision and evaluation in the context of strengthening school culture.* Carlisle, MA: Research for Better Teaching, p. 50.

[15] Duke, D. L. (1995). The move to reform teacher evaluation. In D. L. Duke (Ed.), *Teacher evaluation policy: From accountability to professional development.* Albany, NY: State University of New York Press, p. 6.

[16] Brandt, R. M. (1995). Teacher evaluation for career ladder and incentive pay programs. In D. L. Duke (Ed.), *Teacher evaluation policy: From accountability to professional development.* Albany, NY: State University of New York Press, pp. 28–29.

[17] Joint Committee on Standards for Educational Evaluation, 1988, pp. 6–7.

[18] Frase, L., & Streshly, W. (1994). Lack of accuracy, feedback, and commitment in teacher evaluation. *Journal of Personnel Evaluation in Education, 1*, 47–57, p. 48.

[19] Tucker, P. D., & Kindred, K. P. (1997). Legal considerations in designing teacher evaluation systems. In J. H. Stronge (Ed.), *Evaluating teaching: A guide to current thinking and best practice* (pp. 59–90). Thousand Oaks, CA: Corwin Press, pp. 60–61.

[20] Darling-Hammond, L. (1990). Teacher evaluation in transition: Emerging roles and evolving methods. In J. Millman and L. Darling-Hammond (Eds.), *The new handbook of teacher evaluation: Assessing elementary and secondary school teachers* (pp. 17–32). Newbury Park, CA: Sage, p. 17.

[21] Bacharach, S. B., Conley, S. C., & Shedd, J. B. (1990). Evaluating teachers for career awards and merit pay. In J. Millman and L. Darling-Hammond (Eds.), *The new handbook of teacher evaluation: Assessing elementary and secondary school teachers* (pp. 133–146). Newbury Park, CA: Sage, p. 145.

[22] Stronge, 1997, p. 7.

[23] Helm, V. M. (1997). Conducting a successful evaluation conference. In J. H. Stronge (Ed.), *Evaluating teaching: A guide to current thinking and best practice* (pp. 251–269). Thousand Oaks, CA: Corwin Press.

[24] McLaughlin, M. W. (1990). Embracing contraries: Implementing and sustaining teacher evaluation. In J. Millman and L. Darling-Hammond (Eds.), *The new handbook of teacher evaluation: Assessing elementary and secondary school teachers* (pp. 403–415). Newbury Park, CA: Sage, p. 403.

[25] Airasian, P. W. (1993). Teacher assessment: Some issues for principals. *NASSP Bulletin, 77*(555), 55–65; Poston, W. K., Jr., & Manatt, R. P. (1993). Principals as evaluators: Limiting effects on school reform. *International Journal of Educational Reform, 2*(1), 41–48.

[26] Bridges, E. M. (1992). *The incompetent teacher: Managerial responses.* Washington, DC: The Falmer Press; Conley, D. T. (1987). Critical attributes of effective evaluation systems. *Educational Leadership, 44*(7), 60–64; Duke, D. L. (1990). Developing teacher evaluation systems that promote professional growth. *Journal of Personnel Evaluation in Education, 4*, 131–144; Poston, W. K., Jr., & Manatt, R. P. (1993). Principals as evaluators: Limiting effects on school reform. *International Journal of Educational Reform, 2*(1), 41–48.

[27] McLaughlin, 1990, p. 410.

[28] Conley, D. T. (1987). Critical attributes of effective evaluation systems. *Educational Leadership, 44*(7), 60–64.

[29] McLaughlin, 1990, p. 411.

[30] Murphy, J. A., & Pimentel, S. (1996). Grading principals: Administrator evaluations come of age. *Phi Delta Kappan, 78*, 74–81.

[31] McLaughlin, 1990, p. 406.

[32] This section is adapted from: Tucker, P. D., Stronge, J. H., & Gareis, C. R. (2002). *Handbook on Teacher Portfolios for Evaluation and Professional Development.* Larchmont, NY: Eye On Education, pp. 67–68.

[33] Valencia, S. (1990). A portfolio approach to classroom reading assessment: The whys, whats, and hows. *Reading Teacher, 43*, 338–340.

[34] Stufflebeam, D. L. (1983). The CIPP model for program evaluation. In G. Madaus, M. S. Scriven, & D. L. Stufflebeam (Eds.), *Evaluation models: Viewpoints on educational and human services in evaluation* (pp. 117–141). Boston: Kluwer-Nijhoff.

[35] Scriven, M. (1994). Duties of the teacher. *Journal of Personnel Evaluation in Education, 8*, 151–184.

[36] Wolf, K. (1991). The schoolteacher's portfolio: Issues in design, implementation, and evaluation. *Phi Delta Kappan, 73*, 129–136

[37] Stronge, J. H. (1995). Balancing individual and institutional goals in educational personnel evaluation: A conceptual framework. *Studies in Educational Evaluation, 21*, 131–151, pp. 145–146.

2

Teacher Evaluation: Background and Context

The centrality and importance of teacher effectiveness in the ongoing pursuit of quality educational experiences for children are unquestionable. Although curricula, resources, and other variables are important considerations, instructional expertise is at the heart of the learning enterprise. The ability to judge and develop teacher effectiveness with skill, therefore, is essential in fostering the kinds of schools we all want for our children.

The classroom teacher, as the most visible professional working within schools, has been evaluated in some manner for as long as we have had schools. Often the process was informal and based on general satisfaction of the community, but over the years, evaluation has evolved into the highly structured and formalized procedures used in most school systems today. In this chapter, we provide a historical background on how evaluation models have developed, and possibly improved, over the years, with discussion of the resulting models of evaluation that are in use today. In particular, we address the following questions:

♦ What is the history of teacher evaluation?

♦ How has the role of the teacher changed over time?

♦ What are the major frameworks for evaluating teacher performance?

♦ What are the different models of teacher evaluation?

♦ What are the standards for quality personnel evaluation?

What Is the History of Teacher Evaluation?

The tradition of teacher evaluation in this country dates back to the colonial period, when citizen groups periodically toured the schools to hear recitations by students and ensure that teachers properly managed classrooms.[1] In the 1800s, administrative positions became more common, and responsibility for evaluation was assumed by master teachers or full-time administrators within the school; however, typically it was informal in nature with no written procedures.[2] By 1925, "various kinds of teacher efficiency ratings"[3] were being used by a majority of larger city school systems, and almost all public school systems had written evaluation procedures by the 1970s.[4]

Prior to the 1970s, the focus of teacher evaluation was primarily summative. Principals made their judgment about the teachers' performance and recommended retention or dismissal with little or no feedback to teachers for improving their practice. "Clearly, this approach was one of the chief reasons for teacher discontent."[5] Beginning in the early 1970s, authors[6] advocated a more formative approach to evaluation that would provide teachers with guidance on how to improve and would engage them in the evaluation process as participants as opposed to subjects. These suggestions for change were grounded in an assumption that greater involvement would positively affect teachers' perceptions of evaluation, reducing the inherent threat of the process, which would promote greater teacher commitment to the development and improvement of instructional skills.[7] Teachers certainly endorsed this viewpoint; a survey at the time by the National Education Association found that teachers overwhelmingly (93%) favored the use of evaluation for the purpose of improving teacher performance.[8]

Since that time, "many school districts have endeavored to incorporate elements of formative evaluation into their total process."[9] Based on a survey of 1,000 teachers conducted in the mid-1990s, most school systems have shifted to a more formative process. Teachers reported that performance evaluations were used to a moderate or great extent in their schools for the following formative purposes:

♦ Guide improvement of teacher skills (91%)

♦ Recognize and reinforce teaching excellence (81%)

♦ Help teachers focus on student outcomes (79%)

♦ Plan in-service education activities (67%)

In contrast, the summative use of performance evaluations was noted by less than half of the teachers as being used to "a moderate or great extent," and the discharge of incompetent teachers was reported by only 45% of the teachers. Strikingly, 78% of the teachers indicated that dismissal *should* be one purpose of evaluation in their school systems.[10]

The current educational context for teacher evaluation is one in which the public's demand for greater accountability and the teaching profession's interest in improving its professional standing duel for center stage. The former calls for performance standards and tangible measures of student achievement, while the latter emphasizes the need for support of the fundamental decision-making quality of teaching that is context-specific and sometimes defies specific standards. With its emphasis on standards *and* professionalism, the National Board for Professional Teaching Standards (NBPTS) has attempted to reconcile these two competing goals. It has recognized that "teaching is at the heart of education, and the single most important action the nation can take to improve schools is to strengthen teaching."[11] Strategies to enhance teaching and thus improve schools encompass a range of efforts from those at the national level such as the NBPTS to those at more local levels such as state and district teacher evaluation systems.

How Has the Role of the Teacher Changed Over Time?

The fundamental role of the teacher seems ageless in many regards. It would be hard to conceive of a "teacher" without the requisite skills to communicate a certain body of knowledge in such a manner that students could understand and learn the material. There is a fundamental expectation for subject matter expertise and the ability to plan lessons to convey that information and associated skills. Additional expectations have taken on greater saliency in the last few years, however, and they are reflected in newer sets of teacher evaluation criteria.

◆ *Assessment*—In today's information age, the fundamental requirement of an education has heightened the need to facilitate *every* child's success in school. Teachers are now expected to assess and support the learning needs of children such that there is optimal student achievement. No longer are traditional, summative tests sufficient; there is a need for a range of checkpoints to assess prior learning and increasing levels of mastery over time. Sophisticated assessment skills for children with special needs, limited English, and a host of other risk factors have become integral to strong instructional skills.

◆ *Communication and community relations*—The role of the teacher today extends beyond the classroom, across the school and into the community. Principals are encouraging greater collaboration among teachers to enhance the curriculum and to develop schools as learning communities. Research by Joyce Epstein[12] and others has documented the positive effect of family involvement on student achievement, and schools are beginning to develop more systematic approaches to how they work with parents and other community members. Effective communication both within and outside the school requires good interpersonal skills and a willingness to collaborate with others.

◆ *Ongoing development*—Given the rapidly changing world in which we live, it is foolhardy to believe that learning ends with formal schooling. Teachers must reflect on their practice and strive to enhance the skills and knowledge necessary to be effective with students. Teachers, like other professionals, must pursue ongoing professional development as a means to grow and learn as individuals and to enrich their classrooms and schools with their acquired expertise.[13]

These expectations are reflected in the expanded role definitions that will be discussed in the next section.

What Are the Major Frameworks for Evaluating Teacher Performance?

In 1986, the National Commission on Teaching and America's Future issued its final report[14] summarizing the changing nature of society and the resulting demands on schools and their teachers. It was a comprehensive report that explored the challenges and possibilities for reforming every stage of a teaching career, from preparation to career ladders. As a result, many initiatives were launched to strengthen the teaching profession, one of which was the Interstate New Teacher Assessment and Support Consortium (INTASC). Members of the consortium include state education agencies, higher education institutions, and national educational organizations. INTASC was sponsored by the Council of Chief State School Officers and was established to enhance collaboration among states interested in rethinking and reforming teacher assessment for initial licensing as well as for preparation and induction into the profession.

Interstate New Teacher Assessment and Support Consortium (INTASC) Standards

The standards embody the knowledge, skills, and dispositions that all teachers need to practice as they begin teaching. More specific standards for a variety of subject areas and levels of schooling, such as mathematics or special education, have been developed or will be developed in the near future. The overall framework and underlying assumptions, such as performance-based assessment, are consistent with the National Board for Professional Teaching Standards, which offers certification for more experienced practicing teachers. The core INTASC Standards are listed in Figure 2.1.

Figure 2.1

Interstate New Teacher Assessment and Support Consortium Core Standards[15]

Standard 1, Subject Matter & Content Pedagogy

The teacher understands the central concepts, tools of inquiry, and structures of the discipline(s) he or she teaches and can create learning experiences that make these aspects of subject matter meaningful for students.

Standard 2, Student Development & Learning

The teacher understands how children and youth learn and develop, and can provide learning opportunities that support their intellectual, social, and personal development.

Standard 3, Diverse Learners

The teacher understands how students differ in their approaches to learning and creates instructional opportunities that are adapted to learners from diverse cultural backgrounds and with exceptionalities.

Standard 4, Multiple Instructional Strategies

The teacher understands and uses a variety of instructional strategies to encourage students' development of critical thinking, problem solving, and performance skills.

Standard 5, Learning Environment

The teacher uses an understanding of individual and group motivation and behavior drawn from the foundational sciences of psychology, anthropology, and sociology to develop strategies for organizing and supporting individual and group work.

Standard 6, Communication

The teacher uses knowledge of effective verbal, nonverbal, and media communication techniques to foster inquiry, collaboration, and supportive interaction in the classroom.

Standard 7, Planning Instruction

The teacher plans and manages instruction based upon knowledge of subject matter, students, the community, and curriculum goals.

Standard 8, Assessment

The teacher understands and uses formal and informal assessment strategies to evaluate and ensure the continuous intellectual, social, and physical development of the learner.

Standard 9, Reflective Practice & Professional Development

The teacher understands the central concepts, tools of inquiry, and structures of the discipline(s) he or she teaches and can create learning experiences that make these aspects of subject matter meaningful for students.

Standard 10, Collaboration with Colleagues & Families

The teacher communicates and interacts with parents/guardians, families, school colleagues, and the community to support students' learning and well-being.

These ten core standards are further defined by multiple indicators of (a) knowledge, (b) dispositions, and (c) performances. The following are examples of each, under Standard 1:

Knowledge

♦ The teacher understands how students' conceptual frameworks and their misconceptions for an area of knowledge can influence their learning.

Dispositions

♦ The teacher has enthusiasm for the discipline(s) s/he teaches and sees connections to everyday life.

Performances

♦ The teacher effectively uses multiple representations and explanations of disciplinary concepts that capture key ideas and link them to students' prior understandings.

National Board for Professional Teaching Standards

Three years after *A Nation at Risk*, in 1986, the Carnegie Task Force on Teaching as a Profession issued a pivotal report, *A Nation Prepared: Teachers for the 21st Century*. Its leading recommendation called for the establishment of a National Board for Professional Teaching Standards (NBPTS). The following year, the National Board for Professional Teaching Standards was established to develop standards for the advanced certification of highly skilled veteran teachers, much like those found in other professions. The National Board and INTASC, both established in 1987, are "united in their view that the complex art of teaching requires performance-based standards and assessment strategies that are capable of capturing teachers' reasoned judgments and that evaluate what they can actually do in authentic teaching situations."[16]

Since its inception, the NBPTS has developed more than 20 sets of subject area standards for multiple student levels and certified over 10,000 teachers as highly qualified in their specialty area. More than 40 states and many local school systems now offer financial recognition for National Board Certification. The primary goal of the NBPTS is to "identify and recognize teachers who effectively enhance student learning and demonstrate the high level of knowledge, skills, abilities and commitments reflected in the following five core propositions."[17] The five core propositions that underpin the work of the National Board, with illustration of how they link to the INTASC standards addressed earlier, are listed in Figure 2.2. Each of the propositions is described in further detail with more performance-based indicators of practices indicative of the stated beliefs. For example, the first belief statement is followed by this elaboration:

Accomplished teachers are dedicated to making knowledge accessible to all students. They act on the belief that all students can learn. They treat students equitably, recognizing the

Figure 2.2
NBPTS Five Core Propositions

NBPTS Five Core Propositions	Related INTASC Standard(s)
Teachers are committed to students and their learning.	2
Teachers know the subjects they teach and how to teach those subjects to students.	1
Teachers are responsible for managing and monitoring student learning.	3, 4, 5, 6, 7, 8
Teachers think systematically about their practice and learn from experience.	9
Teachers are members of learning communities.	10

individual differences that distinguish one student from another and taking account of these differences in their practice. They adjust their practice based on observation and knowledge of their students' interests, abilities, skills, knowledge, family circumstances, and peer relationships.[18]

Taken together, the INTASC Standards for capable, beginning teachers and the NBPTS Certification for more accomplished, experienced teachers provide a vision for the teaching profession of what highly qualified teachers know, believe, and practice.

What Are the Different Models of Teacher Evaluation?

A wide variety of teacher evaluation models may be found in use in local school systems across the country; despite the variation in specific models, however, many common features may be identified. The following list explains several major types of evaluation models, with the recognition that in practice, evaluation systems frequently reflect a combination or hybrid of multiple approaches.

◆ *Teacher Trait Model*—This model is characterized by a checklist of desirable attributes for teachers, such as "enthusiastic," "fair," and "creative." According to a 1988 publication by the Educational Research Service,[19] 32% of schools used this approach despite its emphasis on pre-existing personality traits that may not be amenable to improvement efforts.

◆ *Process-Oriented Model*—This model is most familiar to educators because it focuses on the instructional "processes" taking place in the classroom that can be easily observed by supervisors/administrators. Frequently, observational data are organized by specific teaching behaviors that research has shown to be correlated positively with student achievement, such as the Hunter model.

◆ *Duties-Based Evaluation*—A duties-based approach to evaluation is based on specific tasks or requirements of the job. For example, one duty might be the frequent assessment of student learning; in this model, however, the evaluation criteria would not specify the precise strategies for student assessment.

◆ *Accountability*—An accountability approach to evaluation typically links judgment about teacher performance to student achievement of instructional objectives or other outcome measures. In 1988, the Educational Research Service found that this approach was used in 35% of the schools nationally,[20] and we can only assume that this percentage has increased as a result of the accountability movement across the country.

◆ *Goals-Based Evaluation*—This evaluation approach is similar to the business model of Managing By Objectives (MBO) and is typically used by school systems in combination with other models. It is often viewed as especially appropriate for more experienced teachers who set their own goals for professional development and are then evaluated based on their goal attainment.

◆ *Professional Growth Model*—A professional growth model of evaluation shifts the focus to individual teachers and their development as professionals. Observers provide ongoing, formative feedback for improving teaching skills that are identified by the teacher as areas of interest or need.

◆ *Hybrid*—As previously noted, hybrid evaluation models are the most common because school systems typically do not use a pure form of any of the six models listed above, but rather a unique combination that integrates multiple purposes and methodologies. Often, more prescriptive models are used for less experienced teachers and more open-ended models for more experienced and accomplished teachers.

Figure 2.3
Models of Teacher Evaluation

Teacher Evaluation Models	Positive Features	Negative Features
Teacher Trait Model	◆ Quick and easy ◆ Time honored ◆ Discretionary judgment for the administrator ◆ Minimal professional contact required	◆ Subjectivity in rating presence and degree of attribute (e.g., creativity) ◆ Not a direct reflection on teaching performance ◆ Difficulty in offering assistance for professional growth
Process-Oriented Model[21]	◆ Specific, behavioral indices for evaluation ◆ Common language for principals in describing elements of a lesson ◆ Promotion of research-based teaching behaviors	◆ Prescriptive in terms of behaviors to be promoted and assessed ◆ Possible emphasis on style variables over job responsibilities ◆ Restrictive for experienced teachers
Duties-Based Evaluation[22]	◆ Satisfaction of legal requirement for being job-related ◆ Avoidance of questions regarding teaching style	◆ Difficulty in obtaining agreement on duties ◆ Questions arise about the relative importance of each duty
Accountability[23]	◆ Popular with the general public and politicians ◆ Focus on educational outcomes ◆ Clear expectations for improved student learning	◆ Assumption that teacher performance is a direct, causal factor in student performance and behavior ◆ Limited by the validity of assessment measures
Goals-Based Evaluation[24]	◆ Promotion of teacher involvement and reflective practice ◆ Use of multiple data sources as input in the self-evaluation process	◆ Greater time commitment ◆ Goals are idiosyncratic and not necessarily related to organizational goals ◆ Open-ended in nature and may not withstand legal challenge
Professional Growth Model[25]	◆ Promotion of professionalism and professional growth ◆ Empowering of individual teacher ◆ Strong formative purpose	◆ No accountability to the school ◆ No specific connection to organizational goals or performance
Hybrid[26]	◆ Unique combination of strategies to suit multiple purposes and school contexts ◆ Tiered systems can address the differing needs of individuals in the schools	◆ Cumbersome to develop ◆ Difficult to balance different purposes such as personal growth and academic accountability

Figure 2.3 summarizes positive and negative features of these seven evaluation models.

As noted in Figure 2.3, every evaluation model has weaknesses as well as strengths; thus, there is no one perfect approach. Carefully crafted hybrids can minimize weaknesses by combining strategies that naturally compensate for each other. The key consideration, however, should be the match of a particular model or combination of models to the needs and goals of a particular school district. The model should reflect that community's values and beliefs about teaching, and more importantly, about learning. The time and effort committed to personnel evaluation should support and advance school improvement and accountability efforts; otherwise, it becomes a wasted opportunity.

What Are the Standards for Quality Personnel Evaluation?

In the previous section, a variety of teacher evaluation models were presented that highlighted differences in possible approaches. While the design of a new evaluation system can vary considerably depending on the purposes and values of a given school district, there are certain key characteristics that define a legally sound and ethical system. As a starting point, a quality teacher evaluation system should reflect the standards developed by the Joint Committee on Standards for Educational Evaluation: *propriety, utility, feasibility*, and *accuracy*.[27] A brief overview of how these four categories of standards can be incorporated in teacher evaluation is provided in Figure 2.4 and is followed by more detailed discussion of each category.

Propriety Standards

Propriety Standards "require that evaluations be conducted legally, ethically, and with due regard for the welfare of evaluatees and clients of the evaluations."[32] Ultimately, teacher evaluation should support the primary principle that schools exist to serve students. The five Propriety Standards are as follows:

- ◆ P-1, Service Orientation—Teacher evaluation should promote sound education and help fulfill the school system's mission so that the educational needs of students, community, and society are met.
- ◆ P-2, Formal Evaluation Guidelines—Guidelines for the teacher's evaluation should be agreed upon and communicated in appropriate written form (e.g., negotiated contract).
- ◆ P-3, Conflict of Interest—Conflicts of interest should be identified and properly dealt with to avoid compromising the process and results of teacher evaluation.
- ◆ P-4, Access to Personnel Evaluation Reports—Teacher should be provided ready access to results of his/her evaluation.
- ◆ P-5, Interactions with Evaluatees—The teacher evaluation process should always be conducted in a professional manner so as to enhance, and not damage, reputations and performance.

Utility Standards

"Utility Standards are intended to guide evaluations so that they will be informative, timely, and influential."[33] The collective evaluations of all employees should relate individual performance to the overarching organizational goals. This concept of utility is illuminated in five specific standards:

- ◆ U-1, Constructive Orientation—The intent and practice of teacher evaluation should be constructive in order to assist the teacher in continuing to develop as a professional.
- ◆ U-2, Defined Uses—The intended uses of the evaluation process should be agreed upon in advance in order to facilitate understanding and mutual benefit.
- ◆ U-3, Evaluator Credibility—Teacher evaluation should be conducted credibly and professionally so that the results of the evaluation are respected and used.
- ◆ U-4, Functional Reporting—Evaluation reports should be clear, timely, accurate, and germane in order to enhance practical value.

Figure 2.4

Application of the Personnel Evaluation Standards to Teacher Evaluation

Standards	Description of the Standards	Application to Teacher Evaluation
Propriety Standards	Evaluations should be legal, ethical, and conducted with concern for the welfare of both the evaluatees and their clients.[28]	◆ Written policy inclusive of criteria and procedures ◆ Job-related evaluation criteria ◆ Prior notification before evaluation begins ◆ Legal compatibility with statutory mandates ◆ Equitable treatment of all teachers
Utility Standards	Evaluations should be offered in a timely manner, useful format, and with information that the evaluatee can use to improve performance.[29]	◆ Detailed and focused feedback that enhances instruction for children ◆ Constructive suggestions that allow sufficient time for improvement ◆ Process promotes growth
Feasibility Standards	Evaluation systems must be reasonable to use in terms of the time and resources required to conduct the evaluation, in addition to providing valuable feedback.[30]	◆ Practical procedures for both teachers and administrators ◆ Perception of meaningful evaluation as a priority for the school system, with adequate support
Accuracy Standards	Information collected during the evaluation must be valid and precise in order to draw conclusions about job performance.[31]	◆ Written documentation of all communications regarding performance ◆ Recommendations based on patterns of behavior ◆ Substantiation for personnel recommendations that are made

◆ U-5, Follow-up and Impact—There should be appropriate follow-up to ensure that the results of the evaluation are understood and that appropriate steps are taken for assistance, as needed.

Feasibility Standards

The Feasibility Standards state that evaluation systems should be "as easy to implement as possible, efficient in their use of time and resources, adequately funded, and viable from a number of other standpoints."[34] An evaluation system that satisfies the Feasibility Standards will be applicable specifically to teachers, and, at the same time, it will be sensitive to the practical issues related to proper evaluation within the school system. The Feasibility category includes three specific standards:

◆ F-1, Practical Procedures—Teacher evaluation should be planned and implemented so that the process yields needed information while minimizing disruption and costs.

- F-2, Political Viability—A collaborative process should be employed in designing and implementing teacher evaluation to make the process more constructive and viable.
- F-3, Fiscal Viability—Adequate resources should be provided in order for teacher evaluation to be implemented effectively and efficiently.

Accuracy Standards

Accuracy Standards state that information must "be technically accurate and that conclusions [must] be linked logically to the data."[35] The eight standards within the Accuracy category can be summarized as follows:

- A-1, Defined Role—Teacher evaluation should be based on well-defined job responsibilities.
- A-2, Work Environment—Teacher evaluation should reflect an integrated system in which contextual issues are taken into consideration.
- A-3, Documentation of Procedures—The use of multiple data sources should be included in the design of teacher evaluation procedures.
- A-4, Valid Measurement—Teacher evaluation criteria and procedures should be appropriate for their intended audience.
- A-5, Reliable Measurement—The teacher evaluation system should include consistent and acceptable assessment procedures.
- A-6, Systematic Data Control—Systematic and accurate analysis of data should be considered essential for a fair teacher evaluation system.
- A-7, Bias Control—The provision of proper training to supervisors who conduct evaluations can enhance fairness in both evaluation processes and outcomes.
- A-8, Monitoring Evaluation Systems—The implementation of the teacher evaluation system should be monitored, refined, and improved over time.

The Personnel Evaluation Standards serve as guidelines for the legal and ethical construction of an overall evaluation system.

Summary

The field of teacher evaluation has a long history of practice but a brief period of rigorous study and attention. Evaluation practice has suffered from bias, questionable criteria, and limited substance; in the past fifteen years, however, there has been a professionally rich development of standards for both what it means to be a teacher and what quality evaluation should involve. The INTASC Standards provide a framework for guiding the work of novice teachers, and NBPTS Certification offers a structure for assessing the work of accomplished teachers. Together they establish the goal posts between which the majority of teachers practice on a daily basis and create a professionally sound foundation for teacher evaluation.

This foundation can then be built upon with the appropriate combination of evaluation models to match the professional needs of teachers and the instructional goals of school systems. The Goals and Roles Evaluation Model is a model that integrates and balances the multiple purposes for teacher evaluation and is presented in the next chapter along with a wealth of tools to be found in Parts II and III of this *Handbook*. In the remaining chapters, we will guide you through the steps to develop a legally sound and meaningful evaluation system.

Chapter 2 References

[1] Tracy, S. J., & MacNaughton, R. (1993). *Assisting and assessing educational personnel: The impact of clinical supervision*. Boston: Allyn and Bacon.

[2] Blumberg, A., & Greenfield, W. (1980). *The effective principal: Perspectives on school leadership*. Boston: Allyn and Bacon.

[3] Shinkfield, A. J., & Stufflebeam, D. (1995). *Teacher evaluation: Guide to effective practice*. Boston: Kluwer Academic, p. 13.

[4] Stemnock, S. K. (1969). *Evaluating teacher performance* (Educational Research Service Circular No. 3). Washington, DC: National Education Association.

[5] Shinkfield & Stufflebeam, 1995, p. 22.

[6] See, for example, Bolton, D. L. (1972). *Selection and evaluation of teachers*. Berkeley, CA: McCutchen; House, E. R. (1973). *School evaluation: The politics and process*. Berkeley, CA: McCutchen.

[7] Shinkfield & Stufflebeam, 1995.

[8] National Education Association, Research Division. (1972). *Evaluating teacher performance* (Educational Research Service Circular No. 2). Washington, DC: Author.

[9] Shinkfield & Stufflebeam,1995, p. 22.

[10] Nolan, M. J., Rowand, C., & Farris, E. (1994). *Public elementary teachers' views on teacher performance evaluations.* Washington, DC: U.S. Department of Education, Office of Educational Research and Improvement.

[11] National Board for Professional Teaching Standards. (1990). *Toward high and rigorous standards for the teaching profession.* Detroit, MI: Author, p. 5.

[12] Epstein, J. L., Sanders, M. G., Salinas, K. C., Simon, B. S., Rodriguez-Jansorn, N., & Van Voorhis, F. L. (2002). *School, family, and community partnerships* (2nd ed.). Thousand Oaks, CA: Corwin Press.

[13] See the National Board for Professional Teaching Standards' website at: http://www.nbpts.org

[14] National Commission on Teaching & America's Future. (1996). *What matters most: Teaching for America's future.* New York: Author.

[15] See http://www.ccsso.org/intasc.html

[16] See http://www.ccsso.org/intasc.html

[17] See http://www.nbpts.org/about/coreprops.cfm

[18] See http://www.nbpts.org/about/coreprops.cfm

[19] Educational Research Service. (1988). *Teacher evaluation: Practices and procedures.* Arlington, VA: Author.

[20] Educational Research Service, 1988.

[21] Hunter, M. (1984). Knowing, teaching, and supervising. In P. L. Hosford (Ed.), *Using what we know about teaching.* Alexandria, VA: Association for Supervision and Curriculum Development.

[22] Scriven, M. (1994). Duties of the teacher. *Journal of Personnel Evaluation in Education, 8,* 151-184.

[23] See McNeil, J. (1971). *Toward accountable teachers.* New York: Holt, Rinehart, Winston; Popham, W. (1973). *Evaluating instruction.* Englewood, NJ: Prentice-Hall.

[24] Redfern, G. (1972). *How to evaluate teachers: A performance objectives approach.* Worthington, OH: School Management Institute; Stiggins, R. J., & Duke, D. (1988). *The case for commitment to teacher growth: Research on teacher evaluation.* Albany: State University of New York Press.

[25] Iwanicki, E. F. (1981). Contract plans: A professional growth-oriented approach to evaluating teacher performance. In J. Millman (Ed.), *Handbook of teacher evaluation* (pp. 203-228). Beverly Hills, CA: Sage.

[26] Danielson, C. (1996). *Enhancing professional practice: A framework for teaching.* Alexandria, VA: Association for Supervision and Curriculum Development; Stronge, J. H. (Ed.). (1997). *Evaluating teaching: A guide to current thinking and best practice.* Thousand Oaks, CA: Corwin Press.

[27] Joint Committee on Standards for Educational Evaluation. (1988). *The personnel evaluation standards: How to assess systems of evaluating educators.* Newbury Park, CA: Sage.

[28] Joint Committee on Standards for Educational Evaluation, 1988, p. 11.

[29] Joint Committee on Standards for Educational Evaluation, 1988, p. 45.

[30] Joint Committee on Standards for Educational Evaluation, 1988, p. 71.

[31] Joint Committee on Standards for Educational Evaluation, 1988, p. 83.

[32] Joint Committee on Standards for Educational Evaluation, 1988, p. 21.

[33] Joint Committee on Standards for Educational Evaluation, 1988, p. 45.

[34] Joint Committee on Standards for Educational Evaluation, 1988, p. 71.

[35] Joint Committee on Standards for Educational Evaluation, 1988, p. 83.

3

The Goals and Roles Evaluation Model

Several models for evaluation were presented in the previous chapter, each with advantages and possible utility in a given set of circumstances. For purposes of discussion, each model was described in its pure form, to highlight differences and unique characteristics. For practical purposes, however, hybrid models often offer greater flexibility and appeal based on their breadth of focus and range of strategies employed. The Goals and Roles Evaluation Model[1] presented in this chapter is one such hybrid model that combines important features such as organizational planning and assessment, explicit role expectations, performance feedback, and an improvement focus at both the organizational and individual level.

The Goals and Roles Evaluation Model is a practical, research-based model of personnel evaluation that is squarely rooted in the premise of individual-institutional improvement and that focuses on the unique contributions made by each educator to the accomplishment of the school system's mission. It is solidly based on:

♦ evaluating performance in the context of organizational goals, as advocated in Chapter 1,

♦ using multiple data sources for documenting performance,

♦ facilitating open communication, and

♦ basing evaluation on clearly defined job expectations.

The authors believe it is an optimal model for developing or redesigning evaluation systems to reflect current thinking and best practice in personnel evaluation.

This chapter offers a description of the model along with background on the theoretical and practical support for it from the educational literature. The discussion specifically addresses the following questions:

♦ What are the underlying assumptions?

♦ What is the purpose of the model?

♦ What are the key features?

♦ What are the basic steps in the process?

What Are the Underlying Assumptions?

The Goals and Roles Evaluation Model reflects systems thinking and recognizes that the improvement efforts of individuals must be embedded in larger organizational change efforts, aligned with the goals of the organization, and supported actively by the organization. As noted by Castetter, "a performance appraisal system has its genesis in the broad purposes of the organization."[2] As such, a quality evaluation system should encourage the improvement of professional educators as a means of improving the school system as a whole. Key underlying assumptions also include the following:

♦ A school's goals are met through the *collective performance* of all personnel.

♦ An effective evaluation system promotes the *growth and development* of the individual and the school.

♦ A well-defined evaluation system provides for a *more objective* evaluation based on observable, job-related results, and its purposes are clearly established for the individual professional.

♦ A clearly articulated evaluation system makes the school more accountable to its public and is *legally defensible* in its treatment of all employees.

♦ The *entire staff* of the school should be included in a comprehensive evaluation system.

♦ The administrators and employees mutually should agree upon the design of an evaluation system through honest and open *communication*.

♦ The school personnel have a legal and ethical right to understand the *criteria* used to evaluate their performance.

♦ A *unified* evaluation process for all personnel is a more efficient use of school resources and administrative and staff time than multiple evaluation systems.

♦ All employees deserve well-defined job descriptions, systematic performance feedback, and appropriate *opportunities for improvement*.

What Is the Purpose of the Model?

The two primary purposes of any personnel evaluation system should be *performance assessment* (i.e., summative focus) and *performance improvement* (i.e., formative focus). On the one hand, there is a professional and ethical responsibility for schools to ensure that educators are fulfilling their roles in a competent and conscientious manner, particularly in the current context of accountability. It is equally important, however, for an evaluation system to provide constructive, detailed feedback to foster continuous professional improvement and development for individuals. Hence, a meaningful evaluation system must be both outcome-oriented and improvement-oriented. In order to provide an evaluation system that facilitates accomplishment of the school's goals (i.e., accountability orientation) and professional growth of the employee (i.e., improvement orientation), the Goals and Roles Evaluation Model emphasizes the relationship between expected job performance and actual job performance.

The evaluation model is designed to accomplish the following:

♦ To contribute to the successful achievement of the goals and objectives of the whole school system.

♦ To improve the quality of instruction by assuring accountability for classroom performance.

♦ To provide a basis for instructional improvement through productive teacher appraisal and professional growth.

♦ To create a collaborative process for evaluation between teacher and administrator that promotes self-growth, instructional effectiveness, and improvement of overall job performance.

What Are the Key Features?

The Goals and Roles Evaluation Model emphasizes the dynamic and integrative nature of evaluation in an educational environment committed to systematic growth and development. For organizations to grow, they must clearly articulate their *goals*, which are then achieved through the collective performance of individuals in their respective *roles* as teachers, principals, specialists, and many others. This evaluation model builds directly on the interrelatedness of organizational expectations and job performance. Thus, integral parts of this process are establishing organizational goals, defining each job with a set of performance standards that reflect the organization's goals, setting criteria for assessing job performance, documenting and evaluating performance, and relating performance to the original goals.

The Goals and Roles Evaluation Model includes the following distinguishing characteristics:

♦ *Use of straightforward, understandable language*

Performance expectations are stated in plain, understandable language to facilitate clarity. The use of straightforward language is encouraged throughout the development process of a new evaluation system, especially in the design of products such as evaluation handbooks, evaluation forms, and training materials.

♦ *Adaptability*

The Goals and Roles Evaluation Model is designed to be both comprehensive and adaptable for use with a variety of educational positions. You will find in *Part III: Tools You Can Use* that the Model has been adapted for use with classroom teachers, English second language (ESL) teachers, gifted/talented enrichment teachers, preschool teachers, reading specialist teachers, reading recovery teachers, and special education resource teachers. We have attempted to build on this key feature of adaptability by:

- accentuating the use of a uniform framework for evaluating all personnel positions,
- developing the basic building blocks (i.e., validated duties and responsibilities for instructional positions) so that they can be customized for multiple positions and settings, and
- designing assessment strategies and processes that account for the different levels of professional growth of educators.

♦ *Systematic approach to evaluation*

It simply is not feasible for school principals (the individuals primarily charged with the responsibility for conducting evaluations in most local schools) or other evaluators to implement multiple evaluation systems with different requirements, guidelines, and methods. The six-step evaluation cycle of the Goals and Roles Evaluation Model provides an efficient, standardized method for implementing evaluation. While assessment forms and processes must be differentiated for the various instructional positions, the evaluation model and protocol can be standardized. This combination of standardizing the evaluation framework and customizing its application to fit the needs of specific positions allows for a more reliable and easy-to-use evaluation system while, at the same time, accounting for important distinctions in roles and responsibilities of various instructional personnel.

♦ *Emphasis on communication throughout the evaluation process*

Personnel evaluation systems should reflect the fundamental role that effective communication plays in every aspect of the evaluation process. Since the ultimate goal of any evaluation is to continue successful programs or improve less successful ones, communication in the forms of public disclosure and evaluator-evaluatee discussion is essential. Thus, opportunities for systematic communication between evaluators and instructional personnel are built into the assessment and evaluation system.

♦ *Legally and technically sound evaluation system*

While a conceptually sound and legally and technically correct evaluation system will not guarantee effective evaluation, one that is flawed and irrational most assuredly *will* guarantee failure. The Goals and Roles Evaluation Model is designed as an evaluation system that is conceptually, legally, and technically sound, to promote the likelihood of achieving such desirable outcomes as the three described in the guiding assumptions of the Joint Committee on Standards for Education Evaluation[3]:

• provide effective service to students and society;

• establish personnel evaluation practices that are constructive and free of unnecessary threatening or demoralizing characteristics; and

• facilitate planning for sound professional development experiences.

♦ *Use of multiple data sources*

The design of the Goals and Roles Evaluation Model emphasizes multifaceted assessment techniques for documentation of job performance. The use of multiple sources of information:

• increases the validity of an evaluation for any professional educator,

• allows for differing documentation needs based on job responsibilities of particular positions (e.g., classroom teacher vs. school counselor), and

• permits differentiation of performance for personnel at different points in their careers (e.g., novice and advanced).

While formal observation can provide a significant data source, too frequently it has represented the sole source of data collection under clinical supervision evaluation models. Other methods that could be considered for the collection of information on performance include:

• Client surveys (i.e., students, parents, subordinates, and peers),

• Portfolio development, and

• Other pertinent sources (e.g., artifact analysis—performance logs, service records, case notes, lesson plans).

The proper use of multiple data sources in performance evaluation can dramatically improve the utility (e.g., through better performance feedback) of the evaluation system. Additionally, the use of multiple data sources can enhance the validity of the process, and offer a more legally defensible basis for evaluation decisions.

What Are the Basic Steps in the Model?

The Goals and Roles Evaluation Model provides a logical framework for school systems to connect school improvement efforts with the contributions of individual educators. Schools improve through the daily work of faculty and staff whose roles are clearly defined and supported by the existing organizational priorities. By reflecting on the following questions, school systems can identify future directions and develop an evaluation system that supports that process.

The dynamic nature of the development and implementation phases of the Goals and Roles Evaluation Model, with progress through individual steps, is depicted in Figure 3.1. The following is a more detailed description of the six steps of the Goals and Roles Evaluation Model.

STEP 1: Identify System Goals. Evaluation is the process of determining value relative to stated objectives. Therefore, determining the needs of the organization is a prerequisite for all remaining steps, if the evaluation process is to be relevant to the organization's mission and, ultimately, accountable to the public. Such relevance becomes possible when goals are translated into operational terms. A direct relationship should exist between the needs of the educational organization and the programs that should be established, maintained, or modified to fulfill those needs.

STEP 2: Develop Job Performance Standards. Just as the assessed needs of the organization serve to clarify the expectations of all programs, the program expectations and standards for performance serve to define the professional responsibilities associated with the role of the teacher. Program goals, such as improving learning for all students, need to be translated into job

Figure 3.1
Goals and Roles Evaluation Model

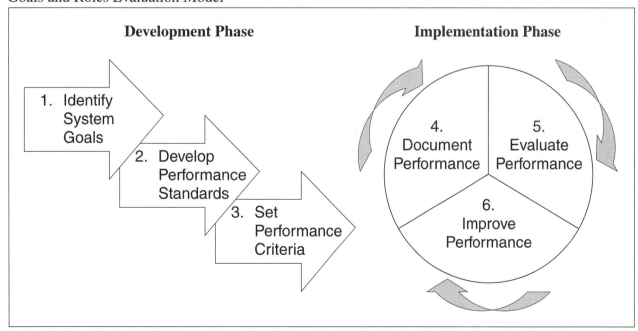

Used with permission of James H. Stronge.

performance standards such as "The teacher recognizes individual learning differences and is able to differentiate instruction to meet diverse student needs." These job performance standards must then be aligned with specific performance indicators that serve as behavioral evidence that the responsibility is met. Such performance indicators should be observable and measurable behaviors that reflect each responsibility.

STEP 3: Set Performance Criteria. Standards, to be appropriate and valid as evaluation tools, must be accompanied by realistic criteria for evaluation based on the resources or lack thereof in a given setting. Performance criteria address how well a job is to be done, how often it is to be done, and, ultimately, whether it is done at all. The standards themselves, as developed in Step 2 above, represent the expectations for each person fulfilling a position; criteria that indicate levels of performance above and below the standards are developed in Step 3. Setting such criteria

represents a critical step in the Development Phase, because it constitutes the definition of acceptable performance, and it also contributes to the legal defensibility of the evaluation system.

STEP 4: Document Performance. The evaluator, with the assistance of the evaluatee, is responsible for collecting information from other supervisors, colleagues, and clients, and for synthesizing the information for use in the evaluation process. It is important to involve individuals in the evaluation process who possess the professional expertise to address practice issues. This ensures credibility and accountability for quality programs.

STEP 5: Evaluate Performance. The vehicle for this crucial step in the evaluation process is typically the evaluation conference. The conference provides a forum in which a person's documented job performance and achievements are compared with previously established goals and objectives, using previously determined

Figure 3.2

Steps in the Goals and Roles Evaluation Model

DEVELOPMENT PHASE	
Step 1: **Identify System Needs**	Determine the mission and goals of the school and school system.
Step 2: **Develop Job Performance Standards**	Translate the goals into position expectations, reflected in job performance standards and related performance indicators for each individual staff member.
Step 3: **Set Performance Criteria**	Determine criteria to assess level(s) of performance within each job's performance standards.
IMPLEMENTATION PHASE	
Step 4: **Document Performance**	Record sufficient information about the individual's performance to support ongoing professional development and to justify personnel decisions.
Step 5: **Evaluate Performance**	Compare the individual's documented job performance with established job performance standards.
Step 6: **Improve and Maintain Performance** **& Professional Service**	Emphasize individual and program improvement through accountability and professional development in this step, which brings the process full cycle.

standards for measuring the level of that performance. The difference between the standards and actual performance, reflecting a "discrepancy" in expectations, serves as a basis for the conduct review process. What to do with the discrepancy depends on the purpose of the evaluation as well as the degree of the discrepancy. If the evaluation has been formative in nature, it is used to restructure, improve, or modify the evaluatee's performance. If the evaluation has been summative, further improvement becomes only one of a variety of possible decisions and actions.

STEP 6: Improve Performance. Improving and maintaining professional service may take the form of a variety of personnel decisions, including assistance of personnel in improving their performance, personnel transfers, and, when necessary, termination. This step suggests the importance of professional development that balances the interests of the individual and the interests of the school.

Step 6 brings the evaluation process full circle by using the results of the discrepancy analysis in Step 5 to improve or maintain professional service. For professionals who meet or exceed established standards, Step 6 provides an opportunity to identify new goals or higher levels of proficiency related to current ones. For teachers who do not meet established standards, it is important to analyze the reasons why a discrepancy exists. In some cases, goals and standards may be unrealistic given the available resources and circumstances. If the professional has failed to meet reasonable goals and standards, the discrepancy analysis provides a diagnosis of specific problems with job performance. This information is helpful in developing a plan for improvement and remediation (which involves another cycle of Steps 4, 5, and 6).

Summary

Figure 3.2 summarizes the steps in the development and implementation of the Goals and Roles Evaluation Model.

The Goals and Roles Evaluation Model was developed to structure a quality personnel evaluation process and address many of the shortcomings of existing evaluation models. An underlying premise of the model is that evaluation should be integrated into the fabric of school life by embedding it in school improvement goals and linking it to professional improvement. It is firmly grounded in clear, job-related evaluation criteria, multiple performance data sources, and legally defensible procedures. Most importantly, it emphasizes the importance of collaboration among teachers and administrators; honest, direct communication; and commitment to constructive feedback as means for professional growth. As noted by Michael Fullan:

"The challenge is to improve education in the only way it can be—through the day-to-day actions of empowered individuals."[4]

Chapter 3 References

[1] Stronge, J. H. (Ed.). (1997). *Evaluating teaching: A guide to current thinking and best practice.* Thousand Oaks, CA: Corwin Press.

[2] Castetter, W. B. (1981). *The personnel function in educational administration* (3rd ed.). New York: Macmillan, p. 239.

[3] Joint Committee on Standards for Educational Evaluation. (1988). *The personnel evaluation standards: How to assess systems for evaluating educators.* Thousand Oaks, CA: Corwin Press.

[4] Fullan, M. (1997). *What's worth fighting for in the principalship?* New York: Teachers College Press, p. 47.

4

Developing Teacher Performance Standards

Before we can hope to develop a meaningful performance evaluation system, it is essential that we understand the overarching organizational goals. As described in Chapter 3, identifying system goals (Step 1 in Figure 4.1) should be considered a prerequisite to actually developing the evaluation system itself. Since our purpose here, however, is to discuss the design of a quality teacher evaluation system, we will move beyond identifying system goals and begin the design process with Step 2: Developing Performance Standards.

Figure 4.1

Goals and Roles Evaluation Model: Developing Performance Standards

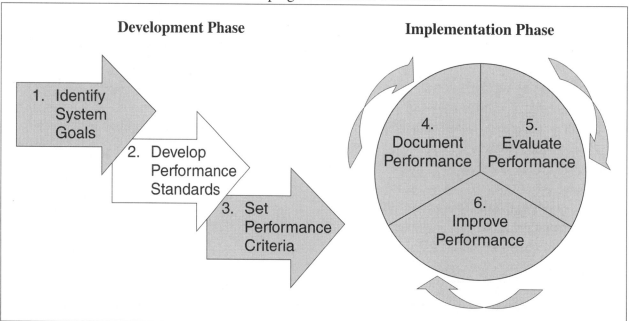

Used with permission of James H. Stronge.

The foundation for an effective teacher evaluation system—in fact, for any performance evaluation system—is the identification of well-defined job performance standards. Before we can ever hope to document and evaluate performance, it is first necessary to define *what* teachers should know and be able to do. By first defining *what* we expect the teacher to do, we are able to eliminate superfluous or unimportant evaluation dimensions and, instead, focus squarely on vital teacher roles and responsibilities. Thus, job performance standards for teachers serve as the foundation of the entire evaluation system.

In this chapter we offer guidance in deciding what should be the major focus of the teacher's job and in designing performance standards that accurately reflect quality teacher work. The place of developing teacher performance standards within the overall framework of the *Goals and Roles Evaluation Model* is highlighted in Figure 4.1. Specifically, we address the following questions:

- What is the job of the teacher?
- What are performance standards?
- What research supports teacher performance standards?
- What are the steps in developing teacher performance standards?
- What teacher performance standards are recommended for use?

What Is the Job of the Teacher?

Teach'er, n. *1. One who teaches or instructs[1]*

While human resource departments regularly develop and provide job descriptions for an array of educational positions, interestingly, the job of teacher often is neglected. Perhaps because we believe that we so readily understand what it means to be a teacher, or perhaps because it is such a complex and encompassing job, we just do not go to the trouble of providing an operational definition. Yet an effective evaluation of performance against job expectations requires a clear definition of those expectations.

One useful method of beginning the process of defining the role of a teacher is through a job description. Such a job description must:

- be an accurate *general* description of the teacher's role,
- serve as a basis upon which the teacher's evaluation can be built, and
- be rationally connected to the *specific* duties and responsibilities contained within the teacher's performance evaluation.[2]

A sample teacher job description is provided in Figure 4.2.

What are Performance Standards?

Overview

The foundation of a unified teacher evaluation system is the use of clearly described and well-documented job performance standards for all educators. In order for a performance evaluation to be fair and comprehensive, it is necessary to describe the performance standards of teachers and other professionals with sufficient detail and accuracy so that both educators and their supervisors can reasonably understand the job expectations. In essence, a set of performance standards is a detailed job description.

As reflected in the *Handbook*, this detailed description of major performance responsibilities upon which the evaluation will be based includes a three-tiered description of

- Domains (i.e., areas of responsibility)
- Performance standards (i.e., job responsibilities)
- Performance indicators (i.e., sample behaviors)

Figure 4.3 provides a graphic depiction of the three levels.

Domains

Domains provide the general framework for describing major aspects of the work of educators. Basically, domains are categories of teacher performance standards (i.e., job responsibilities or duties), and serve as logical clusters for those performance standards.

Figure 4.2

Sample Teacher Job Description

> ### *"Teacher"*
>
> #### *Primary Function*
> The teacher provides classroom leadership and instruction to promote student progress. The teacher complies with all school board policies, state codes, and mandates set forth by the State Board of Education through the Department of Education.
>
> #### *Qualifications*
> - Possesses certification and qualifications as set forth by the Board of Education.
> - Possesses and maintains professional qualifications and personal attributes as set forth by the school board and the school.
> - Demonstrates a commitment to professional ethics and growth.
>
> #### *Organizational Relationships*
> The teacher reports to the school principal and bears responsibility for planning instruction, assessment, student safety, classroom management, learning environment, communications, community relations, and student achievement. All employees of the school district perform their duties at the direction of the superintendent.

Figure 4.3

Three-Tiered System for Performance Standards

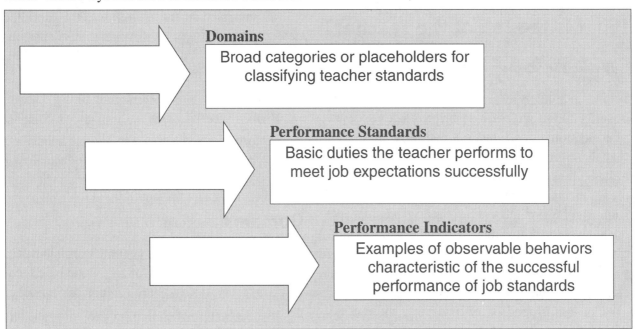

Domains
Broad categories or placeholders for classifying teacher standards

Performance Standards
Basic duties the teacher performs to meet job expectations successfully

Performance Indicators
Examples of observable behaviors characteristic of the successful performance of job standards

Used with permission of James H. Stronge.

Classroom teachers. For teachers, domains or categories of job performance standards may include such areas of responsibility as the following:

♦ *instruction,*

♦ *assessment,*

♦ *learning environment,*

♦ *communications and community relations,* and

♦ *professionalism.*

Figure 4.4 provides definitions for a five-domain teacher evaluation system based on these five areas.

Schools or school systems may wish to alter the domain list to meet specific needs or help stakeholders reach consensus. For example, some school districts choose to incorporate the standards for *Communication/Community Relations* under other domains (e.g., communicating student progress under the *Assessment* domain, communicating classroom rules and procedures under the *Learning Environment* domain, or communicating with parents and colleagues under *Professionalism*). Alternative headings also may be selected (e.g., *Classroom Management* and *Learning Environment,* or *Planning and Instructional Delivery* instead of *Instruction*).

Resource teachers. Too often educators have been subjected to the use of evaluation systems

Figure 4.4
Definitions of Classroom Teacher Domains

Domain	Definition
Instruction	*Instruction* is an ongoing and reflective process for facilitating the acquisition of knowledge, skills, and understanding. This domain encompasses both organizing for instruction and delivery of instruction. The major standards include planning and implementing a variety of activities consistent with instructional objectives and selecting instructional methods compatible with student abilities and learning styles.
Assessment	*Assessment* is the process of systematically gathering, reporting, and using a variety of data in an unbiased and consistent manner to measure and improve student performance. This domain includes the standards for conducting evaluation and providing feedback to students that encourages student progress and measures student achievement.
Learning Environment	*Learning Environment* reflects the development and effective use of resources, routines, and procedures that support a positive classroom climate and promote student learning. This domain includes the teacher's standards for planning and demonstrating effective routines and procedures that create a safe, organized, and productive learning environment.
Communication/ Community Relations	The *Communication/Community Relations* domain includes the standards for effective teacher communication within the classroom and between the classroom and others, as well as the standard for encouraging parent and community involvement.
Professionalism	The *Professionalism* domain defines the standards for demonstrating a commitment to professional ethics and growth and for complying with division policies and procedures.

that simply do not fit. For example, it is fairly common practice for school districts to employ a single teacher evaluation system with counselors, library/media specialists, school psychologists, and other specialists as well as teachers. This kind of forced fit just does not work; in fact, frequently the best response on a summative evaluation form for many of these educators on the evaluation criteria is "Not Applicable."

The mismatch between the educator's job and the evaluation system need not be so extreme as trying to make a teacher evaluation system fit a school psychologist; the problem can exist for selected groups of resource teachers who are not primarily classroom-based. Consider the primary roles of teachers such as special education resource teachers, gifted/talented enrichment teachers, Reading Recovery teachers, reading specialists, and similar specialists. Indeed, these individuals are clearly teachers—and their positions are teaching positions—but they are specialty teachers. In addition to delivering direct

instruction to students, their roles often require them to spend significant amounts of time with program coordination, student assessment, collaboration with other educators on behalf of students, and other such responsibilities. Consequently, the core set of classroom teacher domains and performance standards may not come close to actually defining their work. For these reasons, we have chosen to include in the *Handbook* separate sets of performance domains and standards for selected resource teaching positions. The separate set of performance domains for resource teachers is summarized in Figure 4.5.

Performance Standards

Performance standards are the job responsibilities or duties performed by a teacher. They are organized under the identified domains. The performance standards within each domain represent the major job responsibilities in which the

Figure 4.5

Definitions of Resource Teacher Domains

Domain	Definition
Program Management	*Program management* involves planning, coordinating, and organizing the program, facilitating change as needed.
Assessment	The *Assessment* domain includes using data to measure and improve student performance and/or program effectiveness.
Direct Services/ Instruction	*Direct Services/Instruction* include a variety of instructional and/or intervention services to meet the direct instructional needs of students.
Collaboration	The *Collaboration* domain includes collaborating and/or consulting with school personnel, parents, and others to facilitate and coordinate the delivery of services to students.
Professionalism	The *Professionalism* domain defines the standards for demonstrating a commitment to professional ethics and growth and for complying with division policies and procedures.

Please note: While we have addressed the unique needs of selected groups of teachers, we purposely have omitted other professional educator positions, such as administrators, counselors, library/media specialists, school nurses, school psychologists, and the like. These positions are included in other evaluation handbooks in this series published by Eye On Education.

Figure 4.6

Sample Teacher Performance Standards

Teacher Standard I-1: Knowledge of Subject Matter

    I-1: The teacher demonstrates current and accurate knowledge of subject matter covered in the curriculum.

Teacher Standard A-1: Use of Student Assessments

    A-1: The teacher uses a variety of appropriate assessments to measure student achievement.

---

teacher engages. The performance standards—not the domains—form the basis for the development of job descriptions and, thus, should also form the basis for job evaluation.

The teacher performance standards provide greater specification of role expectations than the domains but are broader in nature than discrete, observable behaviors. In other words, they provide greater clarity on the precise nature of each domain but do not provide a specific behavior or set of behaviors that would be directly amenable to assessment. Two examples of performance standards for teachers are given in Figure 4.6.

Performance Indicators

The assumption upon which a system of teacher performance standards is built is that teachers—regardless of what their particular assignments might be—are far more alike than they are different. Nonetheless, while the use of a common set of instructional performance standards tends to work very well for most teachers, preK-12, the actual work of a high school teacher (for example, a chemistry teacher) differs markedly from that of a fourth grade teacher. Likewise, the role of a chemistry teacher is different from those of other high school teachers (for example, a Spanish teacher or even a biology teacher). Practically speaking, however, it would be virtually impossible to create and implement an evaluation system with separate sets of

performance standards for every grade level, subject matter, or other teacher distinction that exists in a school district. Yet if we do not account for important differences in teacher roles and responsibilities, the evaluation process becomes completely irrelevant. So how do we adjust for these important differences in teacher work? It is through the customization of the performance indicators—the most specific level in the three-tiered hierarchy.

While domains and performance standards describe the essence of the job, a more specific unit of performance—performance indicators—is needed for actual documentation of the accomplishments of the teacher. Performance standards constitute the basic units of the job and, as described above, are organized within broadly defined domains. However, neither domains nor performance standards lend themselves readily to direct classroom observation or measurement.

Performance indicators are used in the teacher evaluation system to do just what the term implies—*indicate*—in observable behaviors, the types and quality of performance associated with performance standards. A performance indicator is a typical behavior that can be observed or documented to determine the degree to which an employee is fulfilling a given performance standard. Figure 4.7 offers examples of performance indicators that are associated with the two performance standards provided in the previous section.

Figure 4.7

Sample Teacher Performance Indicators

Teacher Standard—Instruction Domain

I-1: The teacher demonstrates current and accurate knowledge of subject matter covered in the curriculum.

Sample Performance Indicators

The teacher

- bases instruction on goals that reflect high expectations, understanding of the subject, and the importance of learning.
- demonstrates the ability to engage and maintain student attention and interest.
- links objectives for instruction to prior student learning
- exhibits knowledge and demonstrates skills relevant to the subject area(s) taught.
- demonstrates an ability to make topics and activities meaningful and relevant to student learning.

Teacher Standard - Assessment Domain

A-1: The teacher uses a variety of appropriate assessments to measure student achievement.

Sample Performance Indicators

The teacher

- assesses student performance based on instructional objectives.
- continuously monitors student progress before, during, and after instruction through frequent and systematic assessment.
- demonstrates competence in the use of acceptable grading, ranking, and scoring practices in recording student achievement.
- uses multiple assessment strategies including teacher-made, criterion-referenced, and standardized tests.
- uses oral, non-verbal, and written forms of assessment to measure student performance.
- includes information on student participation, performance, and/or products in assessment.

It is important to note that performance indicators are merely *examples* of behaviors. While sample lists of performance indicators are provided for each teacher standard that we have included in the *Handbook*, these lists are not intended to be exhaustive. Rather, they are merely examples of typical behaviors that may serve as an indication that a teacher meets the given standard. Evaluators and teachers are encouraged to review the lists of performance indicators and to customize them—supplementing, modifying, or reducing as appropriate—for a particular teacher work assignment or situation.

What Research Supports Teacher Performance Standards?

Much has been written about the qualities of effective teachers, ranging from general observations that apply to all educators to subject

Figure 4.8

Research Supporting Teacher Domains[3]

Selected Research	Domains				
	Instruction	Assessment	Learning Environment	Communications & Community Relations	Professionalism
Black & Howard-Jones, 2000				•	•
Buttram & Waters, 1997	•				
Check, 1999					
Collinson, Killeavy, & Stevenson, 1999			•	•	•
Cotton, 2000	•	•	•	•	
Covino & Iwanicki, 1996	•		•		
Darling-Hammond, 2001	•				
Emmer, Evertson, & Anderson, 1980	•	•	•	•	
Ferguson & Womack, 1993					•
Fetler, 1999	•				•
Good & Brophy, 1997	•	•	•		
Johnson, 1997	•	•	•	•	•
Mason, Schroeter, Combs, & Washington, 1992	•	•	•	•	
McBer, 2000	•		•		•
Peart & Campbell, 1999	•	•	•	•	•
Stronge, 2002	•	•	•	•	•
Wang, Haertel, & Walberg, 1993	•	•	•		
Wright, Horn, & Sanders, 1997	•	•			

area-specific or population-specific characteristics. The knowledge, skills, and dispositions of effective teachers that recur in the literature are presented here as supporting points for the domains, performance standards, and performance indicators identified as teacher job responsibilities. Figure 4.8 organizes the selected research on characteristics of effective teachers by domains commonly found in teacher evaluation.

Effective teachers are knowledgeable about their content area, student growth and development, instructional strategies and resources, and assessment.[4] These educators possess skills for planning lessons, establishing routines and procedures for a smoothly operating classroom, managing student behavior, and communicating with colleagues, parents, and students.[5] Teacher disposition leaves a lasting impression on students, as it makes the professional accessible to students through the use of humor, fairness, respect, and compassion.[6] Teacher job descriptions often focus on the knowledge and skills

Figure 4.9
Performance
Standards:
Alternative
Terminology

Recommended Terms	Alternative Terms
Domain	◆ Area or Responsibility ◆ Category ◆ Division ◆ Field ◆ Placeholder
Performance Standard	◆ Job duty ◆ Performance responsibility ◆ Performance expectation ◆ Function
Performance Indicator	◆ Quality indicator ◆ Sample behavior

components of the profession, which are easier to evaluate. However, effective teachers combine technical skills and resources, knowledge of students, and understanding of content with their own personalities to offer meaningful instructional experiences to their pupils. Furthermore, highly effective teachers facilitate learning for all students, with their classrooms demonstrating high levels of student achievement regardless of the range of learners in their classrooms.[7] Since teacher evaluation, ultimately, is about documenting performance levels and supporting quality teaching, it is essential that we base the teacher's performance evaluation on documented teacher effectiveness research.

What Are the Steps in Developing Performance Standards?

Selecting Terminology

An early step in designing or customizing a unified performance evaluation system is to reach consensus regarding terminology. The terms in the *Handbook on Teacher Evaluation* were selected because, based on considerable field testing, they have been found to be relatively clear, straightforward, and applicable to a variety of teacher and other educational positions. Schools or school systems, however, may select different terms to meet their own unique organizational requirements or to further customize the Goals and Roles Evaluation Model (as described in Chapter 3). Sample alternative terms are listed in Figure 4.9.

Determining Content for Performance Standards

The next step in developing a comprehensive set of teacher performance standards is for stakeholders to reach consensus on the content of the domains, performance standards, and performance indicators that will form the foundation of their customized evaluation process. The specific performance standards that are to be implemented, however, should reflect a close alignment with the school or district needs. While we have recommended selected sets of teacher performance standards in the *Handbook*, it is important to involve teachers, principals, central office administrators and supervisors, and perhaps community members in selecting or developing the set of standards to be used. This participatory, inclusive process not only will assist with needed customization that better reflects the needs of the given school community, but also will increase buy-in and support from all constituents. Therefore, it is essential for each organization to build

Figure 4.10

Recommended Sets
of Teacher
Performance
Standards

Teacher Performance	Type of Performance Standards	
	Classroom Teacher	Resource Teacher
Classroom Teacher—Five Domains	•	
Classroom Teacher—Four Domains	•	
English Second Language (ESL) Teacher		•
Gifted/Talented Enrichment Teacher		•
Preschool Teacher		•
Reading Specialist Teacher		•
Reading Recovery Teacher		•
Special Education Resource Teacher		•

on prior work and to involve representative stakeholders in the process of developing the most desirable set of teacher performance standards.

We have attempted to develop the various sets of teacher performance standards included in Part II of the *Handbook* as comprehensively as possible. However, in developing the performance indicators—the third tier and most specific aspect of the standards—we have tried to be extensive but not exhaustive. Consequently, there may be performance indicators that reflect a particular circumstance that should be added. On the other hand, there likely will be performance indicators that you choose to eliminate. In the final analysis, what you hope to achieve is a description of a teaching position that is as complete and accurate as possible.

What Teacher Performance Standards Are Recommended for Use?

The *Handbook on Teacher Evaluation* provides eight complete sets of teacher performance standards. The teaching positions for which we have developed separate sets of performance domains and standards are summarized in Figure 4.10.

Part II of the *Handbook* provides the actual detailed sets of teacher performance standards. The domains, standards, and performance indicators included in Part II are functional, comprehensive, research based, and field tested. Decision-makers at local schools or districts can select—or customize as needed—one or more of the recommended sets of teacher performance standards that best fit the needs of the district and the specific roles. We do suggest that a single set of standards be selected for all classroom teachers and, possibly, separate sets selected for the specialty teaching positions, such as resource teachers.

Summary: How Should Teacher Performance Standards Be Used?

As indicated earlier, the teacher's standards serve as the basis against which teacher performance is measured. Taken as a whole, the performance standards are meant to be as comprehensive as possible in reflecting what a teacher's job encompasses. However, we do not intend that an entire list be implemented verbatim, for several reasons. In order for a teacher to fulfill all of the performance standards identified in the *Handbook* to the fullest extent, it would require the proverbial 110% effort. Actually, it would probably require closer to 210%! Consequently, supervisors and teachers must make decisions related to specific professional development goals and manageable ways of demonstrating performance of the standards.

Now that we have reviewed the process and content for determining the *what* of teacher evaluation, we turn our attention to the *how* in documenting performance in Chapter 5.

Chapter 4 References

[1] McKechnie, J. L. (Ed.). (1983). *Webster's new twentieth century dictionary* (2nd ed.). New York: Simon & Schuster, p. 1871.

[2] DiPaola, M. F., & Stronge, J. H. (2003). *Superintendent evaluation handbook*. Lanham, MD: The Scarecrow Press.

[3] Black, R. S., & Howard-Jones, A. (2000). Reflections on best and worst teachers: An experiential perspective of teaching. *Journal of Research and Development in Education, 34*(1), 1–12; Buttram, J. L., & Waters, J. T. (1997). Improving America's schools through standards-based education. *Bulletin, 81*(590), 1–5; Collinson, V., Killeavy, M., & Stevenson, H. J. (1999). Exemplary teachers: Practicing an ethic of care in England, Ireland, and the United States. *Journal for a Just and Caring Education, 5*(4), 349–366; Cotton, K. (2000). *The schooling practices that matter most.* Portland, OR: Northwest Regional Educational Laboratory and Alexandria, VA: Association for Supervision and Curriculum Development; Covino, E. A. & Iwanicki, E. (1996). Experienced teachers: Their constructs on effective teaching. *Journal of Personnel Evaluation in Education, 11,* 325–363; Darling-Hammond, L. (2001). The challenge of staffing our schools. *Educational Leadership, 58*(8), 12–17; Educational Review Office. (1998). *The Capable Teacher.* Retrieved online at ttp://www.ero.govt.nz/Publications/eers1998/98n02hl.htm ; Emmer, E. T., Evertson, C. M., & Anderson, L. M. (1980). Effective classroom management at the beginning of the year. *The Elementary School Journal, 80*(5), 219–231; Ferguson, P. & Womack, S. T. (1993). The impact of subject matter and education coursework on teaching performance. *Journal of Teacher Education, 44,* 55–63; Fetler, M. (1999). High school staff characteristics and mathematics test results. *Educational Policy Analysis Archives, 7*(9). Retrieved from http://olam.ed.asu.edu/v7n9; Good, T. L., & Brophy, J. E. (1997). *Looking in classrooms* (7th ed.). New York: Addison-Wesley; Johnson, B. L. (1997). An organizational analysis of multiple perspectives of effective teaching: Implications for teacher evaluation. *Journal of Personnel Evaluation in Education, 11,* 69–87; Mason, D. A., Schroeter, D. D., Combs, R. K., & Washington, K. (1992). Assigning average-achieving eighth graders to advanced mathematics classes in an urban junior high. *The Elementary School Journal, 92*(5), 587–599; McBer, H. (2000). *Research Into Teacher Effectiveness: A Model of Teacher Effectiveness.* (Research Report #216). England: Department for Education and Employment; Peart, N. A. & Campbell, F. A. (1999). At-risk students' perceptions of teacher effectiveness. *Journal for a Just and Caring Education, 5*(3), 269–284; Stronge, J. H. (2002). *Qualities of effective teachers.* Alexandria, VA: ASCD

[4] Ferguson & Womack, 1993; Fetler, 1999; Mason, et al., 1992; McBer, 2000

[5] Cotton, 2000; Emmer, et al., 1980; Good & Brophy, 1997; Stronge, 2002

[6] Black & Howard-Jones, 2000; Peart & Campbell, 1999

[7] Wright, S. P., Horn, S. P., & Sanders, W. L. (1997). Teacher and classroom context effects on student achievement: Implications for teacher evaluation. *Journal of Personnel Evaluation in Education, 11,* 57–67.

5

Using Criteria to Rate Teacher Performance

Figure 5.1

Goals and Roles Evaluation Model: Designing Performance Criteria

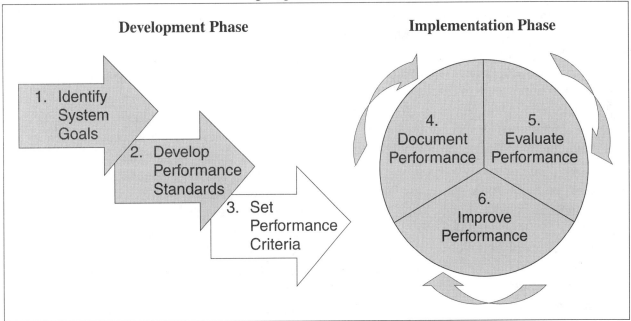

Used with permission of James H. Stronge.

There are two major considerations in assessing the quality of a teacher's performance: the actual job responsibility or performance of job standards (the *what*) and the way in which the work is performed (the *how well*). As we discussed in Chapter 4, the identified performance standards provide a description of *what* is expected of the teacher. However, the set of performance standards alone is not adequate to ensure a quality evaluation system. We also need to know *how well* the teacher fulfills her/his job.[1] In this chapter we explore the *how well* aspect needed for designing and implementing a quality teacher performance evaluation system.

This chapter addresses the ways and means for using established criteria in rating teacher performance. The place of designing and using criteria within the overall framework of the *Goals and Roles Evaluation Model* is illustrated in Figure 5.1. Specifically, the following questions are addressed:

- What are the intended outcomes of teacher evaluation?
- What assessment tools can be used in providing formative feedback?
- What types of rating scales can be used in summative evaluation?
- What is a performance appraisal rubric and how is it used?

What Are the Intended Outcomes of Teacher Evaluation?

In Chapter 1, we briefly touched on fundamental purposes for the teacher evaluation when we described an improvement-accountability continuum. This important issue bears elaboration here as we move into a discussion of how to use criteria to rate the teacher's performance. Again, a comprehensive teacher evaluation system should be rooted in two broad purposes:

- It should be *outcome-oriented*, contributing to the teacher's goals and to the mission of the program, school, and/or total school system (i.e., accountability or summative focus).[2] School or school district purposes should form the basis for all organizational action. As Castetter stated, "a performance appraisal system has its genesis in the broad purposes of the organization."[3]
- It should be *improvement-oriented*, contributing to the personal and professional development needs of the teacher as well as improvement within the school organization (i.e., improvement or formative focus).[4] Stufflebeam captured well the improvement emphasis in evaluation when he wrote that the purpose of evaluation is "not to prove but to improve."[5] While a teacher evaluation system should be focused on results, it also must be focused on supporting and helping teachers improve their own performance.

What Assessment Tools Can Be Used in Providing Formative Feedback?

Performance Indicators and Formative Feedback

In Chapters 3 and 4, we introduced the concept of a three-tiered system for describing the teacher's performance standards. Performance indicators—the third tier in the three-tiered system—are used in the teacher evaluation system to do just what the term implies—*indicate*—in observable behaviors, the types and quality of performance associated with performance standards.

Sample performance indicators (listed for all sets of standards included in Part II of the *Handbook*) are examples of observable, tangible behaviors that reflect the performance of a standard. In other words, the performance indicators tell the evaluator and the teacher the type of observable actions that constitute acceptable performance. A teacher or an evaluator, then, can use the sample performance indicators to clarify the behavior (the *what*) that meets each standard. Conversely, negative behaviors can draw attention to areas that need improvement. Drawn from examples in Chapter 4, Figure 5.2 illustrates the kind of performance indicators that can be used as "look-fors" and "red flags" for a given teacher standard.

While performance indicators can be very useful in illuminating what to look for in teacher performance, they are *not* a glorified check list that equals effective teaching. Never assume that if all performance indicators are found, it automatically means that a teacher is producing quality work; also, if some performance indicators are missing, do not assume the teacher is producing inferior work. Teaching is far too complex to confine to a simple list. Rather, performance indicators are most useful when used as a guide for the kinds of behavior and evidence that typically are seen in classrooms.

Figure 5.2

Sample Teacher Performance Indicators Used as "Look-fors" and "Red Flags"

Teacher Standard—Instruction Domain

    I-1: The teacher demonstrates current and accurate knowledge of subject matter covered in the curriculum.

Sample Performance Indicators – Look-fors

The teacher

- bases instruction on goals that reflect high expectations, understanding of the subject, and the importance of learning.
- demonstrates the ability to engage and maintain student attention and interest.
- links objectives for instruction to prior student learning.
- exhibits knowledge and demonstrates skills relevant to the subject area(s) taught.
- demonstrates an ability to make topics and activities meaningful and relevant to student learning.

Sample Performance Indicators – Red Flags[6]

The teacher

- has difficulty individualizing instruction.
- uses improper oral or written communication.
- does not properly incorporate curriculum objectives into the lesson.
- instructs students using out-of-date materials.
- fails to remain current on discoveries in the subject area, resulting in teaching students inaccurate information.
- demonstrates a lack of knowledge about real life applications of the content.

Interim Reviews and Formative Feedback

One of the most untenable decisions that an evaluator could make would be to withhold performance information until the end of the evaluation, and then reveal the negative results to the teacher. For a variety of reasons, failing to provide regular formative feedback is a critical flaw in the overall process.

- Firstly, if a teacher is doing good work, reinforce it by communicating that fact. Even with adults, positive reinforcement and recognition pay dividends! On the other hand, if the teacher is not doing good work, do not allow him or her to perform poorly or malpractice all year. Help the teacher get better while there is hope and while this year's students can benefit.

- Secondly, not providing ongoing improvement-oriented feedback would be unethical, if not illegal. Several state statutes and many local school board policies require that teachers be given opportunities to improve if the teaching behavior is deemed remediable.

- Finally, there should be no surprises at a summative evaluation conference. Communicate early and often and be clear about strengths and areas for improvement, and then provide clear guidance for making instructional improvements.

Figure 5.3
Teacher Performance Review

---

*Teacher Name*_____   *Evaluator* _____

*School*_____   *School Year* _____

Directions: Evaluators use this form to maintain a running record of evidence documented for each teacher performance standard. Evidence can be drawn from formal observations, portfolio review, and other appropriate sources. This form should be maintained by the evaluator during the course of the evaluation cycle (yearly for probationary teachers: and a three-hear cycle for continuing contact teachers.)

Domain: Instruction

   I-1 The teacher demonstrates current and accurate knowledge of subject matter covered in the curriculum.

Date   *Comments*

_____

_____

_____

_____

Obviously, thoughtful and insightful feedback, early and often, is a hallmark of an effective evaluation system—and of effective evaluators, for that matter. Thus, it is essential that the teacher evaluation system be designed and implemented in such a manner as to foster an ongoing dialogue about quality teacher work. Evaluation is a process, not an event!

In addition to the informal, ongoing discussion between the teacher and evaluator, an interim assessment and conference can be very useful in summarizing and highlighting progress to date, noting areas of strength, and focusing attention on any specific areas for improvement. An interim performance review is intended to provide an initial rating on performance and allows an opportunity for improvement prior to the summative evaluation. In some school districts, this interim report is reviewed during a conference between

the teacher and evaluator to promote professional improvement, but it is not generally forwarded to the personnel office. Also, for some school districts, an interim review is used mid-year (e.g., December or January) each year; for others, it is used in an off-cycle year for a multi-year evaluation cycle (e.g., by January of Year 2 in a three-year evaluation cycle for tenured teachers). Figure 5.3 illustrates a running record format that might be used for an interim review form, and Part III of the *Handbook* includes a performance review form.

What Types of Rating Scales Can Be Used in Summative Evaluation?

There is a fundamental problem with rating scales: They typically are high inference—that is, they are based on subjective opinion that is not anchored in actual evidence. By comparison, documenting student time-on-task or the use of questioning skills by the teacher is relatively low inference.[7] Despite this inherent flaw in rating scales, we do not recommend eliminating their use in teacher evaluation for a number of reasons:

♦ First, determining the quality of performance is more than examining a set of facts; it requires consideration of the context of the work, attitudes, results, and so forth. Thus, evaluation, ultimately, *is* about judgment—albeit judgment based squarely on performance.

♦ Second, the absence of a rating scale can be problematic, too. Consider, for example, the possibility of replacing a rating scale with totally narrative feedback. Indeed, narrative comments are valuable to highlight performance and to illuminate specific behaviors, recommendations, etc. Nonetheless, it would be extraordinarily difficult to achieve any reasonable measure of inter-rater reliability among evaluators and across multiple evaluatees based on these narrative comments.

♦ Finally, because it is so difficult to define "incompetence" operationally, some states have modified or replaced the term in their school codes with definitions that relate to documented evaluations. For example, Virginia modified its statute to state that incompetence means "performance that is documented through evaluation to be consistently less than satisfactory."[8] In California, the term incompetence has been replaced with "unsatisfactory performance" as grounds for a K–12 teacher's dismissal.[9] The use of ratings often is explicitly or implicitly required in state statutes and local policies.

Rather than eliminating the use of rating scales entirely, we recommend modifying how they are designed and implemented. While there are no ways to completely rid rating scales of the inherent flaw of unfounded, high inference judg-

ment, there are ways and means to minimize this aspect of their use. One such method is to more accurately define what the rating scale means in order to guide the evaluator's judgment.

Designing Rating Scales

Obviously, rating scales of various types are widely used in teacher evaluation. Figure 5.4 depicts several typical categories of rating scales based on the number of rating levels, with illustration of terminology used to label the levels in each category. The figure reflects existing teacher evaluation systems that we found in an informal survey of school districts across the country.[10]

The terms included in Figure 5.4 reflect both normative and criterion-referenced terms. Normative-referenced scaling terms would include comparative terms such as "superior," "above average," "average," "below average," and "inferior." By definition, accurate ratings could not result in a majority of a staff's evaluations being "above average" or higher; it would violate the meaning of "average" to have 80% of all teachers evaluated as above average. Using criterion-referenced scaling terms, however, avoids this problem. Given appropriate and clear definitions, terms such as "excellent," "good," "satisfactory," "poor," or "inadequate" could be applicable to any number of teachers. For example, if a school hired all capable and committed teachers and provided quality opportunities for professional growth, it could conceivably rate 60% or more of its staff as "exceeding standard" without violating the validity of its evaluation procedures and standards.[11]

Rating scales can be designed as simply as a dichotomous scale (e.g., pass-fail). While simple to understand and implement, a two-point scale lacks the differentiation needed to encourage professional growth. On the other hand, rating scales with as many as six levels are difficult to operationally define and equally difficult to implement.

Figure 5.4
Common Terminology Used in Rating Scales

Number of Rating Levels	Terminology Options			
2	◆ Meets Expectations ◆ Does Not Meet Expectations	◆ Satisfactory ◆ Unsatisfactory	◆ Acceptable ◆ Unacceptable	
3	◆ Exceeds Expectations ◆ Meets Expectations ◆ Below Expectations	◆ Meets Expectations ◆ Needs Improvement ◆ Unsatisfactory	◆ Excellent ◆ Satisfactory ◆ Unsatisfactory	
4	◆ Exceeds Expectations ◆ Meets Expectations ◆ Performance Needs Improvement ◆ Below Expectations	◆ Exemplary ◆ Effective ◆ Needs Improvement ◆ Unsatisfactory	◆ High Quality Performance ◆ Professionally Competent ◆ Needs Improvement ◆ Ineffective Performance	◆ Excellent ◆ Area of Strength ◆ Needs Improvement ◆ Unsatisfactory
5	◆ Clearly Outstanding ◆ Exceeds Expectations ◆ Meets Expectations ◆ Below Expectations ◆ Unsatisfactory	◆ Superior ◆ Above Expectations ◆ Meets Expectations ◆ Below Expectations ◆ Unsatisfactory	◆ Outstanding ◆ Superior ◆ Satisfactory ◆ Needs Improvement ◆ Unsatisfactory	
6	◆ Superior ◆ Well Above Standard ◆ Above Standard ◆ At Standard ◆ Below Standard ◆ Unsatisfactory	◆ Outstanding ◆ Above Expectations ◆ Meets Expectations ◆ Needs Improvement ◆ Below Expectations ◆ Unsatisfactory	◆ Exemplary ◆ Highly Effective ◆ Effective ◆ Borderline ◆ Ineffective ◆ Highly Ineffective	

Figure 5.5

Sample Definitions for a Four-point Rating Scale

Rating Term	Definition
Performance Exceeds Expectations	The performance of the teacher exceeds required responsibilities, consistently producing exemplary work that optimizes student achievement and behavior.
Performance Meets Expectations	The performance of the teacher consistently fulfills responsibilities, resulting in quality work that impacts student achievement or behavior in a positive manner. *This rating is a high performance criteria and is expected of all teachers.*
Performance Needs Improvement	The teacher inconsistently meets responsibilities, resulting in less than quality work performance and poor student results or behavior.
Performance Is Unsatisfactory	The teacher does not adequately fulfill responsibilities, resulting in inferior work performance and negatively impacting student achievement or behavior.

While there may be legitimate reasons to consider these low or high ranges in rating levels, we recommend designing the teacher evaluation system with a three- or four-point scale. If professional growth and continuous improvement are key considerations, a three- or four-point system is particularly useful because it offers the opportunity to differentiate performance adequately and, at the same time, to explain and justify performance ratings more effectively.

Figure 5.5 provides an example of how a four-point rating scale might be designed and defined. While these definitions do not provide definitive criteria against which performance can be benchmarked, they do generally clarify what is meant by "exceeding performance expectations," "meeting performance expectations," etc.

Using Rating Scales

It is important to consider carefully how a rating scale will be designed and used if it is to add value to a performance evaluation system. A few questions to consider, with some suggested responses, to enhance the utility and feasibility in the design and use of rating scales appear below.

♦ *What scaling terms should be used? How many levels?*

Suggestion: We typically recommend a three- to four-level scaling hierarchy that is criterion-referenced. However, the actual scaling levels, terminology, definitions, etc., should reflect the preferences of the professionals using the system (i.e., evaluators and evaluatees).

♦ *Should a composite rating be given? How will it be determined (i.e., averaging of ratings)?*

Suggestion: An overall judgment about teacher performance may be necessary to make personnel decisions, but a composite rating, as such, has little utility for professional growth and improvement. A composite rating masks specific strengths and weaknesses identified by a quality evaluation process and undermines the intended purpose of professional development.

♦ *Should highest and lowest ratings require written comments or examples?*

Suggestion: Yes. Descriptions of evidence supporting a rating, along with narrative feedback, will add significant value to any rating system. In fact, merely providing a rating of performance without insightful

Figure 5.6

Sample Teacher Evaluation Rating Scale

Teacher Name _____   *Evaluator* _____

School _____   *School Year* _____

Evaluation Code

    E—Performance Exceeds Standard   N—Performance Needs Assistance

    M—Performance Meets Standard   U—Performance is Unsatisfactory

Narrative must be provided for each standard assessed E, N, or U.

Domain: Instruction

I-1 The teacher demonstrates current and accurate knowledge of | E | M | N | U |

      subject matter covered in the curriculum.

_____

_____

_____

_____

_____

Domain: Assessment

A-1 The teacher uses a variety of appropriate assessments to measure | E | **M** | N | U |

      student achievement.

_____

_____

_____

_____

Note: The rating scale is applied at the performance standard level and not to performance indicators.

feedback does little to help teachers grow professionally.

Using the two performance standards we introduced in Chapter 4, Figure 5.6 illustrates how a four-point rating scale might be applied to teacher evaluation. We have based many of the evaluation tools provided in Part III, including summative evaluation forms, primarily on a four-point rating system.

What Is a Performance Appraisal Rubric and How Is It Used?

Defining the terms included in a rating scale is a useful beginning to making the rating of performance more uniform. However, the definitions alone are not enough to facilitate consistency in use. A rating scale, even with reasonably clear definitions of terms, is not adequate to provide guidance to evaluators or evaluatees regarding what a performance rating really means in practical terms. Also, simply using a rating scale—with or without definitions of terms—opens the door for free ranging, undocumented, subjective, and idiosyncratic use of evaluator judgment.

One solution to this problem is the use of a performance appraisal rubric, or as it is often referred to in evaluation literature, a behavioral summary scale. A behavioral summary scale:

> . . . takes the approach that it is better to anchor performance rating scales with more general or abstract benchmarks rather than very specific behaviors. To develop these general statements, the highly specific incidents representing a given level of performance on a particular category can be examined for the underlying thread of common behavioral components.[12]

Typically, a *Performance Appraisal Rubric (PAR)* guides evaluators in assessing how well a teacher's work is performed in relation to a given performance standard. The PAR is provided to increase reliability and, thereby, fairness among evaluators. An example of a PAR is presented in Figure 5.7 for classroom teachers and in Figure 5.8 for resource/specialty area teachers.

As illustrated above, the *Performance Appraisal Rubric* provides a scoring rubric for judging performance quality (i.e., rating *how well* the teacher is performing). The use of the PAR is included in the overall rating process as follows:

Step 1: The appropriate set of performance standards for use in the teacher evaluation system is determined *a priori.*

Step 2: The evaluator reviews documentation collected throughout the evaluation cycle to rate work performance. Data collection and feedback regarding performance occur at specified points in the evaluation cycle to monitor the process and to keep teachers informed regarding progress in meeting their performance standards.

Step 3: The accumulated performance data are measured against the PAR to determine the most appropriate rating for a given performance standard.

It is important to understand that in using general—more abstract—criteria like those presented in a PAR, documented performance for a given teacher performance standard typically will not fall neatly into one of the scoring options (meets expectations, exceeds expectations, etc.). The fact is that even the best teachers can have an off day; thus, there could be bits of evidence that the teacher's performance does not measure up. Therefore, it is important to base a performance rating—even when using a PAR—on the *preponderance of evidence.* A second important point to make in the use of a PAR is that it will not eliminate the application of judgment regarding how well a teacher performs her or his job; rather, a PAR is designed to *guide* the application of judgment. Selected sets of complete *Performance Appraisal Rubrics* for both classroom teachers and specialty position teachers are included in Part III of the *Handbook.*

Figure 5.7

Performance Appraisal Rubric for Instruction Domain for Classroom Teachers

Exceeds Expectations	Meets Expectations	Needs Improvement	Unsatisfactory
The teacher seeks and exhibits high level of knowledge of the subject(s) taught and continually updates curriculum materials.	**I-1: The teacher demonstrates current and accurate knowledge of subject matter covered in the curriculum.**	The teacher lacks comprehensive knowledge of the subject(s) taught or does not stay updated with changes in the subject area.	The teacher lacks knowledge of the subject area and does not stay current or follow the curriculum.
The teacher capitalizes on student interests and needs to achieve the desired student performance on the current district curriculum.	**I-2: The teacher plans instruction to achieve desired student learning objectives that reflect the current district curriculum.**	The teacher inconsistently plans instruction to support student success on the current district curriculum.	The teacher fails to plan instruction that reflects the current curriculum.
The teacher demonstrates awareness, sensitivity, and knowledge in responding to different student needs (e.g., instructional, developmental, and physical).	**I-3: The teacher recognizes and plans for individual learning differences and differentiates instruction to meet student needs.**	The teacher inconsistently makes accommodations for student needs.	The teacher does not differentiate instruction and/or does not make appropriate accommodations for students.
The teacher identifies, modifies, and creates instructional materials that support student learning and the district curriculum.	**I-4: The teacher uses materials, technology, and resources compatible with students' needs and abilities that support the current district curriculum.**	The teacher minimally integrates technology and/or inconsistently selects appropriate materials and resources to support student learning.	The teacher does not differentiate materials, technology, and resources to support students' accessing and succeeding in learning the district curriculum.
The teacher actively involves the students in making connections with prior knowledge, experiences, and other subject areas.	**I-5: The teacher links present content/skills with past and future learning experiences, other subject areas, and real world experiences/applications.**	The teacher makes superficial connections to prior student knowledge and experiences.	The teacher instructs students on the subject(s) taught in isolation of other experiences, subjects, and knowledge.
The teacher facilitates student learning through effective use of questioning, organization, performance expectations, and instructional strategies.	**I-6: The teacher uses a variety of instructional strategies that promote student learning.**	The teacher lacks variety in the instructional approaches used.	The teacher rarely deviates from a single instructional strategy (e.g., lecture).

Figure 5.8

Performance Appraisal Rubric for Assessment for Resource and Specialty Area Teachers

Exceeds Expectations	Meets Expectations	Needs Improvement	Unsatisfactory
The resource/specialty teacher provides both statistical and anecdotal evidence of successful objective completion.	**A-1: The resource/specialty teacher assesses and documents attainment of program objective(s).**	The resource/specialty teacher maintains a record of program objective completion, but has weak or incomplete documentation.	The resource/specialty teacher does not complete necessary documentation of program objectives.
The resource/specialty teacher is adept at selecting, using, and interpreting data from instruments or records and serves as a resource to others to improve their skills.	**A-2: The resource/specialty teacher demonstrates proficiency in administering, scoring/evaluating, and interpreting data from instruments or records.**	The resource/specialty teacher knows when and where to seek assistance with instruments or data interpretation and accesses assistance when needed.	The resource/specialty teacher does not appropriately administer or accurately interpret data from instruments or records.
The resource/specialty teacher pre-assesses students, seeks additional information, and makes informed decisions regarding the intervention or evaluation of the intervention/program.	**A-3: The resource/specialty teacher uses assessment information for decision making.**	The resource/specialty teacher makes decisions based heavily on perception with little consideration of other assessment information.	The resource/specialty teacher's decision making does not show evidence of the use of assessment data.
The resource/specialty teacher is a reflective practitioner who continually improves the delivery of services through evaluating multiple sources of feedback and data.	**A-4: The resource/specialty teacher uses evaluation to improve the delivery of services.**	The resource/specialty teacher inconsistently uses evaluation information to improve the delivery of services.	The resource/specialty teacher does not use evaluation to improve performance.

Summary

Designing the criteria by which teacher performance is assessed creates a means to standardize how feedback will be given. When applying criteria to a teacher's performance, the evaluator is considering the job responsibilities and assigning a judgement of quality to the work completed. By addressing both what the teacher is supposed to do and the degree to which the standards were addressed, teachers and administrators can use the evaluation to improve performance. Establishing an evaluation system that contains components such as rating scales and performance appraisal rubrics *is not* a guarantee that teacher performance will improve. However, it is a powerful tool to document teachers' performance on specific standards. Evaluation can also serve as a means for educators to reflect upon the feedback given and set annual goals for the next evaluation cycle.

The process of measuring performance against the standards and performance criteria, as noted above, depends on extensive evidence of performance gathered systematically by the individuals involved in the process. This key step of documenting performance is discussed in the next chapter.

Chapter 5 References

[1] DiPaola, M. F., & Stronge, J. H. (2003). *Superintendent evaluation handbook.* Lanham, MD: The Scarecrow Press.

[2] Stronge, J. H. (1997). Improving schools through teacher evaluation. In J. H. Stronge (Ed.), *Evaluating teaching: A guide to current thinking and best practice* (pp. 1–23). Thousand Oaks, CA: Corwin Press.

[3] Castetter, W. B. (1981). *The personnel function in educational administration* (3rd ed.). New York: Macmillan, p. 239.

[4] Stronge, 1997.

[5] Stufflebeam, D. L. (1983). The CIPP model for program evaluation. In G. Madaus, M. S. Scriven, & D. L. Stufflebeam (Eds.), *Evaluation models: Viewpoints on educational and human services in evaluation* (pp. 117–141). Boston, MA: Kluwer-Nijhoff, p. 117.

[6] Adapted from Stronge, J. H. (2002). *Qualities of effective teachers.* Alexandria, VA: Association for Supervision and Curriculum Development.

[7] McGreal, T. I. (1990). The use of rating scales in teacher evaluation: Concerns and recommendations. *Journal of Personnel Evaluation in Education, 4,* 41–58.

[8] Virginia Department of Education. (2000). Virginia school laws. Charlottesville, VA: Michie, p. 208. (VA Code §22.1-307).

[9] California Education Code §44932(a)(4).

[10] Informal survey based on a convenience sample of school district teacher evaluation rating scales.

[11] Stronge, J. H., & Helm, V. M. (1991). *Evaluating professional support personnel in education.* Newbury Park, CA: Sage.

[12] McGreal, 1990, p. 48.

6

Documenting Teacher Performance

Figure 6.1

Goals and Roles Evaluation Model: Documenting Performance

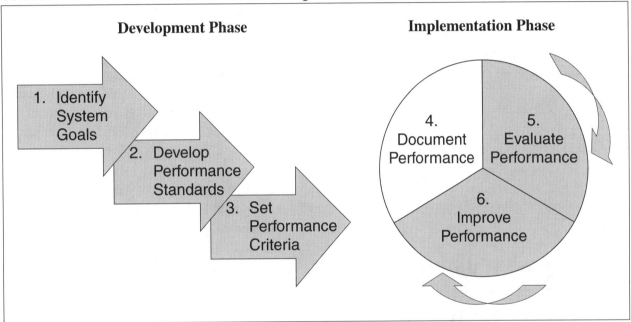

Figure 6.1 used with permission of James H. Stronge

Teacher evaluation in education historically has relied heavily—and often solely—on direct observation. Traditionally, evaluation of teachers consisted primarily of a supervisor (principal or department head) dropping in on a teacher's class once a year and writing a few words about the teacher's enthusiasm or organization. The written "evaluation" was then filed and probably never read or used again unless there were performance problems leading to termination activity.

Later, the clinical supervision model came to dominate teacher evaluation. In this system, a supervisor trained in the model met with the teacher in a pre-observation conference before observing, and then conducted a post-observation conference, in which the supervisor highlighted the teacher's strengths and weaknesses. Yet the sole basis for performance evaluation was still the supervisor's observation. In fact, under this system, being observed was synonymous with being evaluated. More recently still, evaluation has shifted its focus towards specific, research-based teaching behaviors. But how are these behaviors documented?

If we are to offer a fuller, more comprehensive picture of teacher performance, we must consider the use of multiple data sources in documenting performance. This chapter addresses the ways and means of using multiple data sources in teacher evaluation. The place of documenting performance within the overall framework of the *Goals and Roles Evaluation Model* is illustrated in Figure 6.1. Specifically, we concern ourselves with the following fundamental questions:

♦ So what is wrong with observation-only teacher evaluation systems?

♦ From whom should teacher performance data be collected?

♦ What data sources should be used in teacher evaluation?

♦ What are the benefits of using multiple data sources in teacher evaluation?

♦ What guidelines should be followed in developing and using multiple data sources in teacher evaluation?

So What Is Wrong with Observation-only Teacher Evaluation Systems?

As noted earlier, one of the most common methods for evaluating classroom teachers, in recent decades, has been a clinical supervision model consisting of a pre-conference, observation, and post-conference. In a study conducted by the Educational Research Service,[1] 99.8% of American public school administrators used direct classroom observation as the primary data collection technique. However, primary reliance on formal observations in evaluation poses significant problems (e.g., artificiality, small sample of performance) for teacher evaluation.[2]

A teacher evaluation system that relies primarily on formal observation is not well balanced: "it just isn't possible to get a full, fair, or even accurate picture of a teacher's performance merely with classroom visits—even with visits more frequent than two or three times a year."[3] Classroom observation as the sole basis for performance evaluation has limited utility and can even be questioned as a valid and reliable means of evaluating teachers, especially for those whose assignments are not totally based in classroom instruction and related tasks. In support of this contention that observation-only evaluations are flawed, Figure 6.2 identifies key concerns and is followed by an elaboration of these key points.

♦ *Limited performance evidence.* Classroom observation visits, even three to four visits per year for a full hour each, typically represent less that one-half of one percent of actual teaching performance. For example, if teachers work 180 days for six hours a day, they will have worked 1,080 hours in a year; yet the evaluation is based on four one-hour observations, just 0.37% of the time taught! For administrators who observe once a year, the evaluation would be based on 60 minutes out of the 64,800 minutes the teacher taught. Thus, observation-only systems offer only a limited glimpse of teacher performance. Such limited measures of performance tend to be unreliable because they reflect such a small sample size.

♦ *Artificial nature of observation.* When special lessons are prepared for a planned classroom observation visit, they may not necessarily reflect typical classroom teaching. Thus, formal classroom observation can be an artificial view of what really occurs in the classroom on a day-to-day basis.

♦ *Classroom responsibilities only.* Teachers are responsible for far more than direct classroom instruction. For instance, they are

Figure 6.2

Limitations of Observation-only Teacher Evaluation Systems

> *Observation only . . .*
> - *offers limited evidence about teacher work.*
> - *can provide an artificial view of teacher effectiveness.*
> - *assesses classroom, but not other, responsibilities.*
> - *focuses on teaching processes, but not products.*
> - *is an inspection approach to evaluation.*

expected to use student assessment more comprehensively than ever before, to carry out effective communications with parents and others, and to reflect multiple aspects of professionalism. The complexity of professional roles in today's schools requires a performance evaluation that reflects that complexity.

- *Process, not product.* Observation tends to measure specific teaching processes well (e.g., instructional skills such as questioning skills, classroom management). By the same token, however, it does not reflect teaching results (e.g., student products, student achievement). If both process and product evaluations are desired, then observation-only misses the mark.

- *Inspection approach to evaluation.* While observation does provide insight into many important aspects of teaching, it is, nonetheless, an inspection model in which the evaluator

passes judgment on the teaching performance. This inspection emphasis tends to de-emphasize the professionalism of teachers.

From Whom Should Teacher Performance Data Be Collected?

There are a variety of sources from which to collect evaluative input about a teacher's performance. Figure 6.3 depicts several individuals and groups that may be able to contribute meaningful insights into the teacher's performance. This "360 degree" data collection process (i.e., involving everyone who surrounds the employee, from client to supervisor) is used widely in the business world. It frequently is used for faculty in higher education and for principals and superintendents at the K-12 level. Following is a brief discussion of the nature of data to be collected from each of the various constituencies.

Figure 6.3

Providing Input into Teacher Performance

Individual Providing Input	Type of Information Typically Provided		
	Classroom or Other Observation	Portfolio or Other Artifacts	Client Surveys
Teacher: Self Evaluation		•	
Peers and Other Colleagues	•		
Students and Parents			•
Supervisor	•	•	

Teacher Self-evaluation

Self-evaluation historically has had little to commend it, especially for accountability or institutional decision-making purposes. The literature contains contradictory findings about the accuracy of self-evaluations and the consistency of self-evaluations with those of the employee's supervisor. Numerous sources, however, have begun to recognize the potential of self-evaluation for two purposes:

♦ for professional development, and
♦ as one component of the total evaluation portrait in a multi-faceted data collection system.[4]

Peers and Other Colleagues

Another valuable source for feedback regarding a teacher's performance can be other teachers, curriculum specialists, and other professionals with expertise in the teacher's field. For example, having a science curriculum specialist assist with observations and data collection related to science teaching can lend a valuable dimension to understanding the content work of the teacher. A key issue to consider with peer and specialist review is whether the information collected will be used for formative purposes (improvement-oriented), summative purposes (outcome-oriented), or both. This decision regarding the purpose(s) of peer/specialist feedback should be decided in advance of any data collection and then should be clearly communicated to everyone involved in the evaluation process.

Students and Parents

While evaluation by students is common in higher education, it is relatively infrequent in elementary and secondary schools. However, carefully constructed survey instruments—focusing not on personality but on specific job behaviors important to successful teacher performance—can elicit input from an important constituency.

Depending on the philosophy of the school district and the intended use of the data, it may be appropriate to solicit feedback from parents or from community individuals. As with students, however, it is vital to focus on specific performance responsibilities that parents are in a position to know. For example, parents likely can respond to a question such as "Does the teacher communicate with me about my student's performance?" but are probably far less able to answer a question such as "What is the classroom environment like?"

Supervisor

Finally, of course, the principal or other supervisor should have direct input in teacher data collection through classroom observations and other appropriate means. But unlike most teacher evaluation systems, where the observation is synonymous with evaluation, we recommend that principals base their evaluation on an analysis of the total evaluation portrait. This comprehensive performance portrait can consist of input from peers, students, perhaps parents and/or other individuals external to the school, and from the teacher's self-evaluation, which includes the portfolio of job artifacts gathered during the evaluation cycle. If the total data collection process has been well designed, there should be ample data of considerable breadth and depth as a basis upon which to make a well-founded, fair, and objective evaluation.

What Data Sources Should Be Used in Teacher Evaluation?

Although teacher evaluation traditionally has relied heavily—almost exclusively—on formal classroom observation for documentation,[5] a quality teacher evaluation system cannot simply depend upon observation alone. Rather, an evaluation system that builds upon multiple sources of performance evidence provides multiple ways of knowing *what* work assignments a teacher engages in and *how well* she or he achieves those assignments. As noted in earlier publications,[6] key types of recommended data sources include those described in Figure 6.4.

Observation

Direct classroom observation can be a useful way to collect information on teacher performance; as a stand-alone data collection process, however, it has major limitations. If the purpose of a teacher evaluation system is to provide a comprehensive picture of performance in order to guide professional growth, then classroom observations should be only one piece of the information collected.[7] Furthermore, observations themselves can take on a variety of forms and can be conducted in a variety of settings—ranging from quick, drop-by classroom visits to formal, pre-planned observational reviews. This range of performance observation possibilities might generally be classified as *systematic* (i.e., formal) or *incidental* (i.e., informal).

Systematic observation. In *systematic observation*, the supervisor conducts a semi-structured, planned observation—either announced or unannounced—of a teacher who is presenting a lesson to students or a program to staff or some other client group. Evaluators can use formal observations as one source of information to determine whether a teacher is meeting expectations for performance standards. Typically, the evaluator provides feedback about the observation during a review conference with the teacher.

Incidental observation. *Incidental observation* is less direct and structured than systematic observation. Informal observations are intended to provide more frequent information on a wider variety of contributions made by teachers in the classroom or to the school community as a whole.

This type of informal observation might include making walk-through classroom visits, observing instruction for a short duration (say, 10–15 minutes), and observing work in non-classroom settings at various times throughout the school year.[8] For example, an informal observation might include briefly visiting a classroom during a science lab experiment or observing a teacher participating in a faculty meeting or committee meeting. An important factor for evaluators to remember when collecting incidental observation data is to focus on specific, factual descriptions of performance. Also, it is important to obtain a representative sampling of performance observations.[9]

We provide multiple teacher observation forms in Part III of the *Handbook*. Specifically, we offer a variety of styles of forms, including both formal and informal, from which appropriate forms can be adapted for use in a particular school setting. Figure 6.5 shows part of a teacher performance review that can be maintained by an administrator to document specific examples of when a particular performance standard was observed. Figure 6.6 shows how the performance indicators can be used as commonly observable behaviors to assist evaluators in quickly recording performance standards observed.

Figure 6.4

Data Sources for Teachers

Data Type	Description
Observation	Formal classroom observation and informal ongoing anecdotal observation of performance
Teacher portfolios	Artifacts of performance, including performance logs, lesson plans, reflections on performance, etc.
Client surveys	Surveys of students, parents, peers, and others
Student performance data	Measures of student progress, including standardized test scores, classroom assessments, and student products

Figure 6.5
Teacher Performance Review

Domain: Learning Environment		
L-1 The teacher communicates and maintains clear expectations about behavior, classroom procedures, and academic achievement.		_Evidence of Standard_
Date	_Comments_	

Teacher Portfolios

Another important source for obtaining documentation of a teacher's performance is analysis of artifacts (i.e., the collection of written records and documents produced by the teacher as a part of his or her job responsibilities). Artifacts for a special education teacher, for example, might include copies of IEPs developed (with identifying information removed), lesson plans related to those IEPs, syllabi developed or adapted for a given class, and representative samples of student work. Additional artifacts that are likely to be available and meaningful as part of a data collection process that is intended to accurately reflect the teacher's job performance could include the following:

♦ lesson plans,

♦ instructional materials,

♦ student assessments,

♦ forms developed and/or used for record keeping,

♦ significant correspondence and memos,

♦ schedules, logs, or calendars of activities, and

♦ evidence of professional development.

Organizing teacher portfolios. A portfolio represents a formalized process for organizing and reviewing artifacts. [10] A useful description of a teaching portfolio for the purposes of evaluation

Figure 6.6
Formal Observation Record

Domain: Communication/Community Relations
C-1: The teacher communicates effectively with students and models standard English.
• uses standard English grammar when communicating with students
• uses precise language, acceptable oral expression, and written communication
• explains concepts and lesson content to students in a logical and sequential appropriate manner
• gives clear and appropriate directions
• models various effective communication strategies for conveying ideas and information for a variety of learning styles
• emphasizes major points of concern by using techniques e.g., repetition and verbal or non-verbal cues
• actively listens and responds constructively
Comments _____

Figure 6.7

Teacher Portfolio Organization

Organizing the Teacher Portfolio Based on Performance Domains

Instruction

Assessment

Learning Environment

Communications and Community Relations

Professionalism

is that a portfolio is a collection of materials by and about a teacher that is limited in scope, yet whose specific contents remain the choice of the teacher.[11] For use in teacher evaluation, a well organized, formal portfolio can be more revealing, thoughtful, and reflective than the mere collection of various artifacts.[12]

Using a teacher's established performance standards is a simple and logical way to organize teacher portfolios. For example, referring to the five domains of teaching identified in Chapter 4 and listed in Figure 6.7, a teacher's portfolio would be organized into distinct sections, one section for each domain. Then the specific teacher performance standards that comprise each of these five domains would constitute subsets for the organization of the portfolio. An individual teacher who is assembling her or his portfolio would select artifacts that document each of the performance standards for which she or he is accountable.[13]

Contents for teacher portfolios. Since teacher portfolios can be organized around the teacher performance standards for which a teacher is held accountable, it makes sense to select artifacts carefully with the standards in mind. Figure 6.8[14] includes four examples of teacher performance standards and how selected artifacts could be used to document those standards.

Portfolio data can and should be collected by the teacher. Thus, the portfolio collection and review process becomes a type of structured self-assessment, especially when reflection *about* performance, written by the teacher, is included in the portfolio. A good way to emphasize self-

reflection in portfolios is by including a brief narrative written by the teacher, highlighting major accomplishments and areas for continued growth.[15]

It is important to recognize that the materials and information contributed by the teacher to the performance portfolio do not necessarily entail significant additional record-keeping. Rather, the use of materials and records that naturally come from teaching should be emphasized. If a portfolio becomes merely a paper chase, it invariably misses the marks of professional growth and improved performance evaluations.[16]

Client Surveys

In recent years there has been a growing movement for teachers and other educators to adopt 360-degree assessment principles that are often used in business and industry.[17] A 360-degree evaluation focuses on soliciting feedback from students, parents, and other members of the school community regarding the work of the teacher.[18] The use of client surveys provides an opportunity to consider perceptions of these key stakeholders on the classroom learning experience. It should be noted that while we offer support for the use of client surveys—including student and parent surveys—even in their best form, client surveys should be viewed as only one source in a multi-data collection system of assessment. In the following section, we highlight the use of student and parent surveys.

Students. Student feedback can be a viable source of information that enhances our understanding of

Figure 6.8

The Interrelationship Between Teacher Job Standards and Portfolio Artifacts

Sample Teacher Responsibility	↔	Sample Artifacts
The teacher demonstrates current and accurate knowledge of subject matter covered in the curriculum.	↔	◆ Course syllabus ◆ Unit lesson plans ◆ Annotated bibliography of related journal articles
The teacher provides a variety of ongoing and culminating assessments to measure student performance.	↔	◆ Teacher-made tests or quizzes ◆ Explanation of grading procedures ◆ Sample of grade recording system
The teacher communicates clear expectations about behavior to students and parents.	↔	◆ Explanation of classroom management procedures ◆ Teacher-student communications
The teacher participates in an ongoing process of professional development.	↔	◆ List of in-service activities ◆ Example of a product created from a professional development activity

teaching and learning and, thus, can serve as a valuable addition to the teacher evaluation picture. One of the arguments for involving students in providing evaluation feedback is that they are the primary consumers of the teacher's services.[19] One writer noted that " . . . no other individual or group has [the] breadth, depth, or length of experience with the teacher . . . [and] . . . teachers look to their students rather than to outside sources for indications of their teaching performance."[20]

As direct participants in the teaching-learning process, students are the major clients of teachers, and they are in the key position to provide information about teacher effectiveness. Most importantly, students are the only group among teachers who have direct knowledge about classroom practices on a regular basis. Figure 6.9 provides a sample from a student survey, and Part III of the *Handbook* includes three separate student surveys that can be adapted for use.

Parents. As with students, parents can provide useful information about teacher performance. If parent surveys are to be used, however, it is critical that the surveys be designed to ask parents *only* information they are in a position to know. For

example, do not ask them about what occurs in the classroom because their feedback can only be second-hand—based on information they receive from their child. If information about the classroom is desired, ask students—not their parents. Instead, ask parents about what they are in a position to know, such as homework assignments and teacher communication to the home. Figure 6.10 illustrates how a parent survey might be designed. Additionally, Part III of the *Handbook* includes a parent survey that can be adapted as needed.

A caution about using client surveys. While 360-degree feedback can be an insightful practice for use in teacher improvement and evaluation, there are several pitfalls that must be avoided. To begin, while client surveys can provide an important perspective on the teacher's performance, they should be used as only one component in the evaluation system. Also, evaluators should recognize that inviting students, parents, or peers to provide feedback regarding teacher performance provides merely that—feedback.[21] It is not synonymous with a final, summative evaluation.

Another concern relates to *how* the results will be used. In colleges and universities, it is

Figure 6.9

Sample Items from Student Survey (Grades 4–5)

	Yes	*Sometimes*	*No*
EXAMPLE: I like listening to music.			
1. My teacher listens to me.			
2. My teacher gives me help when I need it.			
3. My teacher shows us how to do new things.			
4. I know what I am supposed to do in class.			
5. I am able to do the work in class.			
6. I learn new things in my class.			

Used with permission: Eye On Education

common practice to use student surveys as a direct measure of teaching effectiveness. This is a type of high-stakes evaluation environment in which merit pay, tenure, and promotion are partially based on the survey results. In preK-12 school settings, this high-stakes approach to client surveys is highly unusual. A more common approach is to require the use of surveys, but to have the results made available only to the teacher. A "for your eyes only" approach:

♦ makes the client surveys strictly formative in nature,

♦ allows for their use to inform the teacher directly about relative strengths and weaknesses, but

♦ does not incorporate the surveys into the summative evaluation decision-making process, as the administrator does not view them.

While a potentially useful source of information is lost to summative decision making in a "for your eyes only" approach, advantages that are gained include decreased cost to administer, less threat to teachers, and a far higher acceptance of the use of client surveys.

Figure 6.10

Sample Items from Parent Survey

The teacher generally:	*Check One*	*Comments*
1. makes me feel comfortable in contacting her/him.	☐ Yes ☐ Sometimes ☐ No ☐ NA	
2. communicates in an understandable way.	☐ Yes ☐ Sometimes ☐ No ☐ NA	

Used with permission: Eye on Education

Student Achievement and Measures of Student Progress

Given the central role that teachers and other educational professionals have always played in successful schools, connecting teacher performance and student performance is a logical extension of the educational reform agenda.[22] "The purpose of teaching is learning, and the purpose of schooling is to ensure that each new generation of students accumulates the knowledge and skills needed to meet the social, political, and economic demands of adulthood."[23]

For many teachers, direct measures of student performance can be directly documented. A value-added—or gain score—approach can be used that documents their influence on student learning. Simply put, a value-added teacher assessment system can be summarized as:

Student Learning End Score

$$\frac{-\ Student\ Learning\ Beginning\ Score}{Student\ Gain\ Score}$$

Whenever student success is linked to teacher success, regardless of the measures of student performance that might be assessed, it is essential to ascertain a direct link between the teacher's performance and students' performance.[24] It is not sufficient merely to identify how a teacher might indirectly influence a student's achievement on a given performance measure. To illustrate this important issue, consider the following:

while graduation rates and SAT scores most certainly are linked to school factors, connecting these measures to any one employee, in almost all cases, simply is not possible. If employee success is to be meaningfully linked to student success, then it is imperative that a causal link be clearly established.[25]

The following list summarizes ten key considerations for incorporating student achievement or other measures of student performance in a teacher evaluation system.[26]

---

1. *Use student learning as only one component of a teacher assessment system that is based on multiple data sources.*

Measures of student learning are vitally important to judging the effectiveness of teachers and schools, but they should never take the place of professional judgment. The use of test results in teacher evaluation can be viewed as a complement to traditional supervision based on classroom observations and other pertinent data sources that capture the complexity of the teacher's role.

2. *When judging teacher effectiveness, consider the context in which teaching and learning occur.*

There are circumstances when teachers have done everything possible at the classroom level to enhance instruction, but teaching conditions, such as the lack of materials or student turnover, prevent maximum benefit by children. Consideration should always be given for the wide array of variables beyond the control of individual teachers.

3. *Use measures of student growth versus a fixed achievement standard or goal.*

A growth orientation requires the use of pre- and post-testing to determine progress versus the attainment of predetermined pass rates or proficiency levels based on a single sample of performance. True measures of learning should focus on growth in knowledge and skills, not on student aptitude.

4. *Compare learning gains from one point in time to another for the same students, not different groups of students.*

Implicit in the concept of gain scores is the assumption that similar tests will be used to measure student learning across time on an individual basis. When multiple measures of student learning are aggregated across the same class of students, we believe a reasonably fair measure of teacher effects is generated.

5. *Recognize that gain scores have pitfalls that must be avoided.*

Even when measures of student growth are used, it is important to interpret gain scores properly. In particular, a statistical artifact known as the regression effect needs to be considered. It results in a tendency for students starting with low performance levels to show larger gains than warranted and students with higher performance to show lower gains. Both groups move toward the mean or average performance. Additionally, a ceiling effect on the test will interfere with students who start with high scores, as the ceiling makes it difficult to show continued high gain scores as students "top out."

6. *Use a timeframe for teacher assessment that allows patterns of student learning to be documented.*

If teachers are to be held accountable for student learning, then it is critical that patterns of student learning over time be established. Single measures of learning only provide a snapshot of performance on a given day; multiple measures over the course of a year are necessary to provide information for establishing a reliable growth pattern.

7. *Use fair and valid measures of student learning.*

Reliability, validity, freedom from bias, and fairness are obvious concerns and conditions for connecting student assessment to teacher evaluation. These criteria for test selection are essential conditions for a proper testing program and become doubly important when they may have implications for personnel decisions.

8. *Select student assessment measures that are most closely aligned with existing curriculum.*

Standardized tests should be selected based on their general or predominant alignment with the articulated curriculum. The more closely aligned the assessment measures are with the curriculum, the more accurate they are as a gauge of student learning.

9. *Do not narrow the curriculum and limit teaching to fit a test unless the test actually measures what should be taught.*

Another unintended but predictable consequence of selecting standardized tests that are not aligned with the curriculum is the distortion of the curriculum to meet the demands of the test. Curriculum and instruction should drive assessment, not the reverse.

10. *Use measures of student learning to improve teaching, learning, and whole schools.*

Measures of student learning can provide valuable feedback on the learning of individual students, the teaching of specific subjects, and the effectiveness of instructional strategies and programs. They should be used in a constructive manner to help everyone in schools to improve and grow.

A number of school systems and states have begun the process of linking student learning to the evaluation of teachers. Methodologies vary widely from statistically complex and highly systematic[27] to approaches individually tailored to the teacher or school.[28] We have included in Part III of the *Handbook* a sample form for documenting student academic and performance growth that can be used district-wide or on a teacher-by-teacher basis.

What Are the Benefits of Using Multiple Data Sources in Teacher Evaluation?

Given the multi-faceted nature of teachers' positions, it seems almost transparently obvious that their performance should be documented with multi-faceted data. Additionally, there are numerous advantages to collecting performance evaluation data from a variety of sources. Some of these advantages include the following:[29]

Increased validity. Validity (i.e. appropriateness) is increased almost by definition when we increase the components of performance being evaluated. The information used in making decisions about personnel should be a valid measure of actual job performance and, thus, should include information on all major dimensions of the teacher's job. Using a variety of indicators of performance provides more accurate information than collecting a single example of performance possibly could.[30]

Increased reliability. Reliability (i.e., consistency) typically increases with an increase in sampling size. Therefore, evaluations based on multi-faceted data collection will dramatically improve the reliability of the evaluation compared with one-shot formal observations because of the increased sampling of performance from multiple perspectives. Additionally, we increase the likelihood that performance strengths and weaknesses can be cited and corroborated by several sources of data.

Decreased subjectivity. When the evaluator bases the performance evaluation not solely on one or more direct observations but on the entire performance portrait obtained by analyzing input from the teacher, the teacher's students, peers, and others with whom the teacher works, the threat of subjectivity is lessened. Calling on multiple sources of data provides a more solid foundation upon which to base objective evaluative judgments.

Increased comfort level of both evaluator and teacher. By removing the sole burden on the evaluator, both parties find some reassurance in the fact that the final evaluation is based on input from numerous other individuals and sources.

Expanded performance portrait. By including input from multiple observations, portfolios, client surveys, measures of student progress, and other pertinent information sources, a more realistic picture of performance can be painted. By incorporating assessment of both in-class and out-of-class activities, the use of multiple data sources provides important input that is omitted in evaluation that relies primarily on teaching observations.

Additional benefits of using multiple data sources in the teacher evaluation process include opportunities:

♦ to document performance that is more closely related to actual work,

♦ to collect data in more naturally occurring situations, and

♦ to integrate primary and secondary data sources in the evaluation.

All in all, the extra trouble that comes from collecting and using multiple sources of teacher performance data is easily offset by the expanded value in the teacher evaluation process and results.

What Guidelines Should Be Followed in Developing and Using Multiple Data Sources in Teacher Evaluation?[31]

The following guidelines can be useful in planning and implementing a teacher evaluation system that incorporates multiple data sources.

♦ *Communication is important.* Grant Wiggins,[32] in writing about the use of portfolio assessment with students, made a point that is germane to our discussion of the use of multiple data sources with teachers: Procedures must be developed through a collaborative, public forum in which the audience and client are involved. Throughout the evaluation process, including the development of procedures for use of multiple data sources, teachers have every right to be involved in and to know as much about the evaluation system as possible.

♦ *Relate individual performance to school goals.* Designing an evaluation system that relies on authentic data must begin by matching goals of the school organization with the interests of students, teachers, administrators, parents, and the larger community. In order to have compatibility between the teacher and the organization, procedures must identify individual strengths and reflect society's intellectual values. "Determining the needs of the organization is a prerequisite for all remaining steps if the evaluation process is to be relevant to the organization's mission and, ultimately, responsive to the public demands for accountability."[33]

♦ *The context of evaluation must be taken into account.* Understanding and accounting for the context of the evaluation is another critical factor in developing sound evaluation systems.[34] Authentic assessment as reflected in the use of multiple data sources involves frequent reviews and feedback about work; it is not a one-shot formal classroom observation, but ongoing, systematic data collection, formal and informal, over time.

♦ *The overall evaluation system should facilitate professional growth.* Teacher evaluation with an improvement orientation is intended to provide recognition for noteworthy performance, along with immediate and intermediate feedback for performance improvement and correction where needed. The use of multiple data sources contributes significantly to this overall effort in that it broadens the evaluator's and teacher's awareness of what has been accomplished and of where specific strengths and weaknesses in performance exist. This recognition, in turn, can lead to improvement strategies.

Summary

Direct observation as the sole basis for performance evaluation has limited utility and can even be questioned as a valid and reliable means of evaluating classroom teachers. We contend that multiple data sources are essential to a fair and valid teacher evaluation system. However, it is vital to remember that collecting feedback regarding teacher performance from a variety of people is not synonymous with evaluation; it is merely the collection of information upon which evaluation should be based.

We hope by now that we have convinced our readers of the value and validity of properly using multiple data sources in teacher evaluation. The complexity of professional roles in today's schools requires a performance evaluation that reflects that complexity.

Chapter 6 References

[1] Educational Research Service. (1988). *Teacher evaluation: Practices and procedures.* Arlington, VA: Author.

[2] Medley, D. M., Coker, H., & Soar, R. S. (1984). *Measurement-based evaluation of teacher performance.* New York: Longman.

[3] Tucker, P. D., Stronge, J. H., & Gareis, C. R. (2002). *Handbook on teacher portfolios for evaluation and professional development.* Larchmont, NY: Eye On Education, p. 56.

[4] See, for example, Airasian, P. W., & Gullickson, A. (1997). Teacher self-evaluation. In J. H. Stronge (Ed.). *Evaluating teaching: A guide to current thinking and best* practice (pp. 215–247). Thousand Oaks, CA: Corwin Press; Mohrman, J. M., Jr., Resnick-West, S. M., & Lawler, E. E., III. (1989). *Designing performance appraisal systems: Aligning appraisals and organizational realities.* San Francisco, CA: Jossey-Bass; Teel, K.S. (1980). Performance appraisal: Current trends, persistent progress. *Personnel Journal, 59*(4), 296–301; 316.

[5] Educational Research Service, 1988.

[6] See: Stronge, J. H. (1997). Improving schools through teacher evaluation. In J.H. Stronge (Ed.), *Evaluating teaching: A guide to current thinking and best practice* (pp. 1–23). Thousand Oaks, CA: Corwin Press; Stronge, J. H., & Helm, V. M. (1991). *Evaluating professional support personnel in education.* Newbury Park, CA: Sage.

[7] Stronge & Helm, 1991.

[8] Harrington-Lueker, D. (1996). Chuck the checklist. *Executive Educator, 18* (6), 21–24.

[9] Stronge & Helm, 1991, pp. 175–177.

[10] Wheeler, P. H. (1993). *Using portfolios to assess teacher performance* (EREAPA Publication Series No. 93-7). (ERIC Document Reproduction Service No. ED 364 967); Wolf, K., Lichtenstein, G., & Stevenson, C. (1997). Portfolios in teacher evaluation. In J. H. Stronge (Ed.), *Evaluating teaching: A guide to current thinking and best practice* (pp. 193–214). Thousand Oaks, CA: Corwin Press.

[11] Tucker, P. D., Stronge, J. H., & Gareis, C. R. (2002). *Handbook on teacher portfolios for evaluation and professional development.* Larchmont, NY: Eye On Education; Wolf, K. (1996). Developing an effective teaching portfolio. *Educational Leadership, 53*(6), 34–37.

[12] Gareis, C. R. (1999). Teacher portfolios: Do they enhance teacher evaluation? (located in CREATE News section). *Journal of Personnel Evaluation in Education, 13*, 96–99.

[13] Tucker, Stronge, & Gareis, 2002.

[14] Used with permission: Tucker, Stronge, & Gareis, 2002.

[15] Stronge, J. H. (in press). Evaluating educational specialists. In D. Nevo & D. Stufflebeam (Eds.), *The International Handbook of Educational Evaluation.* Boston, MA: Kluwer Academic Press.

[16] Tucker, Stronge, & Gareis, 2002.

[17] DiPaola, M. D., & Stronge, J. H. (2003). *The handbook on superintendent evaluation.* Lanham, MD: Scarecrow Press.

[18] Manatt, R. P. (2000). Feedback at 360 degrees. *The School Administrator Web Edition.* Available at http://www.aasa.org/publications/sa/2000_10/Manatt.htm.

[19] Stronge, J. H., & Ostrander, L. (1997). Client surveys in teacher evaluation. In J. H. Stronge (Ed.), *Evaluating teaching: A guide to current thinking and best practice* (pp. 129–161). Thousand Oaks, CA: Corwin Press.

[20] Follman, J. (1992). Secondary school students' ratings of teacher effectiveness. *The High School Journal, 75*, 168–178, p. 169.

[21] Stronge & Ostrander, 1997, p. 153.

[22] See, for example: Mendro, R. L. (1998). Student achievement and school and teacher accountability. *Journal of Personnel Evaluation in Education, 12*, 257–267.

[23] McConney, A. A., Schalock, M. D., & Schalock, H. D. (1997). Indicators of student learning in teacher evaluation. In J. H. Stronge (Ed.), *Evaluating teaching: A guide to current thinking and best practice* (pp. 162–192). Thousand Oaks, CA: Corwin Press, p. 162.

[24] Stronge, 2003.

[25] Stronge, 2003.

[26] Stronge, J. H., & Tucker, P. D. (2000). *Teacher evaluation and student achievement.* Washington, DC: National Education Association.

[27] See Stronge, J. H., & Tucker, P. D. (2000). *Teacher evaluation and student achievement.* Washington, DC: National Education Association.; Webster, W. J., & Mendro, R. L. (1997). The Dallas value-added accountability system. In J. Millman (Ed.), *Grading teachers, grading schools: Is student achievement a valid evaluation measure?* (pp. 81–99). Thousand Oaks, CA: Corwin Press; Wright, S. P., Horn, S. P., & Sanders, W. L. (1997). Teacher and classroom context effects on student achievement: Implications for teacher evaluation. *Journal of Personnel Evaluation in Education, 11*, 57–67.

[28] Tucker, P. D., & Stronge, J. H. (2001). Measure for measure: Using student results in teacher evaluation. *American School Board Journal, 88*(9), 34–37.

[29] Taken from Stronge & Helm, 1991.

[30] Valencia, S. (1990). A portfolio approach to classroom reading assessment: The whys, whats, and hows. *Reading Teacher, 43*(4), pp. 338–340.

[31] Taken from unpublished work by James H. Stronge and Virginia M. Helm.

[32] Wiggins, G. (1991). Standards, not standardization: Evolving quality student work. *Educational Leadership, 48*(4), 18–26.

[33] Stronge, J. H. (1995). Balancing individual and institutional goals in educational personnel evaluation: A conceptual framework. *Studies in educational evaluation, 21*(2), 131–151, p. 141.

[34] Stufflebeam, D. L. (1983). The CIPP model for program evaluation. In G. Madaus, M. S. Scriven, & D. L. Stufflebeam (Eds.) *Evaluation models: Viewpoints on educational and human services in evaluation* (pp. 117–141). Boston: Kluwer-Nijhoff.

7

Implementing a Teacher Performance Evaluation System

Figure 7.1

Goals and Roles Evaluation Model: Evaluating Performance

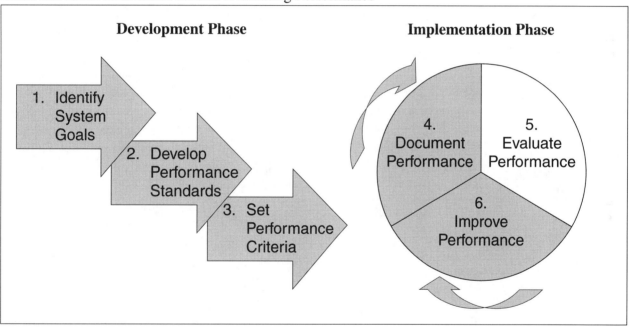

Used with permission from James H. Stronge

Chapters 1 through 6 have provided both background on teacher evaluation and the basic building blocks for the development of a quality evaluation system. In Chapters 1 through 3, we discussed the purposes of teacher evaluation, existing frameworks for understanding the work of teachers, and models of evaluation. In Chapters 4 through 6, we described specific performance standards, performance rubrics, and strategies for the documentation of teacher performance. Research demonstrates the importance of job-related criteria, clearly articulated expectations regarding the quality of perform-ance, and multiple sources of information to document performance in effective teacher evaluation systems. These elements are necessary but not sufficient to ensure effectiveness, however; the context of implementation is key to maximizing the potential of a technically sound evaluation system. Issues such as organizational commitment to teacher quality, evaluator training, and tangible support for teacher improvement are critical for transforming evaluation from a bureaucratic activity into a meaningful strategy for school improvement.

Implementation—the actual evaluation of job performance—is Step 5 in the *Goals and Roles Evaluation Model* and is addressed in the subsequent sections of this chapter. Given that every step builds on the previous ones, it is assumed that careful consideration has been given to the development of the evaluation system (Development Phase: Steps 1–3) and methods for documenting performance have been identified (Implementation Phase: Step 4). The place of evaluating performance within the overall context of the model is illustrated in Figure 7.1.

In this chapter, we will address the key implementation issues that are fundamental to the contextual realities that affect any new initiatives. Specifically, we will address the following questions related to teacher evaluation:

♦ What policy should guide the performance evaluation of the teacher?

♦ What procedures should be established?

♦ How do you help teachers improve performance?

♦ What training is required to implement the performance evaluation of teachers?

What Policy Should Guide the Performance Evaluation of the Teacher?

No matter how much autonomy teachers and administrators might enjoy, ultimately life in schools is determined by policy. Teachers and administrators are expected to implement the multiple layers of policy that affect every aspect of schools from student discipline to accreditation. "Policy" can be a slippery term used to refer to rules or guidelines from a central office. A useful definition for policy is "official action for a specified purpose or purposes that is deliberated and decided upon by individuals or groups vested with legitimate authority."[1] For schools, legitimate authority exists at the federal, state and local level. At the federal level, the most notable source of policy would be the U. S. Department of Education. At the state level, the state Department of Education (or Department of Public Instruction) and Board of Education are primary policymakers. At the local level, the Board of Education is responsible for setting policy.

Policy regarding teacher evaluation is set at both the state and local levels. Although there is usually a top-down flow of policy to the local level, sometimes local events or constituencies influence the development of state policy.[2] Approximately half of the states have enacted laws pertaining to teacher evaluation,[3] and while some states merely require the evaluation of school personnel, others have established statewide evaluation systems. In most states, the legislature mandates certain aspects of the process and leaves the specifics of teacher evaluation policy and practice to the local boards.[4]

As the definition above suggests, policy should define the specific purpose or purposes of an activity. Because policy is "deliberated and decided upon," it also reflects the beliefs and values of those who share in the development process about key elements of that process and the underlying ideas. Some of the central themes that have swirled through teacher evaluation policy during the last twenty years have been accountability, professional development, professionalism, and pay for performance.[5] Figure 7.2 offers an example of local school board policy for a small school system with no collective bargaining. The purposes of evaluation are clearly defined, as well as the manner in which it is to be conducted. The policy also suggests a collaborative approach to evaluation that informs

Figure 7.2
Sample Policy Statement 1

Williamsburg-James City County Public Schools, Virginia
Policies and Procedures Manual

Subject: Evaluation of Teachers
Purposes of the Evaluation System
The primary purposes of the Williamsburg-James City County Public Schools Teachers' Evaluation System are improvement and maintenance of quality professional performance, as well as promotion of the Williamsburg-James City County School Division's mission and goals. Evaluation is both a means and an end. As a means, it is a process of communication, personal support, feedback, adjustment, and growth for both the individual and the organization. As an end, it represents the basis for documenting evidence for the retention, improvement, promotion, and dismissal of personnel.[6]

the work of teachers as well as the school system. In contrast, the policy statement in Figure 7.3 comes from a large, urban school district with collective bargaining; yet there are many similarities between the two. The statement in Figure 7.3 also clearly defines the purposes of evaluation and identifies "good teaching" as an organizational priority. Both statements are general in nature, which is recommended in public policy, focusing on overall purposes without addressing the specifics of evaluation criteria and procedures. This approach provides the school system with direction but permits revisions and

adjustments as necessary so that procedures are flexible and responsive to shifting demands or new thinking about the purposes and processes of evaluation.

What Procedures Should Be Established?

Evaluation procedures should be straightforward and identify who will be evaluated, by whom, how often, and by what means. Most important, however, the procedures should provide credible and useful information to the teacher on

Figure 7.3
Sample Policy Statement 2

The School Board of Miami-Dade County, Florida
Permanent Personnel

Evaluation—Teacher
The Board recognizes that the teaching process is extremely complex and that the appraisal of this process is a difficult and technical function. But, because it is universally accepted that good teaching is the most important element in a sound educational program, teacher appraisal shall be accomplished.

Appraisal of teaching service should serve the following purposes: 1) Aid the individual teacher to grow professionally; 2) Raise the standards of the teaching profession as a whole; and 3) Raise the quality of instruction and educational services to the children of the community.[7]

Figure 7.4

Considerations for Evaluation Procedures

Tasks	Who	What	When
Meetings: Pre- and Post-Event	Principal	Observations	*Probationary*
Classroom Visits and Reports	Assistant Principal	Portfolios	*Teachers*
Review of Portfolios	Department Head	Student Learning	Planning
Administration and Review of Student Learning Measures: Pre- and Post-Assessments	Peer Coach	Measures	Interim
	Central Office	Annual Goals	Final
	Supervisor	Client Surveys	
Annual Goals: Drafting and Review	Teacher	Documentation:	
Administration and Review of Surveys		◆ Lesson plans	
		◆ Grades	
Review of Documentation		◆ Testing	
Review of Self-evaluation		◆ Parent Contacts	
Summative Evaluations		◆ Professional Development	
		Self-evaluation	

his/her practice, if evaluation is to improve teaching and educational quality.[8] In addition, it is essential that evaluation procedures are legally sound and hold up under careful scrutiny. This is especially important in the case of a recommendation for dismissal, ensuring that there has been sufficient documentation and due process to withstand legal review.[9]

Various aspects of Step 5, "Evaluate Performance," in the Goals and Roles Evaluation Model will be discussed in the following sections. Figure 7.4 summarizes the major components of most evaluation procedures. The possible combinations and variations are almost limitless and permit school systems to tailor procedures to their own purposes, resources, and legal mandates.

Who will be evaluated and by whom?

Almost all school systems require regular, formal evaluation of everyone who works within the school. The principal is the supervisor who typically conducts the evaluation of professional staff within the school building,[10] but it is important to establish clarity about who is responsible for writing the final evaluation report and who else might play a role in providing feedback to the professional and input in the summative decision-making process. School systems and individual schools vary in how supervisors are assigned roles in the evaluation process depending on the talents and preferences of the administrative staff. Common evaluation assignments include the following:

◆ The principal is responsible for all summative evaluations. Assistant principals, department heads, central office supervisors, and/or peer coaches may provide input based on observations or review of materials such as lesson plans, assessment data, annual goals, and individualized education plans, but final judgments about performance are made by the principal.

◆ The principal and the assistant principal(s) share responsibility for summative evaluations. Each administrator is assigned instructional staff to observe and evaluate for summative purposes. Assignments can be made based on experience in working with certain individuals, subject matter expertise, or other considerations.

♦ Central office supervisors may be responsible for the evaluation of specialized positions (e.g., Head Start teachers, gifted teachers) with input from the building administrators and colleagues who collaborate with the specialist. This arrangement is particularly common when the professionals serve more than one school or their position expectations are substantially different from those of other educators in the building.

While each of the above arrangements has merits, the key to successful practice is the participation of multiple supervisors in the assessment of performance. Researchers in the field and legal experts recommend the involvement of more than one person to judge teacher quality and performance.[11] A more broad-based approach to evaluation enhances its credibility with teachers and its validity for making important personnel decisions, particularly when they may be adverse ones.

How often and when will evaluations be done?

In addition to identifying the participants in the evaluation process, evaluation procedures should provide an approximate timeline and the steps to be taken (e.g., minimum number of observations).[12] Teachers should be able to expect that written evaluation procedures will guide the process for the most part, but it is important that the evaluation procedures be realistic and somewhat flexible in nature. For example, a range of dates versus specified dates provides adequate notice for teachers of when to anticipate visits yet allows for unexpected events and conflicts in the scheduling of observations and meetings. Most researchers and practitioners agree, however, that once an observation has been conducted, it is common courtesy to schedule a feedback session or conference as soon as possible and definitely within five days.

Teacher evaluation procedures need to accommodate the wide spectrum of teacher abilities, from the expert masters who seek professional stimulation in their work to the struggling newcomers who require directive intervention and coaching. In response, many school systems have developed differentiated evaluation procedures for non-tenured/probationary and tenured/continuing contract teachers. Typically procedures are more prescriptive, involving more frequent and closer supervision, for less experienced teachers and more self-directed for capable, experienced teachers. Less experienced teachers tend to be observed more frequently and receive annual evaluations, often required by state statute. More experienced teachers are observed less regularly, if at all, and are evaluated every three to four years.[13] Teachers with tenure/continuing contract status may have the option of selecting more independent strategies for documenting performance, such as professional goal setting, peer coaching, and action research projects, in addition to or instead of observations.

As a result of different evaluation activities for non-tenured/probationary teachers and tenured/continuing contract (e.g., formal observation schedule), the timeline for evaluation differs. Figures 7.5 and 7.6 detail sample evaluation schedules for each.

Non-tenured/Probationary Teachers. In this case, the procedures for evaluating the performance of non-tenured/probationary teachers rely on a minimum of two observations per year, as specified in Figure 7.5, as well as the development and review of annual goals, student performance measures, portfolios, and other pertinent data. Observations may be conducted and feedback provided by anyone designated by the evaluator (e.g., teacher leader, curriculum specialist). In this example, one formal observation

Figure 7.5

Annual Evaluation Schedule for Non-tenured/Probationary Teachers

Data Collection Procedure	Form	Evaluator	Teacher	Due Date
Annual Goal for Student Achievement	Annual Goal Form	Reviews/ Approves	Selects/ Develops	October 1
Formal Observation & Conference (minimum 2)	Formal Observation Record	•		October 15 November 1
Informal Observation (ongoing) (minimum 2)	Informal Observation Form	•		February 15
Summative Evaluation, Portfolio Review, and Conference	Summative Form	•		February 28

is required during each of the first two quarters in each year of probation.

Tenured/Continuing Contract Teachers. In Figure 7.6, the collection of information to assess continuing contract teacher performance relies upon the same information sources as for non-tenured/probationary teachers. Tenured/continuing contract teachers are observed a minimum of one time each year prior to the end of the third quarter. Additional observations may occur at any point in the evaluation cycle. The figure details the timeline for a three-year evaluation cycle of tenured/continuing contract teachers.

Timelines such as those shown above differ depending on a number of contextual variables including the complexity in the evaluation process, negotiated agreements, contract dates, and the school year calendar. It is especially important to complete the evaluation process for non-tenured/probationary teachers so that decisions about offering them contract renewal or continuing contract status can be made in a timely manner. Obviously, the precise due dates for each stage of the evaluation process need to be aligned with state legal requirements, provisions in negotiated agreements, and local school board policy.

By what means will evaluations be made?

At its most fundamental level, evaluation is a "process by which the acceptability of teacher performance is judged."[14] Acceptability is a relative term and can only be judged with the assistance of tools such as performance standards (Chapter 4), performance criteria (Chapter 5), and performance data (Chapter 6). Research by Duke and Stiggins[15] indicated that clear performance criteria and standards were correlated with evaluation systems in which teachers perceived they had grown professionally. Therefore, technically sound criteria and standards not only meet the legal criteria of reasonable, job-related expectations but also provide the necessary specificity for professional development.

Evaluation procedures should specify what is expected of instructional personnel, how well they are expected to fulfill these tasks, and how their performance will be documented. In Chapter 6, we advocated the use of multiple, broad-based sources of information for documenting performance, including formal and informal observations, client surveys, self-evaluation, artifacts of performance, professional

Figure 7.6

Annual Evaluation Schedule for Tenured/Continuing Contract Teachers

Year	Data Collection Procedure	Form	Evaluator	Teacher	Due Date
Year 1&2	Annual Goal for Student Achievement	Annual Goal Form	Reviews/ Approves	Develops	October 1
	Formal Observation, Portfolio Review, Conference (minimum 1)	Formal Observation Record	•		March 15
	Informal Observations (ongoing)	Informal Observation Form	•		
Year 3	Annual Goal for Student Achievement	Annual Goal Form	Reviews/ Approves	Develops	October 1
	Formal Observation, Portfolio Review, and Conference (minimum 1)	Formal Observation Record	•		March 15
	Informal Observation (ongoing)	Informal Observation Form	•		
	Summative Evaluation Conference	Summative Form	•		March 30

goals, and portfolios. Based on a recent survey, the evidence usually used for teacher evaluations by secondary principals was classroom observation (96.4% of the time); examination of teachers' written lesson/unit plans (56% of the time); examination of teacher assessments, assignments, and tasks (51% of the time); student achievement on standardized tests (23% of the time); and pre- and post-test benchmark assessments (20% of the time).[16] Observing performance in a number of settings in addition to the classroom (e.g., parent conferences or IEP meetings) and collecting documentation of work that is not readily observable enhances the breadth and depth of the evaluator's knowledge, the credibility of the summative evaluations, and the usefulness of what the teacher learns about his or her performance.

Evaluation then becomes a process of comparing a teacher's documented job performance with established duties and acceptable levels of performance based on this information. This step requires periodic formative evaluation conferences as well as an end-of-cycle summative evaluation. Providing feedback throughout the evaluation cycle enables the teacher to identify areas of performance that are exemplary as well as performance areas that should receive attention while there is ample time for improvement. Furthermore, this practice ensures adequate notice of strengths and deficiencies, leading to a fair summative evaluation in which there should be no surprises.

How Do You Help Teachers Improve Performance?

Improving and maintaining quality professional service may include a variety of human

Figure 7.7

Goals and Roles Evaluation Model: Improving Performance

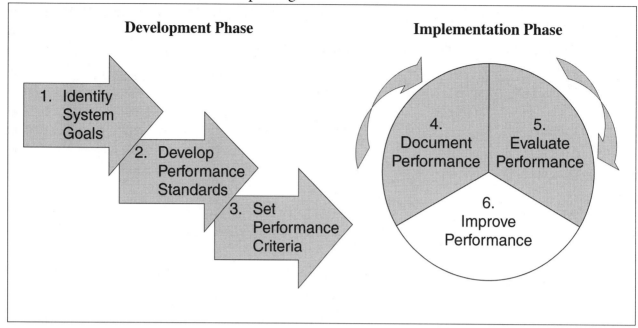

Used with permission of James H. Stronge

resource actions and support efforts (e.g., staff development, mentoring). The fundamental purpose of the evaluation process is to improve both the individual's and the organization's performance and to advance the mission and goals of the school system. Step 6 in the Goals and Roles Evaluation Model emphasizes the importance of this aspect of teacher evaluation. It is not sufficient to diagnose and inform teachers of their strengths and weaknesses; efforts must be made to offer assistance in developing new skills and knowledge for more effective teaching. Step 6 in the evaluation cycle offers a time for reflection, analysis, and change that then serves as an entrée into the next cycle.[17] The place of improving performance within the overall framework of the model is illustrated in Figure 7.7.

When evaluation is related to other personnel functions such as staff development and, ultimately, school improvement, it becomes integral to other school functions rather than an isolated event with little or no meaning. For example, if a number of teachers are identified through the evaluation process as needing assistance in a particular area

such as classroom management, a coordinated staff development program could be developed to provide training to all teachers with similar needs. In this way evaluation serves as a needs assessment that informs the staff development program, and both become more meaningful and legitimate.

While induction, mentoring, peer coaching, and professional development programs all help teachers improve and should be coordinated with evaluation efforts, two fundamental strategies for performance improvement that have been utilized in conjunction with teacher evaluation systems will be discussed below, conferencing and goal setting. These two strategies require the following three basic ingredients:

♦ A structure for systematically collecting *data* on relevant performance;

♦ Meaningful *feedback* based on observations and documentation; and

♦ Development of *goals* based on student learning outcomes.

First and foremost, there must be procedures, such as those noted earlier in the chapter, for collecting data in a systematic fashion. From a legal perspective, it is imperative that personnel decisions are not "capricious or arbitrary," but rather based on credible data, preferably from multiple sources and evaluators. Secondly, "the most crucial link between the teacher and the observer occurs when the teacher is provided with information on his or her performance. If growth is to occur, it is most likely to begin with this communication."[18] And finally, future directions must be defined along with strategies for achieving them. Goal setting is a formal strategy for capturing and articulating these plans, but it is also embedded in the other strategy described below.

Conferencing

Conferencing, as an integral component of clinical supervision, is probably the most widely used strategy for assisting teachers in improving performance.[19] It is used by most school systems in conjunction with classroom observation and can be conducted by a range of supervisors, including the principal, department head, mentor, cooperating teacher, or consulting teacher. The broadest function of the evaluation conference is to improve or enhance job performance by engaging in a reflective conversation on the complexities of teaching and learning, but an effective evaluation conference will achieve a number of more specific purposes:

♦ discussion of goals and objectives, both previously established and newly developed;

♦ candid and complete assessment of the teacher's job performance;

♦ acknowledgement of high quality work;

♦ discussion of suggestions for improvement;

♦ clarification of responsibilities;

♦ correction of misinformation and misunderstanding;

♦ explanation of professional growth opportunities for teachers;

♦ problem solving about the teaching assignment in the context of the organization;

♦ discussion of the department or program as a whole; and

♦ warning to employees having serious performance difficulties, with specific recommendations for improvement and notification of consequences for failure to demonstrate appropriate improvement.[20]

The emphasis among these various components of the evaluation conference will depend upon several variables, such as the age and experience of the teacher, the age and experience of the evaluator, and the quality of performance this teacher has demonstrated. For example, if the teacher is relatively new to the job, he or she may view an older, experienced evaluator as an authority figure or expert and consequently may seek—or at least be receptive to—advice, suggestions, and assurance. An important purpose of the evaluation conference in this situation is to provide candid feedback on the teacher's performance and to assist the teacher in improving his or her job performance to acceptable levels.[21]

Goal Setting

The purpose of goal setting is to focus attention on professional or instructional improvement based on a process of determining baseline performance, developing goals, identifying strategies for improvement, and assessing results at the end of the plan's time period. Theorists[22] have proposed that people are motivated by their personal goals; thus, a key strategy in performance improvement is to assist teachers in the shaping and focusing of those goals to align with school-wide and system-wide initiatives. Goal setting can be used as one data source in a teacher evaluation system or as a core component of a professional development model. Given the flexibility of goal setting, it can be implemented with the whole spectrum of teachers, from novice to experienced and from accomplished to struggling, depending on its focus and structure. For struggling teachers, goal setting is more prescriptive and goal attainment is required for continued employment; for accomplished teachers, goal setting becomes more self-directed and can be an alternative approach to traditional observation.

Despite the differences in how goal setting may be used and with whom, we advocate the following purposes of goal setting:

♦ To make explicit the connection between teaching and learning;

♦ To focus attention on student learning outcomes;

♦ To provide a tool for school improvement; and

♦ To improve instructional practices and teacher performance.

Consistent with the Goals and Roles Evaluation Model, there is a strong emphasis on connecting individual teacher efforts with those of the school system to achieve maximum student learning gains.

Most goal setting models involve five basic components:

♦ Identification of a focus or need;

♦ Description of baseline data relevant to the focus or need;

♦ Articulation of a goal or goals;

♦ Listing of strategies for achieving the goal (resources, training, etc.);

♦ Documentation of results and/or evaluation.

Given these broad guidelines, goal setting is a flexible strategy that can be used as an informal or formal part of conferencing, peer assistance, and remediation.

By addressing both formative evaluation, primarily focused on improvement, and summative evaluation, primarily focused on accountability, this section brings the evaluation process full circle. Formative aspects of evaluation include immediate and ongoing feedback that targets performance improvement for stronger and weaker teachers. It should be ongoing throughout the evaluation process, and it is embedded in the Goals and Roles Evaluation Model.

What Training Is Required to Implement the Performance Evaluation of Teachers?

To optimize the effectiveness of a new evaluation system, developers should ensure its integration into existing structures and address the system in professional training programs. Before implementation of a new system, good practice would suggest that all teachers be oriented to the system, provided with copies of the evaluation handbook, and informed about support for implementation. Administrators and supervisors should also receive an orientation. Moreover, ongoing training should be available to answer questions as they arise, to identify potential problem areas, and to build consistency among evaluators. Additionally, modifications in district-level staff development courses and programs can be made to support changes in the new job expectations, such as more varied and authentic student assessment strategies or increased use of technology. When staff training is linked to teacher evaluation in this way, it is another means of fostering a learning community for adults as well as children within a school and system.

More extensive training for evaluators is critical to ensure the development of necessary skills for conducting observations, analyzing performance data, providing constructive feedback, documenting performance, and assisting in improvement.[23] Researchers have noted that typically "principals have been poorly monitored in terms of their supervisory skill in conducting evaluations of teachers [and they] have provided superficial feedback to teachers with little nor no constructive criticism, and a paucity of strategies for improvement."[24] A vivid example of this problem was shared by Guilford County, North Carolina, when the school system decided to work to raise teacher performance by improving teacher evaluation. In their review of personnel evaluations, they found that only .2% of the sample received "unsatisfactory" ratings and 3.7% received "below standards" ratings, with most ratings in the "above standard" range. In light of the district's student achievement, which ranked near the bottom of their peer group at the time, Jerry Weast, the superintendent, instituted Project H.E.L.P. to improve performance evaluation. Results after one year of implementation were very promising, especially in terms of the principals' skill level in assessing and supporting weak teachers.[25]

Guilford County School System exemplifies how school systems can encourage high quality evaluation by holding evaluators accountable for good practice and expecting them to implement procedures in a meaningful manner. This level of commitment means dedicating the necessary time to the task, supporting teachers in the improvement process, communicating to teachers that the process is important, and ensuring that it will be done fairly. Unless fairness and consistency, the two major concerns of teachers, are present in the evaluation process, it will not have the necessary credibility to be taken seriously by them.[26]

Along with pressure to make teacher evaluation a priority, administrators also need support and ongoing training in evaluation skills. Formal training in the process of evaluation should focus on both the procedural and substantive use of the system. The procedural aspects of an evaluation system refer to an understanding of *what to do when*. This would include an understanding of the goals for evaluation, what performance information to collect and how, the appropriate timelines, what standards to use in judging information, and the requirements for developing an improvement plan.

Skills in the substantive features involve the *substance* of the evaluation procedures. A clear understanding of the performance standards determines the actual quality of the evaluation process and influences how an administrator approaches data collection, documentation, data analysis, conferencing, goal setting, report writing, and remediation. Training can help principals become better skilled in all areas of the evaluation process, but especially those that are critical for working with unsatisfactory teachers: identification of instructional problems or weaknesses compared to established performance standards, the suggestion of appropriate strategies to improve, and identification of available resources to assist in the improvement process.[27]

As you might expect, evaluator training has been found to have a positive effect on all aspects of the evaluation process. The greatest improvements were found in the attributes of evaluative feedback.[28] Teachers reported that the amount, depth, and specificity of information given by administrators after they received training increased substantially. In addition, the teachers rated the evaluators as having a greater knowledge of teaching and increased credibility.[29] Evaluation training for administrators ensures integrity in the process and garners teacher confidence in both the administrator and the procedures.

Summary

As Linda Darling-Hammond observed, "teacher evaluation can be a routine, pro forma activity with little utility for shaping what goes on in schools, or it can be an important vehicle for communicating organizational and professional norms and for stimulating improvement."[30] Achieving the latter requires heightened attention to the implementation issues that have been addressed in this chapter. A teacher evaluation system, like any quality program or curriculum, can be undermined or subverted by poor implementation. Without organizational commitment, well-intentioned evaluators with strong interpersonal skills, and a commitment to improvement, even the best system will fail. Some suggestions to make implementation successful are as follows:

♦ Consider evaluation to be a process, not an event.

♦ Create a climate for evaluation that challenges but doesn't threaten.

- ◆ Plan and provide comprehensive training for teachers and evaluators.

- ◆ Try out new strategies with a pilot and revise them until they achieve the desired purposes.

- ◆ Be sure to communicate the importance of evaluation to all involved parties.

- ◆ Ask for and provide assistance when needed.

- ◆ Focus on improvement that enhances student learning.

Unless teacher evaluation helps teachers improve their knowledge and skills so that they can in turn foster optimal student learning, we are unquestionably wasting our time.

Chapter 7 References

[1] Duke, D. L., & Canady, R. L. (1991). *School policy.* New York: McGraw-Hill.

[2] Duke, D. L. (1995). *Teacher evaluation policy: From accountability to professional development.* Albany, NY: State University of New York Press.

[3] McCarthy, M. M., Cambron-McCabe, N. H., & Thomas, S. B. (1998). *Public school law* (4th ed.). Boston: Allyn and Bacon.

[4] National Association of Secondary School Principals. (1993). A legal memorandum: Teacher evaluation. Reston, VA: Author.

[5] Duke, D. L. (1995).

[6] Williamsburg-James City County Public Schools. (2001). *Policies and procedures manual.* Williamsburg, VA: Author.

[7] Miami-Dade County Public Schools. (1998). *School Board Rules* (6Gx13-4A-1.24). Miami, FL: Author.

[8] See Darling-Hammond, L. (1990). Teacher evaluation in transition: Emerging roles and evolving methods. In J. Millman & L. Darling-Hammond (Eds.), *The new handbook of teacher evaluation: Assessing elementary and secondary school teachers.* Newbury Park, CA: Corwin Press; Poston, W. K., Jr., & Mannatt, R. P. (1993). Principals as evaluators: Limiting effects on school reform. *International Journal of Educational Reform, 2*(1), 41–48.

[9] McGrath, M. J. (1993). When it's time to dismiss an incompetent teacher. *The School Administrator, 50*(3), 30–33.

[10] Educational Research Service. (1988). *Teacher evaluation: Practices and procedures.* Arlington, VA: Author.

[11] Frels, K., & Horton, J. L. (1994). *A documentation system for teacher improvement or termination.* (4th ed.). Topeka, KS: National Organization on Legal Problems of Education; Peterson, K. D. (2002). *Teacher evaluation: A comprehensive guide to new directions and practices.* Thousand Oaks, CA: Corwin Press.

[12] Frels, K., Cooper, T. T., & Reagan, B. R. (1984). *Practical aspects of teacher evaluation.* Topeka, KS: National Organization on Legal Problems in Education.

[13] Educational Research Service. (1988).

[14] Duke, D. L. (1987). *School leadership and instructional improvement.* New York: Random House.

[15] Duke, D. L., & Stiggins, R. (1990). Beyond minimum competence: Evaluation for professional development. In J. Millman and L. Darling-Hammond (Eds.), *The new handbook of teacher evaluation: Assessing elementary and secondary school teachers* (pp. 116–132). Newbury Park, CA: Sage Publications.

[16] National Association of Secondary School Principals. (2001). *Priorities and barriers in high school leadership: A survey of principals.* Reston, VA: Author.

[17] Adapted from Stronge, J. H., Helm, V. M., & Tucker, P. D. (1995). *Evaluation handbook for professional support personnel.* Kalamazoo, MI: Project CREATE, The Evaluation Center, Western Michigan University.

[18] Duke, D. L., & Stiggins, R. (1985). *Teacher evaluation: Five keys to growth.* Washington, DC: National Education Association.

[19] Glickman, C. D. (2002). *Leading for leadership: How to help teachers succeed.* Alexandria, VA: Association for Supervision and Curriculum Development.

[20] Adapted from Redfern, G. B. (1980). *Evaluating teachers and administrators: A performance objectives approach.* Boulder, CO: Westview.

[21] The section on conferencing is adapted from: Stronge, J. H., & Helm, V. M. (1991). *Evaluating professional support personnel in education.* Newbury Park, CA: Sage Publications.

[22] Locke, E. A., Cartledge, N., & Knerr, C. S. (1970). Studies of the relationship between satisfaction, goal-setting, and performance. *Organizational Behavior and Human Performance, 5,* 135–158.

[23] Bridges, E. M. (1992). *The incompetent teacher: Managerial responses.* Washington, DC: The Falmer Press; Duke, D. L. (1990); Poston, W. K., Jr., & Mannatt, R. P. (1993).

[24] Poston, W. K., Jr., & Mannatt, R. P. (1993), p. 43.

[25] Weast, J. D., Wright, J. S., & Frye, S. (1996). Raising teacher performance by improving teacher evaluation: Guilford County's Project H.E.L.P. *ERS Spectrum, 14*(3), 3–8.

[26] Bembry, K. (1995). Teachers' perspectives on developing a teacher evaluation system incorporating student outcomes. *Evaluation Perspectives, 5*(3), 11–12.

[27] Conley, D. T. (1987). Critical attributes of effective evaluation systems. *Educational Leadership, 44*(7), 60–64.

[28] Natriello, G. (1984). Teachers' perceptions of the frequency of evaluation assessments of their effort and effectiveness. *American Education Research Journal, 21,* 579–595.

[29] Sweeney, J. (1992). The effects of evaluator training on teacher evaluation. *Journal of Personnel Evaluation in Education, 6,* 7–14.

[30] Darling-Hammond, L. (1990), p. 19.

8

Teacher Evaluation: Where Do We Go From Here?

Teacher evaluation is often approached as a discrete, isolated activity that is disconnected from the central purposes and personnel activities of a school system; and yet, performance evaluation achieves relevance only by becoming an integral component of other system-level initiatives. Quality evaluation has the potential to meet a number of very important objectives for the school and its many constituencies. Drawing upon the *Handbook* in its entirety, we offer the following observations regarding teacher evaluation:

Whole School Improvement

♦ A school's goals are met through the collective performance of all personnel, especially its teachers.

♦ Effective teacher evaluation promotes the growth and development of the individual and the school.

♦ A well-defined teacher evaluation system makes the school more accountable to its public.

♦ A unified evaluation process for all personnel is a more efficient use of school resources and administrative and staff time than multiple evaluation systems.

Fairness to Teachers and Staff

♦ A well-defined teacher evaluation system provides a basis for an assessment that is as objective as possible, based on observable, job-related results, with its purposes clearly established for the individual.

♦ Administrators and teachers should mutually agree upon the design of an evaluation system through honest and open communication.

♦ Teachers have a legal and ethical right to understand the criteria used to evaluate their performance.

♦ The entire staff of the school should be included in a comprehensive evaluation system.

♦ All employees, including teachers, deserve well-defined job descriptions, systematic performance feedback, and appropriate opportunities for improvement.

In this final chapter in Part I of the *Handbook on Teacher Evaluation*, we will attempt to support the above principles by exploring a few final questions:

♦ What are appropriate legal guidelines for teacher evaluation?

♦ What are key issues to consider in revising a teacher evaluation system?

♦ What are evolving directions in teacher evaluation?

What Are Appropriate Legal Guidelines for Teacher Evaluation?[1]

The following guidelines can assist in developing procedures that promote the development of a high quality teacher evaluation system for both formative and summative evaluation purposes. (For additional details regarding formative and summative evaluation purposes, see Chapters 1 and 5.)

Guideline No.1: Adhere strictly to all state and local (statutory and administrative) procedural requirements in evaluating teachers.

The more closely evaluators adhere to all procedural safeguards embedded in teacher evaluation statutes and policies, the more proper and justifiable will be the implementation of the teacher evaluation process and results. Although case law has produced conflicting results regarding some procedural requirements, failure to comply with any specified deadlines or procedures can invalidate the entire evaluation process.[2] When considering state statutory requirements (e.g., deadline for notification, provision for a hearing) the courts generally have invalidated for the slightest procedural error.

When considering local evaluation policies and procedures (e.g., a requirement for a personal conference within 24 hours following a formal classroom observation), the courts have sometimes—but not always—been a bit more lenient.[3] In these instances, the courts typically have considered the total record and, if they found evidence for a good faith effort, they have tolerated minor procedural deviations that otherwise would not have affected the outcome of the evaluation process or results. Nonetheless, the only safe bet is to adhere to *all* procedural requirements. Moreover, it is the fair thing to do.

Guideline No. 2: Inform teachers of all standards, criteria, and procedures for evaluation before implementation.

It is unfair to leave teachers uninformed about evaluation processes; furthermore, it is a denial of due process to impose standards or procedures after the evaluation process has begun— or worse, has been completed. Prior notice enables teachers to know the rules of the game: who will evaluate what and when, as well as by what standards and with what consequences. The Personnel Evaluation Standard P2 describes the need to fully inform employees of evaluation requirements.

> *P2 Formal Evaluation Guidelines: Guidelines for personnel evaluations should be recorded and provided to employees in statements of policy, negotiated agreements, and/or personnel evaluation manuals, so that evaluations are consistent, equitable, and in accordance with pertinent laws and ethical codes.[4]*

Guideline No. 3: The teacher evaluation system must provide objectivity throughout the process.

Objectivity is one of the most crucial components of any evaluation process. Its presence protects all educators, including teachers, from politically or personally questionable, ulterior motives by the evaluator—including motives that reflect discrimination based on race, gender, religion, national origin, age, handicap, or any other category irrelevant to job performance. This important issue of objectivity is clearly reflected in the Personnel Evaluation Propriety Standards which requires that " . . . evaluations be conducted legally, ethically, and with due regard for the welfare of teachers and clients involved in the evaluations."[5] Specifically, Standard P3 is applicable to the issue of objectivity in personnel evaluations:

> *P3 Conflict of Interest: Conflicts of interest should be identified and dealt with openly and honestly, so that they do not compromise the evaluation process and results.*[6]

Discrimination charges may be based on either the evaluation guidelines and policies or the implementation of the evaluation process itself. Such charges may be brought under the U. S. Constitution (e.g., 14th Amendment), federal legislation (e.g., C.R.A., Title VII), or applicable state statutes. It should be noted that United States Supreme Court rulings have focused primarily on violations occurring in hiring decisions rather than evaluation, specifically. However, the principles established can reasonably be expected to apply in evaluation decisions. Simply put: Treating people differently or unfairly without a rational, bona fide occupational reason will not withstand judicial scrutiny. Teachers deserve to be evaluated on their relevant job performance—and nothing else!

Guideline No. 4: Teacher evaluation should document patterns and effects of behavior.

Actual practice in teacher evaluation is replete with examples of administrators who conducted one-time evaluations and made negative evaluation decisions on the basis of a single, isolated incident; unless the findings from this one-shot evaluation are particularly egregious, these decisions all too frequently do not hold up in court. A much better approach is to document *patterns* of performance

and the related *effects* of the performance. Documenting patterns and effects of behavior includes:

- ◆ patterns of repeated inappropriate, ineffective, or otherwise undesirable behaviors, and
- ◆ adverse effects of those behaviors on students or the school.

One way to establish patterns of behavior is to conduct evaluations more, rather than less, frequently. Another is to use multiple evaluators or sources of data to document performance as discussed in Chapter 6.

Guideline No. 5: Determine whether the teacher's behavior is remediable.

Irremediable behavior has been defined by case law as behavior that has a seriously damaging effect on students or the school community or that could not have been corrected even with prior warning. Generally, teaching responsibilities (such as classroom instruction, classroom managaement, etc.) or professionally related behavior on the job is remediable. Generally, only the more extreme personal behavior, whether on or off the job, is irremediable.

Guideline No. 6: When remediable deficiencies are cited, provide clear descriptions of the deficiencies and clear, specific descriptions of the expected corrections or improvements in performance or behavior that the teacher is required to make.

Deficiencies described as "poor relationships with students" or "poor discipline" in the absence of specific examples can be judged as too vague or ambiguous. General criticisms don't indicate what improvements are needed by the teacher. Courts have implied the need for clear statements of the standards of performance that would provide evidence of correction or remediation of the teacher's deficiencies. In addition, a reasonable time period should be given for improvement along with offers of assistance, such as training workshops, reference materials, and coaching. Statutory law in some states prescribes a requirement for, and the exact nature of assistance to be given.

Guideline No. 7: Provide proper assistance to the teacher in need of remediation.

What kind of activities or experiences should be incorporated into a remediation plan that will provide maximum benefit to the teacher? From case law and from evaluation theory, the following activities and experiences can be summarized:

♦ The evaluator and any other supervisory personnel with specialization in the teacher's area of deficiency may make suggestions for improvement.

♦ Require the teacher to be observed by one or more specialists.

♦ Require the teacher to enroll in courses, workshops, or seminars designed to provide the knowledge or skills she or he needs to improve to a satisfactory level.

♦ Require the teacher to videotape his or her performance and view the tapes.

♦ Assign a consulting teacher who is not only qualified but willing and supportive as well.

♦ Request the services of an assistance team.

Ultimately, it is the teacher's responsibility to improve his/her performance based on evaluative feedback, but the school system must provide assistance for the improvement to the extent feasible to demonstrate a good faith effort on their part.

Guideline No. 8: Substantiate fully any personnel decision.

Evaluation summaries must be consistent with and provide sufficient documentation to substantiate personnel decisions. As the teacher's length of service increases so does the expectation of full due process, including 1) rich documentation of unsatisfactory performance, 2) clear delineation of performance expectations for continued employment along with a timeline and strategies for assistance, 3) further documentation on performance after assistance has been offered, and 4) the final personnel decision and the basis

for it. Clear written records facilitate a better understanding of the events by everyone involved in the process.

What Are Key Issues to Consider in Revising a Teacher Evaluation System?

We have devoted most of the attention in the *Handbook* to designing and implementing quality teacher evaluation systems. However, even when the evaluation system is properly developed and implemented, the work isn't finished. Schools change: Expectations rise, new requirements are mandated, innovative research findings emerge, and better ways of working are discovered. As a result of these and many other changes in the vibrant business of schooling, we need to adapt—and that includes the field of teacher evaluation.

♦ *Start with the school's goals in mind.* Over time, if the school or school system changes its direction in a subtle or more substantial way, then a subtle or substantial change in the evaluation system may be necessary in order to have the performance goals of employees best match the desired goals of the organization.

♦ *Balance the needs for professional growth and accountability.* Make sure the evaluation system is designed to yield the desired results. Some schools have teacher evaluation systems that are aimed totally at professional growth at the expense of providing some degree of accountability; others go overboard in emphasizing results. And some teacher evaluation systems, in reality, are neither professional-growth nor results oriented. Just make sure that you have the right mix between professional growth and accountability.

♦ *Base evaluations on the educator's job.* How many times have we heard colleagues comment that their evaluation doesn't even resemble what they really do. Over time, positions like counselors, and even teachers, can shift and make their evaluations less relevant—or even irrelevant. To help guard against this problem, periodically assess the match between the roles of educators and their actual job responsibilities.

♦ *Make certain that collected performance information is useful.* As we have stressed repeatedly throughout the *Handbook*, you should use appropriate and multiple sources of information about the teacher's performance. Also, look for improvements in how to use portfolios, to connect student achievement to teacher evaluation, and to use other innovative practices that are emerging.

♦ *Differentiate the evaluation system and practices based on important contextual issues.* For example, consider changes needed in relation to the purpose of the evaluation (e.g., improvement-only vs. improvement + accountability), expertise level (e.g., novice vs. expert), the positions to be evaluated (e.g., teacher vs. counselor), and other relevant design issues. If you find that important contextual issues are absent from the existing teacher evaluation system, find a way to fix the problem.

♦ *Start again with the school's goals in mind.* When you find any or all of the above qualities of your teacher evaluation system deficient, it may be time to overhaul it. And, when you do restructure the evaluation system, start again with the school's goals as the guide.

What Are Evolving Directions in Teacher Evaluation?

Teacher evaluation has been slow to change, like many other aspects of schools, but concerned educators everywhere are trying new strategies to enhance existing systems. School systems are experimenting with different types of data sources and are involving different people in the process. Some of the trends that have been noted include the following:

♦ *Teacher evaluation and school reform are increasingly intertwined.*[7]

As the focus for accountability has shifted to the school as the unit for meaningful change, principals are recognizing the importance of aligning teacher evaluation and development with overall improvement efforts. In reality, it is only when teacher evaluation becomes integral to the organizational goals of improving instructional practices, as suggested in Chapter 1, that it will have meaning and value for teachers.

♦ *Multiple data sources are being used more frequently to document performance.*[8]

While classroom observations remain the most common method of evaluating teacher performance, many school systems are introducing other strategies that include a variety of supervisors and data sources such as client feedback, student performance data, portfolios, and self-assessment. Use of multiple sources of information provides a fuller and more realistic portrait of a teacher's impact on students and contribution to the school as a whole.

♦ *Involvement of multiple supervisors in the evaluation process.*

Many factors can limit the principal's effectiveness as an evaluator. Two of the most important are available time and subject area expertise. Colleagues often have greater contact with teachers, more specific expertise, and a better appreciation for the contextual variables impacting performance. The involvement of other professionals in the evaluation process, such as team leaders, department chairs, or consulting teachers, can only enrich the specificity and value of the instructional feedback and provide the support necessary for improvement.

♦ *Greater complexity in evaluation design.*[9]

Innovative evaluation systems are being developed that differentiate approaches for accountability and professional development. To some extent, these approaches follow the traditional route requiring more accountability for beginning teachers and less for experienced teachers; but newer approaches have recognized the need for periodic intensive review for all teachers or in special circumstances where experienced teachers are having difficulties. Flexibility and responsiveness characterize the development of newer systems.

♦ *Stronger connections between evaluation and professional development.*

Teacher evaluation should not be seen as a critique of someone's teaching ability but a diagnostic assessment of his/her strengths and weaknesses. Just as we take students where they are and move them forward with instruction, so should we do with teachers. Professional development should not be based solely on what the school system wants teachers to learn but what teachers need to learn for their own professional growth.

♦ *Hierarchy is giving way to collegiality.*[10]

Evaluation is shifting from an activity that is *perpetrated on* teachers to something that is *conducted with* teachers. Teachers are being asked to self-assess and provide documentation on their own accomplishments and professional activities through portfolios or dossiers. Teachers are working with colleagues to develop individualized professional growth opportunities. Teachers are analyzing student test data to determine school, grade, and class level goals for improvement. Relationships within schools are becoming more supportive, trusting, and collegial in an effort to improve whole schools.

♦ *Use of computer software to support and manage the evaluation process.*[11]

There are now computer programs available to help supervisors gather, organize, and evaluate data from multiple sources and print completed documents for feedback and personnel records. Even more useful are comprehensive database systems that automatically consolidate evaluation data across an entire district and offer a wide array of reports for formative and summative purposes.[12] Such a system can help a school district oversee its evaluation procedures, identify staff strengths and weaknesses, and target staff development efforts. Just as the consolidation and reporting of student achievement data can help a school district direct its resources to the students most in need of assistance, consolidation and reporting of teacher evaluation data can do the same for teachers.

Summary

Ultimately, the mission of schooling is to help students succeed—in learning to read, to compute math, to understand their place in history, to appreciate and respect the world around them, to respect democratic principles, and to become productive and thoughtful contributing members of society. And how do schools fulfill these and a host of other valued and valuable purposes of evaluation? Schools fulfill their mission through their employees. High quality teachers, educational specialists, administrators, and other employees lead to high quality schools. In fact, it is only through their employees that schools can hope to fulfill their mission.

So what is the purpose of evaluation? In its most basic form, evaluation is to help teachers and other educators provide the highest quality services and programs possible to students. A quality performance evaluation system, alone, can't transform a school—or even a single employee unless that person chooses to change. However, when properly designed and implemented, a quality teacher evaluation system certainly can be an important catalyst for change and improvement. In the spirit of supporting teachers and other educators in providing quality educational opportunities for students, we offer the *Handbook on Teacher Evaluation*. We hope that our readers find it of value as they pursue one of Thomas Jefferson's loftiest goals: a free education for all of our nation's children.

Chapter 8 References

[1] Adapted from: Stronge, J. H., & Helm, V. M. (1991). Evaluate Performance. In J. H. Stronge and V. M. Helm. *Evaluating professional support personnel in education* (pp. 201–228). Newbury Park, CA: Sage Publications.

[2] Sullivan, K. A., & Zirkel, P. A. (1998). The law of teacher evaluation: Case Law Update. *Journal of Personnel Evaluation in Education, 11*(4), 367–380.

[3] Sullivan & Zirkel, 1998.

[4] Joint Committee on Standards for Educational Evaluation. (1988). *The personnel evaluation standards: How to assess systems for evaluating educators.* Newbury Park, CA: Corwin Press, Inc., p. 28.

[5] Joint Committee on Standards for Educational Evaluation. (1988), p. 21.

[6] Joint Committee on Standards for Educational Evaluation. (1988), p. 32.

[7] Darling-Hammond, L. (1990), p. 17.

[8] Stronge, J. H. (1997). Improving schools through teacher evaluation. In J. H. Stronge (Ed.), *Evaluating teaching: A guide to current thinking and best practice.* Thousand Oaks, CA: Corwin Press.

[9] Duke, D. L. (1995). Conflict and consensus in the reform of teacher evaluation. In D. L. Duke (Ed.), *Teacher evaluation policy.* Albany, NY: State University of New York, pp. 180–181.

[10] Duke, D. L. (1995). Speculations on the future of teacher evaluation and educational accountability. In D. L. Duke (Ed.), *Teacher evaluation policy.* Albany, NY: State University of New York, pp. 180–181.

[11] Tucker, L. A., & Howard, B. (2003, January). *Taking a systematic approach to teacher evaluation: Using SETS software and the SERVE model.* Paper presented at the Program for Research and Evaluation for Public Schools (PREPS) conference, Jackson, MS.

[12] See for example: www.E³info.com

Part II

Roles and Responsibilities

Overview of Part II: Roles and Responsibilities

This section contains the heart of the teacher evaluation system. It presents the domains, associated performance standards, and a wealth of job-specific performance indicators for teachers and six different resource/specialty positions.

Three-Tiered System for Performance Responsibilities

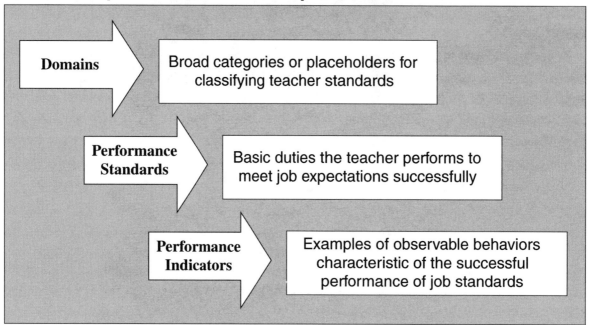

Used with permission of James H. Stronge

Since the jobs performed by classroom teachers and resource/specialty area teachers differ, the domains, performance standards, and performance indicators reflect those differences. Two examples of classroom teacher evaluation systems are presented, one with five domains and the other with four domains. Following the presentation of the classroom teachers' systems are the resource and specialty area teachers' evaluation system domains, standards, and indicators.

The resource/specialty area teachers have a five-domain system presented, which is followed by the performance standards. The domains and standards are the same across all six resource/specialty positions. The standards and the domains are presented first, followed by individual sections for each of the resource/specialty area teachers' positions that contain the tailored performance indicators. The six positions highlighted are:

♦ English Second Language (ESL) Teacher
♦ Gifted/Talented Enrichment Teacher
♦ Preschool Teacher
♦ Reading Recovery Teacher
♦ Reading Specialist Teacher
♦ Special Education Resource Teacher

Only the domains, performance standards, and performance indicators are presented in Part II. Part III contains the performance appraisal rubrics and sample forms for the employee evaluation system.

Classroom Teacher
5 Domains

Classroom Teacher
5 Domains

Instruction

This domain encompasses both organizing for instruction and delivery of instruction. The major standards include planning and implementing a variety of activities consistent with instructional objectives and selecting instructional methods compatible with student abilities and learning styles.

Assessment

This domain includes the standards for conducting evaluation and providing feedback to students that encourages student progress and measures student achievement.

Learning Environment

This domain includes the teacher's standards for planning and demonstrating effective routines and procedures that create a safe, organized, and productive learning environment.

Communication/Community Relations

This domain includes the teacher's standards for effective communication within the classroom and between the classroom and others, as well as the standard for encouraging parent and community involvement.

Professionalism

This final domain defines the standards for demonstrating a commitment to professional ethics and growth and for complying with division policies and procedures.

Performance Standards

Instruction

I-1: The teacher demonstrates current and accurate knowledge of subject matter covered in the curriculum.

I-2: The teacher plans instruction to achieve desired student learning objectives that reflect the current district curriculum.

I-3: The teacher recognizes individual learning differences and differentiates instruction to meet student needs.

I-4: The teacher uses materials, technology, and resources compatible with students' needs and abilities that support the current district curriculum.

I-5: The teacher links present content/skills with past and future learning experiences, other subject areas, and real world experiences/applications.

I-6: The teacher uses a variety of instructional strategies that promote student learning.

Assessment

A-1: The teacher provides a variety of ongoing and culminating assessments to measure student performance.

A-2: The teacher provides ongoing and timely feedback to encourage student progress.

A-3: The teacher uses assessment results to make both daily and long-range instructional decisions.

Learning Environment

L-1: The teacher communicates and maintains clear expectations about behavior, classroom procedures, and academic achievement.

L-2: The teacher maximizes the use of instructional time and resources to increase student learning.

L-3: The teacher demonstrates and models respect toward students and others.

L-4: The teacher organizes the classroom to ensure a safe academic and physical learning environment.

Communication/Community Relations

C-1: The teacher communicates effectively with students and models standard English.

C-2: The teacher works collaboratively with families and community resources to support the success of a diverse student population.

C-3: The teacher initiates and maintains timely communication with parents/guardians, colleagues, and administrators concerning student progress or problems.

Professionalism

P-1: The teacher demonstrates ethical and professional behavior.

P-2: The teacher applies strategies learned from professional development.

P-3: The teacher contributes to the overall school climate by supporting school goals.

Performance Indicators

Instruction

I-1: The teacher demonstrates current and accurate knowledge of subject matter covered in the curriculum.

- The teacher bases instruction on goals that reflect high expectations, understanding of the subject, and the importance of learning.
- The teacher demonstrates the ability to engage and maintain student attention and interest.
- The teacher links objectives for instruction to prior student learning.
- The teacher exhibits knowledge and demonstrates skills relevant to the subject area(s) taught.
- The teacher demonstrates an ability to make topics and activities meaningful and relevant to student learning.
- The teacher exhibits/demonstrates an understanding of technology skills appropriate for the grade level/subject matter.

I-2: The teacher plans instruction to achieve desired student learning objectives that reflect the current district curriculum.

- The teacher selects student objectives for lessons consistent with district guidelines and curriculum.
- The teacher selects learning activities for lessons consistent with district curriculum and student needs.
- The teacher develops lesson plans that are clear, logical, and sequential.
- The teacher plans purposeful assignments for teacher assistants, substitute teachers, student teachers, and others to support student learning.
- The teacher assists students in planning, organizing, and preparing for assignments, long-range projects, and tests.

I-3: The teacher recognizes individual learning differences and differentiates instruction to meet student needs.

- The teacher demonstrates sensitivity, respect, and responsiveness for individual, cultural, religious, and racial differences within the classroom.
- The teacher works with resource/monitoring teachers to implement IEPs and Section 504 plans for identified students.
- The teacher identifies and plans for the instructional and developmental needs of all students, including remedial, high achievers, and identified gifted students.
- The teacher selects material and media that match learning styles of individual students.
- The teacher demonstrates an ability to evaluate and refine existing materials and to create new materials when necessary.

I-4: The teacher uses materials, technology, and resources compatible with students' needs and abilities that support the current district curriculum.

- The teacher selects a variety of materials and media that support the curriculum.
- The teacher integrates available technology into the curriculum.

♦ The teacher selects resources including outside personnel that offer added dimensions to the curriculum.

I-5: The teacher links present content/skills with past and future learning experiences, other subject areas, and real world experiences/applications.

♦ The teacher links current objectives with prior student learning.

♦ The teacher solicits comments, questions, examples, demonstrations, and other contributions from students throughout the lesson.

♦ The teacher matches content/skills taught with the overall scope and sequence of the lesson.

I-6: The teacher uses a variety of instructional strategies that promote student learning.

♦ The teacher communicates clear performance expectations for student learning.

♦ The teacher uses a variety of teaching strategies (e.g., cooperative learning, inquiry, lecture, discussion, problem-based learning).

♦ The teacher uses questioning strategies effectively.

♦ The teacher checks for understanding and modifies instruction accordingly.

♦ The teacher summarizes and reviews major concepts from the lessons.

Assessment

A-1: The teacher provides a variety of ongoing and culminating assessments to measure student performance.

♦ The teacher assesses student performance based on instructional objectives.

♦ The teacher continuously monitors student progress before, during, and after instruction through frequent and systematic assessment.

♦ The teacher demonstrates competence in the use of acceptable grading, ranking, and scoring practices in recording student achievement.

♦ The teacher uses multiple assessment strategies including teacher-made, criterion-referenced, and standardized tests.

♦ The teacher uses oral, non-verbal, and written forms of assessment to measure student performance.

♦ The teacher includes information on student participation, performance, and/or products in assessment.

A-2: The teacher provides ongoing and timely feedback to encourage student progress.

♦ The teacher provides prompt feedback to help students monitor and improve their performance.

♦ The teacher provides meaningful and timely feedback to students and parents about performance and progress.

♦ The teacher communicates and collaborates with colleagues in order to improve student performance.

♦ The teacher collects sufficient assessment data to support accurate reporting of student progress.

♦ The teacher gives performance feedback to students before, during, and after instruction.

A-3: The teacher uses assessment results to make both daily and long-range instructional decisions.

- The teacher uses pre-assessment data to develop expectations for students and for documenting learning.
- The teacher uses results of a variety of formal and informal assessments to plan, monitor, and modify instruction as needed.
- The teacher uses a variety of assessments to monitor and modify instructional content and strategies.
- The teacher uses student assessment data to identify individual and group learning needs.
- The teacher uses informal assessments to adjust instruction while teaching.

Learning Environment

L-1: The teacher communicates and maintains clear expectations about behavior, classroom procedures, and academic achievement.

- The teacher communicates academic and behavioral expectations to students and parents in a clear, concise, and reasonable manner.
- The teacher manages student behavior and provides feedback in a constructive and equitable manner to students and parents.
- The teacher responds in a timely manner to concerns regarding students.
- The teacher relays information about school activities and functions.

L-2: The teacher maximizes the use of instructional time and resources to increase student learning.

- The teacher establishes and utilizes effective routines and procedures.
- The teacher has all materials readily available to allow for a smooth flow of instruction.
- The teacher structures transitions in an efficient and constructive manner.
- The teacher utilizes a variety of available resources to develop engaging instruction.

L-3: The teacher demonstrates and models respect toward students and others.

- The teacher is respectful of students, families, colleagues, and others.
- The teacher models fairness, courtesy, respect, and active listening toward students and others.
- The teacher models concern for students' emotional and physical well-being.

L-4: The teacher organizes the classroom to ensure a safe academic and physical learning environment.

- The teacher creates a physical setting that promotes learning and minimizes disruption.
- The teacher creates a learning environment that encourages student participation, inquiry, and risk-taking.
- The teacher manages emergency situations appropriately.
- The teacher arranges and adapts the classroom setting to accommodate individual and group learning needs.

Communication/Community Relations

C-1: The teacher communicates effectively with students and models standard English.

- The teacher uses standard English grammar when communicating with students.

- The teacher uses precise language, acceptable oral expression, and written communication.
- The teacher explains concepts and lesson content to students in a logical, sequential, and appropriate manner.
- The teacher gives clear and appropriate directions.
- The teacher models various effective communication strategies for conveying ideas and information for a variety of learning styles.
- The teacher emphasizes major points of concern by using techniques such as repetition and verbal or non-verbal cues.
- The teacher actively listens and responds in a constructive manner.

C-2: The teacher works collaboratively with families and community resources to support the success of a diverse student population.

- The teacher shares major instructional goals and classroom expectations with parents.
- The teacher establishes and maintains multiple modes of communication between school and home.
- The teacher initiates communication and responds to parents or guardians concerning student progress or problems in a timely manner.
- The teacher forges partnerships and offers strategies for families to assist in their children's education.
- The teacher uses community resources to enhance student learning and works with the community members in planning and conducting school and community functions.

C-3: The teacher initiates and maintains timely communication with parents/guardians, colleagues, and administrators concerning student progress or problems.

- The teacher communicates in a positive and congenial manner
- The teacher works with school staff and other service providers to reach educational decisions that enhance student learning.
- The teacher adheres to school district policies regarding communication of student information.
- The teacher communicates concerns and problems in a constructive manner maintaining confidentiality as appropriate.

Professionalism

P-1: The teacher demonstrates ethical and professional behavior.

- The teacher maintains a professional demeanor and appearance.
- The teacher carries out responsibilities in accordance with established policies, practices, and regulation in a timely manner.
- The teacher adheres to ethical and professional standards.
- The teacher serves as a positive role model for students and others.

P-2: The teacher applies strategies learned from professional development.

- The teacher uses self-assessment and evaluation feedback to improve performance.

◆ The teacher participates in appropriate professional growth activities (e.g., committees, course work, workshops, conferences) consistent with personal growth and district identified needs.

◆ The teacher explores and applies knowledge and information about effective methods.

P-3: The teacher contributes to the overall school climate by supporting school goals.

◆ The teacher builds professional relationships with colleagues that foster increased student learning.

◆ The teacher shares teaching methods, materials, research, and insights with colleagues.

◆ The teacher serves on school and/or district committees and supports school activities.

◆ The teacher supports the vision, mission, and goals of the school and district and supports community initiatives if appropriate.

◆ The teacher contributes to the profession by serving as a mentor, peer coach, and/or supervisor to pre-service teachers or interns.

Classroom Teacher
4 Domains

Classroom Teacher
4 Domains

Instruction Skills

This domain of performance encompasses both organizing for instruction and delivery of instruction. The major responsibilities include planning and implementing a variety of activities consistent with instructional objectives, selecting instructional methods compatible with student abilities and learning styles.

Assessment Skills

This domain includes the responsibilities for conducting evaluation and providing feedback to students that encourages student progress and measures student achievement.

Learning Environment Skills

The learning environment skills domain includes the teacher's responsibilities for planning and demonstrating effective routines and procedures that create an organized and positive learning environment.

Professionalism

The final domain defines the responsibilities for demonstrating a commitment to professional ethics and growth and for complying with district policies and procedures.

Performance Standards

Domain I: Instructional Skills

Organizing for Instruction:

I-1: The teacher demonstrates current and accurate knowledge of subject matter covered in the curriculum.

I-2: The teacher plans instruction to achieve desired student learning objectives that reflect the current division curriculum.

I-3: The teacher uses materials and resources compatible with students' needs and abilities that support the current division curriculum.

I-4: The teacher links present content/skills with past and future learning experiences, other subject areas, and real world experiences/applications.

Delivery of Instruction:

I-5: The teacher communicates effectively with students.

I-6: The teacher uses instructional strategies that promote student learning.

I-7: The teacher provides learning opportunities for individual differences.

Domain A: Assessment Skills

A-1: The teacher provides a variety of ongoing and culminating assessments to measure student performance.

A-2: The teacher provides ongoing and timely feedback to encourage student progress.

A-3: The teacher uses assessments to make both daily and long-range instructional decisions.

Domain E: Learning Environment

E-1: The teacher maximizes the use of instructional time to increase student learning.

E-2: The teacher demonstrates and models respect toward students and others.

E-3: The teacher organizes the classroom to ensure a safe academic and physical learning environment.

E-4: The teacher communicates clear expectations about behavior to students and parents.

Domain P: Professionalism

P-1: The teacher demonstrates ethical and professional behavior.

P-2: The teacher participates in an ongoing process of professional development.

P-3: The teacher contributes to the overall school climate by supporting school goals.

P-4: The teacher initiates and maintains timely communication with parents/guardians and administrators concerning student progress or problems.

Performance Indicators

Domain I: Instructional Skills

Organizing for Instruction:

I-1: The teacher demonstrates current and accurate knowledge of subject matter covered in the curriculum.

Sample Performance Indicators:

- The teacher exhibits an understanding of the subject areas taught.
- The teacher demonstrates skills relevant to the subject area.
- The teacher utilizes a variety of resources in the subject area.
- The teacher demonstrates an ability to make topics and activities meaningful and relevant to each student.
- The teacher exhibits/demonstrates an understanding of technology skills appropriate for grade level/subject matter.

I-2: The teacher plans instruction to achieve desired student learning objectives that reflect the current district curriculum.

Sample Performance Indicators:

- The teacher selects student objectives for lessons consistent with district guidelines and curriculum.
- The teacher selects learning activities for lessons consistent with district curriculum and student needs.
- The teacher develops lesson plans that are clear, logical, and sequential.
- The teacher plans purposeful assignments for teacher assistants, substitute teachers, student teachers, and others.

I-3: The teacher uses materials and resources compatible with students' needs and abilities that support the current division curriculum.

Sample Performance Indicators:

- The teacher selects a variety of materials and media that support the curriculum.
- The teacher integrates available technology into the curriculum.
- The teacher selects materials and media that match learning styles of individual students.
- The teacher ensures that materials and media are appropriate and challenging for instructional levels.
- The teacher uses materials, media, and equipment that motivate students to learn.

I-4: The teacher links present content/skills with past and future learning experiences, other subject areas, and real world experiences/applications.

Sample Performance Indicators:

- The teacher links current objectives of learning to prior student learning.
- The teacher solicits comments, questions, examples, demonstrations, or other contributions from students throughout the lesson.
- The teacher matches the content/skills taught with the overall scope and sequence of the curriculum.

Delivery of Instruction:

I-5: The teacher communicates effectively with students.

Sample Performance Indicators:

- The teacher uses standard English grammar when communicating with students.
- The teacher uses precise language, acceptable oral expression, and written communication.
- The teacher explains concepts and lesson content to students in a logical and sequential manner.
- The teacher emphasizes major points of concerns by using techniques such as repetition and verbal or non-verbal clues.
- The teacher actively listens and responds in a constructive manner.

I-6: The teacher uses instructional strategies that promote student learning.

Sample Performance Indicators:

- The teacher monitors student understanding and paces the lesson based on achievement.
- The teacher uses a variety of instructional strategies to encourage student achievement.
- The teacher uses questioning strategies to engage students and promote learning.
- The teacher effectively implements a variety of learning activities and experiences consistent with instructional objectives.
- The teacher maximizes student learning by providing opportunities to participate actively and successfully.
- The teacher provides guided and independent practice of skills.
- The teacher summarizes and reviews major concepts from the lesson.
- The teacher provides evidence of measurable student progress.

I-7: The teacher provides learning opportunities for individual differences.

Sample Performance Indicators:

- The teacher identifies and plans for the instructional needs of all students and provides remedial and enrichment activities as necessary.
- The teacher explains content and demonstrates skills in a variety of ways to meet the needs of each student.
- The teacher gives each student an equal opportunity for involvement in learning.
- The teacher holds each student individually responsible for learning.

Domain A: Assessment Skills

A-1: The teacher provides a variety of ongoing and culminating assessments to measure student performance.

Sample Performance Indicators:

- The teacher effectively uses both teacher-made and standardized tests to measure student performance.
- The teacher uses oral, non-verbal, and written forms of assessment to measure student performance.
- The teacher uses authentic assessment to measure student performance.
- The teacher uses available data sources to examine and document student progress.

A-2: The teacher provides ongoing and timely feedback to encourage student progress.

Sample Performance Indicators:

♦ The teacher monitors student progress before, during, and after instruction.

♦ The teacher provides feedback to students and parents about performance and progress within a reasonable time frame.

♦ The teacher uses acceptable grading/ranking/scoring practices in recording and reporting student achievements.

A-3: The teacher uses assessments to make both daily and long-range instructional decisions.

Sample Performance Indicators:

♦ The teacher uses results of a variety of assessments to monitor and modify instruction as needed.

♦ The teacher organizes, maintains, and uses records of student progress to make effective instructional decisions.

♦ The teacher creates and evaluates assessment materials to ensure consistency with current course content.

♦ The teacher utilizes assessments that reflect course content.

♦ The teacher initiates appropriate interventions to address student academic and/or behavioral concerns.

Domain E: Learning Environment

E-1: The teacher maximizes the use of instructional time to increase student learning.

Sample Performance Indicators:

♦ The teacher plans and demonstrates effective routines and procedures.

♦ The teacher structures transitions in an efficient and constructive manner.

♦ The teacher assists students in planning and organizing for assignments, long-range projects, and tests.

♦ The teacher involves the student in learning.

E-2: The teacher demonstrates and models respect toward students and others.

Sample Performance Indicators:

♦ The teacher models caring, fairness, humor, courtesy, respect, and active listening.

♦ The teacher models concern for student emotional and physical well-being.

♦ The teacher seeks and maintains positive interactions with students.

E-3: The teacher organizes the classroom to ensure a safe academic and physical learning environment.

Sample Performance Indicators:

♦ The teacher creates a physical setting that promotes learning and minimizes disruption.

♦ The teacher complies with local, state, and federal safety regulations.

♦ The teacher organizes the classroom to facilitate the monitoring of students' work and to provide assistance.

♦ The teacher manages emergency situations, as they occur, in the school setting.

♦ The teacher creates a learning setting in which the student feels free to take risks.

E-4: The teacher communicates clear expectations about behavior to students and parents.

Sample Performance Indicators:

- ♦ The teacher monitors student behavior and provides feedback in a constructive manner to students and parents.
- ♦ The teacher redirects students who are off-task.
- ♦ The teacher enforces classroom/school rules.
- ♦ The teacher minimizes the effects of disruptive behavior.

Domain P: Professionalism

P-1: The teacher demonstrates ethical and professional behavior.

Sample Performance Indicators:

- ♦ The teacher demonstrates adherence to ethical and professional standards.
- ♦ The teacher selects appropriate channels for resolving concerns and problems while maintaining confidentiality.
- ♦ The teacher maintains professional relations with colleagues and others in the school community.
- ♦ The teacher provides for student confidentiality.

P-2: The teacher participates in an ongoing process of professional development.

Sample Performance Indicators:

- ♦ The teacher participates in professional growth activities including conferences, workshops, course work, and committees, or membership in professional organizations.
- ♦ The teacher explores, disseminates, and applies knowledge and information about new or improved methods of instruction and related issues.
- ♦ The teacher evaluates and identifies areas of personal strength(s) and weakness(es) and seeks improvement of skills and professional performance.

P-3: The teacher contributes to the overall school climate by supporting school goals.

Sample Performance Indicators:

- ♦ The teacher shares teaching insights and coordinates learning activities for students.
- ♦ The teacher serves on school committees and supports school activities.
- ♦ The teacher contributes to the development of the profession by serving as a mentor, peer coach, or supervisor of student teachers.
- ♦ The teacher completes all class and school responsibilities in a timely and effective manner.
- ♦ The teacher carries out duties in accordance with established policies, practices, and regulations.

P-4: The teacher initiates and maintains timely communication with parents/guardians and administrators concerning student progress or problems.

Sample Performance Indicators:

- ♦ The teacher responds promptly to parental concerns.

- The teacher encourages parental involvement within the school.
- The teacher provides information regarding school/community functions to parents/guardians.
- The teacher works with community members in carrying out school and community sponsored functions.

This sample set is from the *Handbook on Teacher Portfolios for Evaluation and Professional Development* written by Pamela D. Tucker, James H. Stronge, and Christopher R. Gareis and published by Eye on Education in 2002.

Resource/Specialty Area Teachers

Resource/Specialty Area Teachers
Domains

Program Management

Program management involves planning, coordinating, and organizing the program, facilitating change as needed.

Assessment

The Assessment domain includes using data to measure and improve student performance and/or program effectiveness.

Direct Services/Instruction

Direct Services/Instruction include a variety of instructional and/or intervention services to meet the direct instructional needs of students.

Collaboration

The Collaboration domain includes collaborating and/or consulting with school personnel, parents, and others to facilitate and coordinate the delivery of services to students.

Professionalism

The Professional domain defines the standards for demonstrating a commitment to professional ethics and growth and for complying with division policies and procedures.

Performance Standards

Program Management

M-1: The resource/specialty area teacher effectively plans, coordinates, and implements a program consistent with established guidelines, policies, and procedures.

M-2: The resource/specialty area teacher manages program resources effectively.

M-3: The resource/specialty area teacher maintains accurate student/program records.

Assessment

A-1: The resource/specialty area teacher assesses and documents attainment of program objective(s).

A-2: The resource/specialty area teacher demonstrates proficiency in administering, scoring/evaluating, and interpreting data from instruments or records.

A-3: The resource/specialty area teacher uses assessment information for decision making.

A-4: The resource/specialty area teacher uses evaluation to improve the delivery of services.

Direct Services/Instruction

D-1: The resource/specialty area teacher demonstrates current, accurate, and comprehensive knowledge consistent with the profession.

D-2: The resource/specialty area teacher provides intervention/instruction that promotes student learning.

D-3: The resource/specialty area teacher seeks, selects, and uses resources compatible with student/program needs.

D-4: The resource/specialty area teacher maintains effective communication and rapport with students.

D-5: The resource/specialty area teacher fosters an organized environment.

Collaboration

C-1: The resource/specialty area teacher consults/collaborates with school personnel.

C-2: The resource/specialty area teacher consults/collaborates with parents and community representatives/agencies.

C-3: The resource/specialty area teacher demonstrates leadership and provides professional development.

Professionalism

P-1: The resource/specialty area teacher demonstrates a professional demeanor and practices ethical standards appropriate to the profession.

P-2: The resource/specialty area teacher participates in a meaningful and continuous process of professional development.

P-3: The resource/specialty area teacher contributes to and supports the profession, the school division, and the effectiveness of the school.

English Second Language Teachers

English Second Language Teachers
Performance Indicators

Program Management

M-1: The resource/specialty area teacher effectively plans, coordinates, and implements a program consistent with established guidelines, policies, and procedures.

The ESL teacher

- exhibits an understanding of language development.
- uses professional literature and current resources.
- models ESL strategies and methods.
- assists schools with identifying/reporting nonnative speakers of English.
- identifies and appropriately places students eligible for ESL services.
- uses the curriculum as a basis for planning and implementing instruction.
- develops lesson plans that are clear, logical, and sequential.
- communicates an understanding of the profession's role within the educational system.

M-2: The resource/specialty area teacher manages program resources effectively.

The ESL teacher

- is accountable for materials and supplies.
- organizes and makes resources available to appropriate users.
- accesses professional and instructional materials efficiently.

M-3: The resource/specialty area teacher maintains accurate student/program records.

The ESL teacher

- organizes/uses an efficient data collection/record keeping system.
- maintains a log (i.e., organized record) of referrals, consultations, and services provided.
- maintains accurate and up-to-date student records.
- maintains student portfolios.
- completes/submits reports in a timely manner.

Assessment

A-1: The resource/specialty area teacher assesses and documents attainment of program objective(s).

The ESL teacher

- organizes and implements a data collection system.
- observes and records student assessments in a systematic manner.
- maintains accurate records of test administration and results.
- reviews data to reflect on program objective(s) completion.
- uses a variety of formal and informal methods for evaluating students.

A-2: The resource/specialty area teacher demonstrates proficiency in administering, scoring/evaluating, and interpreting data from instruments or records.

The ESL teacher

- develops and uses assessment strategies appropriate to the developmental level of the student.
- aligns student assessments with instructional objectives.
- assesses student performance according to criteria based on instructional objectives.
- develops tools and guidelines that help students assess, monitor, and reflect on their own work.
- analyzes and interprets assessment data correctly.
- seeks an assessment environment conducive to maximizing student response.

A-3: The resource/specialty area teacher uses assessment information for decision making.

The ESL teacher

- uses the results of program assessments for student placement and for monitoring instructional growth.
- uses assessment results to identify individual and class learning needs.
- uses informal assessment of student learning to adjust instruction while teaching.

A-4: The resource/specialty area teacher uses evaluation to improve the delivery of services.

The ESL teacher

- administers pre- and post-tests to students receiving ESL services.
- uses multiple assessment strategies
- collects/uses a variety of data to determine the effectiveness of services provided.
- selects and administers individual and group assessments.
- integrates data from a variety of assessment techniques and sources.

Direct Services/Instruction

D-1: The resource/specialty area teacher demonstrates current, accurate, and comprehensive knowledge consistent with the profession.

The ESL teacher

- exhibits an understanding of language development.
- uses professional literature and current resources.
- models ESL strategies and methods.
- assists schools with identifying/reporting nonnative speakers of English.
- identifies and appropriately places students eligible for ESL services.
- uses the adopted curriculum as a basis for planning and implementing instruction.
- develops lesson plans that are clear, logical, and sequential.
- communicates an understanding of the profession's role within the educational system.

D-2: The resource/specialty area teacher provides intervention/instruction that promotes student learning.

The ESL teacher

- serves as an advocate for ESL students.
- recommends accommodations for ESL students.

♦ makes arrangements for interpreters as needed.

♦ plans instruction appropriate to the developmental levels and needs of the students.

♦ plans a variety of activities to encourage maximum student involvement.

♦ plans for and uses appropriate materials, teaching techniques, and resources to enhance instructional activities.

♦ communicates clear, consistent expectations to students.

D-3: The resource/specialty area teacher seeks, selects, and uses resources compatible with student/program needs.

The ESL teacher

♦ provides books and materials that are appropriate and challenging to the students.

♦ uses/integrates technology in ESL services.

♦ selects materials and resources to meet needs of individual students.

D-4: The resource/specialty area teacher maintains effective communication and rapport with students.

The ESL teacher

♦ seeks and maintains a satisfactory working relationship with students.

♦ demonstrates concern for students' emotional and physical well-being.

♦ promotes/models respect for individual and cultural differences.

♦ seeks information about student interests and opinions.

D-5: The resource/specialty area teacher fosters an organized environment.

The ESL teacher

♦ demonstrates an understanding of the influences of physical setting, scheduling, routines, and transitions on student learning.

♦ manages emergency situations as they occur.

♦ arranges/adapts classroom setting to accommodate individual and group learning needs.

♦ maintains an acceptable personal work space.

♦ enforces rules of conduct/standards for acceptable behavior.

Collaboration

C-1: The resource/specialty area teacher consults/collaborates with school personnel.

The ESL teacher

♦ collaborates with school staff and other service providers to reach educational decisions in the best interest of the child and to develop/implement appropriate strategies.

♦ establishes/maintains collaborative relationships with other service providers to facilitate program integration.

♦ serves on school-based committees when requested.

C-2: The resource/specialty area teacher consults/collaborates with parents and community representatives/agencies.

The ESL teacher

♦ communicates with parents concerning student progress/problems.

- serves as a resource for parents regarding the language needs of children.
- responds promptly to parental concerns.
- coordinates/attends parent conferences as needed/requested.
- makes appropriate student referrals to specialists/community agencies.
- promotes parental involvement within the school.
- notifies families of ESL program placement/exit.

C-3: The resource/specialty area teacher demonstrates leadership and provides professional development.

The ESL teacher

- provides information/materials to school/teachers as needed or requested.
- determines staff development needs.
- maintains a professional literature file for dissemination as needed.
- provides in-service/training for school/teachers as needed or requested.
- delivers an organized, appropriate, and informative presentation tailored to the needs of the audience.
- provides leadership for activities related to ESL and/or multicultural education.

Professionalism

P-1: The resource/specialty area teacher demonstrates a professional demeanor and practices ethical standards appropriate to the profession.

The ESL teacher

- maintains a professional appearance.
- relates to co-workers, customers/clients, and others in an ethical and professional manner.
- demonstrates good character and integrity.
- respects confidentiality.
- assumes responsibility for personal actions.
- represents the department/office favorably in the school division/community.
- uses acceptable written and oral language.
- selects appropriate channels for resolving concerns and problems.

P-2: The resource/specialty area teacher participates in a meaningful and continuous process of professional development.

The ESL teacher

- uses self-evaluation to identify personal strengths and weaknesses.
- sets/meets goals to improve job performance.
- participates in professional development opportunities appropriate for the work assignment.
- explores and applies knowledge about new or improved techniques and strategies.
- maintains proper licensure and certification.
- has competency in the use of instructional technology.

P-3: The resource/specialty area teacher contributes to and supports the profession, the school division, and the effectiveness of the school.

The ESL teacher

- is punctual and has good attendance.
- demonstrates appropriate use of employee leave.
- is flexible and open to change.
- supports/assists co-workers/work team.
- is loyal to the organization and advances the mission/goals.
- makes a positive contribution to the overall climate in the workplace.
- supports school/office activities.
- contributes to the development of the profession by serving as a mentor or peer coach/teacher and/or by supervising student teachers and interns when requested.
- participates in professional organizations.

Gifted/Talented Enrichment Teacher

Gifted/Talented Enrichment Teacher
Performance Indicators

Program Management

M-1: The resource/specialty area teacher effectively plans, coordinates, and implements a program consistent with established guidelines, policies, and procedures.

The gifted/talented enrichment teacher

- knows and follows applicable local, state, and federal policies and regulations.
- knows and follows proper school district, department, and/or site procedures.
- demonstrates effective time management and flexibility to allow for direct instruction of students, collaboration with staff and parents, administrative duties, and community service.
- facilitates the extension of state and local curriculum standards and grade-level objectives through differentiated instruction.

M-2: The resource/specialty area teacher manages program resources effectively.

The gifted/talented enrichment teacher

- is accountable for materials and supplies.
- organizes and makes resources available to appropriate users.
- matches/refers materials to best meet the needs of students and teachers.

M-3: The resource/specialty area teacher maintains accurate student/program records.

The gifted/talented enrichment teacher

- organizes/uses an efficient data collection/record keeping system.
- observes and records student assessments in a systematic manner.
- maintains accurate records of test administration and results.
- maintains an up-to-date list of identified gifted students.
- maintains cumulative records of identified gifted students.
- maintains an accurate inventory of materials/equipment.
- completes/submits reports in a timely manner.

Assessment

A-1: The resource/specialty area teacher assesses and documents attainment of program objective(s).

The gifted/talented enrichment teacher

- organizes and implements a data collection system.
- observes and records student assessments in a systematic manner.
- maintains accurate records of test administration and results.
- reviews data to reflect on program objective(s) completion.
- uses a variety of formal and informal methods for evaluating students.
- collects and uses a variety of data to determine program effectiveness.

A-2: The resource/specialty area teacher demonstrates proficiency in administering, scoring/evaluating, and interpreting data from instruments or records.

The gifted/talented enrichment teacher

- ♦ selects/administers appropriate assessment/screening tools that are in compliance with established criteria.
- ♦ processes grade report forms.
- ♦ assesses student performance according to criteria based on instructional objectives.
- ♦ administers selected evaluation instruments appropriately.
- ♦ analyzes and interprets assessment data correctly.

A-3: The resource/specialty area teacher uses assessment information for decision making.

The gifted/talented enrichment teacher

- ♦ interprets/uses data for formal identification or placement purposes.
- ♦ uses assessment data to evaluate program effectiveness.
- ♦ uses assessment for selecting curriculum, materials, and instruction.
- ♦ uses assessment information to improve teaching and learning.

A-4: The resource/specialty area teacher uses evaluation to improve the delivery of services.

The gifted/talented enrichment teacher

- ♦ uses multiple data for determining eligibility.
- ♦ uses a variety of formal and informal methods for evaluating students.
- ♦ integrates data from a variety of assessment techniques and sources.
- ♦ collects/uses a variety of data to determine the effectiveness of services provided.
- ♦ collects data for determining eligibility.
- ♦ processes grade report forms.
- ♦ assesses student interests, talents, and strengths through interest surveys and other means.
- ♦ uses a variety of measures that are appropriate for students, including student self-assessment.
- ♦ uses rubrics and portfolios for student assessment.

Direct Services/Instruction

D-1: The resource/specialty area teacher demonstrates current, accurate, and comprehensive knowledge consistent with the profession.

The gifted/talented enrichment teacher

- ♦ serves as a resource for the school.
- ♦ exhibits an understanding of gifted education.
- ♦ uses professional literature and current resources.
- ♦ makes information and activities meaningful and relevant for high ability learners.
- ♦ uses strategies grounded in current research.
- ♦ incorporates enrichment experiences in the classroom.
- ♦ modifies instructional strategies that differentiate for high ability learners.

D-2: The resource/specialty area teacher provides intervention/instruction that promotes student learning.

The gifted/talented enrichment teacher

- is an advocate for gifted students.
- offers gifted courses appropriate to program level.
- plans exploratory experiences, process skills, and product development for high ability learners.
- implements a continuum of services based on ability levels of students.
- plans exploratory experiences, process skills, and product development for high ability learners.
- modifies instructional strategies to differentiate for high ability learners.
- identifies and plans for the instructional needs of high ability students.
- explains content and demonstrates skills in a variety of ways.
- facilitates students' independent investigations with problem-focusing, plans, resources, products, and audiences.
- provides all high ability students an equal opportunity for involvement in appropriate lessons.

D-3: The resource/specialty area teacher seeks, selects, and uses resources compatible with student/program needs.

The gifted/talented enrichment teacher

- provides materials and activities that are interesting and challenging to high ability learners.
- selects materials and resources to meet needs of individual students.
- uses materials and equipment that motivate students.
- selects resources that are consistent with standard practice and program needs.

D-4: The resource/specialty area teacher maintains effective communication and rapport with students.

The gifted/talented enrichment teacher

- seeks and maintains a satisfactory working relationship with students.
- demonstrates concern for students' emotional and physical well-being.
- promotes/models respect for individual and cultural differences.
- communicates personal enthusiasm to engage students.
- sponsors school-based gifted programs and extracurricular opportunities.
- facilitates the development of student talents and interests.

D-5: The resource/specialty area teacher fosters an organized environment.

The gifted/talented enrichment teacher

- demonstrates understanding of the influence of physical settings, schedules, routines, and transitions on students.
- uses schedules, routines, and transitions to promote development/learning.
- maintains an acceptable personal work space.
- enforces rules of conduct/standards for acceptable behavior.

Collaboration

C-1: The resource/specialty area teacher consults/collaborates with school personnel.

The gifted/talented enrichment teacher

- collaborates with school staff and other service providers to reach educational decisions in the best interest of the child and to develop/implement appropriate strategies.
- collaborates with teachers to determine grades for differentiated instruction.
- establishes/maintains collaborative relationships with teachers and other service providers to facilitate program integration.
- serves on school-based committees when requested.
- assists teachers with curriculum compacting.
- provides alternative studies when requested by the classroom teacher.
- meets regularly with school principal and provides ongoing information updates.
- assists classroom teachers with differentiation of curriculum upon request.
- informs staff of community resources.

C-2: The resource/specialty area teacher consults/collaborates with parents and community representatives/agencies.

The gifted/talented enrichment teacher

- initiates communication with parents concerning student progress/problems.
- serves as a resource for parents and others regarding gifted education.
- coordinates/attends parent conferences as needed/requested.
- facilitates exploratory and other enrichment activities that involve community resources.
- produces newsletters for students, parents, teachers, and administrators.
- provides information for school/PTA publications.
- promotes parental involvement.

C-3: The resource/specialty area teacher demonstrates leadership and provides professional development.

The gifted/talented enrichment teacher

- provides information/materials to school/teachers as needed or requested.
- determines staff development needs.
- maintains a professional literature file for dissemination as needed.
- provides in-service/training for school/teachers as needed or requested.
- delivers an organized, appropriate, and informative presentation tailored to the needs of the audience.
- provides leadership for activities related to gifted education.
- demonstrates appropriate differentiation strategies for teachers.
- provides information pertaining to current enrichment and extension opportunities to students, parents, and school personnel.
- responds to requests for information and concerns in a timely manner.

Professionalism

P-1: The resource/specialty area teacher demonstrates a professional demeanor and practices ethical standards appropriate to the profession.

The gifted/talented enrichment teacher

- maintains a professional appearance.
- relates to co-workers, customers/clients, and others in an ethical and professional manner.
- demonstrates good character and integrity.
- respects confidentiality.
- assumes responsibility for personal actions.
- represents the department/office favorably in the school division/community.
- uses acceptable written and oral language.
- selects appropriate channels for resolving concerns and problems.

P-2: The resource/specialty area teacher participates in a meaningful and continuous process of professional development.

The gifted/talented enrichment teacher

- uses self-evaluation to identify personal strengths and weaknesses.
- sets/meets goals to improve job performance.
- participates in professional development opportunities appropriate for the work assignment.
- explores and applies knowledge about new or improved techniques and strategies.
- maintains proper licensure and certification.
- has competency in instructional technology.

P-3: The resource/specialty area teacher contributes to and supports the profession, the school division, and the effectiveness of the school.

The gifted/talented enrichment teacher

- is punctual and has good attendance.
- demonstrates appropriate use of employee leave.
- is flexible and open to change.
- supports/assists co-workers/work team.
- is loyal to the organization and advances the mission/goals.
- makes a positive contribution to the overall climate in the workplace.
- supports school/office activities.
- contributes to the development of the profession by serving as a mentor or peer coach/teacher and/or by supervising student teachers and interns when requested.
- participates in professional organizations.

Preschool Teachers

Preschool Teachers
Performance Indicators

Program Management

M-1: The resource/specialty area teacher effectively plans, coordinates, and implements a program consistent with established guidelines, policies, and procedures.

The preschool teacher

+ manages caseload and/or scheduling effectively
+ develops a flexible schedule to effectively allow for instruction, collaboration with staff, and parent/community services.
+ manages professional and instructional resources efficiently

M-2: The resource/specialty area teacher manages program resources effectively.

The preschool teacher

+ is accountable for materials and supplies.
+ organizes and makes resources available to appropriate users.
+ accesses professional and instructional materials efficiently.

M-3: The resource/specialty area teacher maintains accurate student/program records.

The preschool teacher

+ establishes annual program goals.
+ communicates understanding of program guidelines, policies, and procedures.
+ uses the early childhood curriculum effectively.
+ prepares, maintains, and updates all active IEPs on an annual basis.

Assessment

A-1: The resource/specialty area teacher assesses and documents attainment of program objective(s).

The preschool teacher

+ organizes and implements a data collection system.
+ observes and records student assessments in a systematic manner.
+ maintains accurate records of test administration and results.
+ reviews data to reflect on program objective(s) completion.
+ uses a variety of formal and informal methods for evaluating students.
+ collects and uses a variety of data to determine program effectiveness.

A-2: The resource/specialty area teacher demonstrates proficiency in administering, scoring/evaluating, and interpreting data from instruments or records.

The preschool teacher

+ organizes and implements a data collection system.
+ observes and records student development in a systematic manner.
+ prepares written diagnostic reports that are comprehensive and objective.

♦ writes educational reports in a timely manner.

A-3: The resource/specialty area teacher uses assessment information for decision making.

The preschool teacher

♦ interprets data for formal identification or placement purposes.

♦ uses assessment to make instructional decisions.

♦ uses assessment information to improve teaching and learning.

A-4: The resource/specialty area teacher uses evaluation to improve the delivery of services.

The preschool teacher

♦ administers assessments in compliance with established procedures.

♦ uses methods of assessment appropriate to the age and experience of young children.

♦ collects meaningful samples of representative work of children.

♦ observes and records children's performance during authentic activities.

Direct Services/Instruction

D-1: The resource/specialty area teacher demonstrates current, accurate, and comprehensive knowledge consistent with the profession.

The preschool teacher

♦ applies theories of child development (both typical and atypical) in various learning situations.

♦ uses professional literature and current resources.

♦ demonstrates an ability to make topics and activities meaningful and relevant.

♦ modifies classroom practices based on current research.

D-2: The resource/specialty teacher provides intervention/instruction that promotes student learning.

The preschool teacher

♦ maintains balance between child-initiated and adult-initiated activities.

♦ incorporates active and quiet activities throughout the daily routine.

♦ provides opportunities for children to make meaningful choices.

♦ makes adaptations to address unique needs and talents.

♦ includes play, exploration, problem-solving, and inquiry to support curiosity and decision-making.

♦ builds on what children know and are able to do to consolidate learning and to foster acquisition of new concepts and skills.

♦ explains content and demonstrates skills in a variety of ways to meet children's needs.

♦ gives all children an opportunity for involvement in learning.

D-3: The resource/specialty area teacher seeks, selects, and uses resources compatible with student/program needs.

The preschool teacher

♦ provides materials and activities that are concrete and relevant to young children.

♦ selects a variety of materials and media that support curriculum.

- uses available technology resources.
- selects materials and resources to meet needs of individual students.
- uses materials and equipment that motivate students to learn.
- identifies and plans for the instructional needs of all students; provides remediation and enrichment as needed.

assists children in developing compensatory skills and techniques.

D-4: The resource/specialty area teacher maintains effective communication and rapport with students.

The preschool teacher

- uses individual/group guidance to develop positive supportive relationships with children.
- helps children use problem solving strategies in resolving conflicts.
- maintains a balance between child and adult talk.
- models caring, fairness, humor, courtesy, and respect.
- listens carefully to children and adapts responses as needed.
- uses a variety of communication strategies, including observing, questioning, repeating, extending, and scaffolding.

D-5: The resource/specialty area teacher fosters an organized environment.

The preschool teacher

- demonstrates understanding of the influence of the physical setting, schedule, routines, and transitions on children.
- uses schedule, routines, and transitions to promote development and learning.
- labels and organizes classroom materials with different levels of complexity.
- maintains classroom materials/equipment in good repair.
- provides materials and equipment in sufficient quantity.

Collaboration

C-1: The resource/specialty area teacher consults/collaborates with school personnel.

The preschool teacher

- communicates assessment results in a professional, accurate manner.
- integrates assessment results with other professionals and parents to develop and implement Individualized Education Plans.
- meets regularly with teachers and other staff involved in early childhood.
- establishes and maintains a collaborative relationship with staff.
- serves as a consultant to child study team.

C-2: The resource/specialty area teacher consults/collaborates with parents and community representatives/agencies.

The preschool teacher

- initiates communication with parents or guardians concerning student progress or problems in a timely manner.
- responds promptly to parental concerns.

- promotes parental involvement within the school.
- provides useful information about the school to parents and community members.
- cooperates with community members in carrying out school and community-sponsored functions.
- links families with community services, based on identified priorities and concerns.
- communicates regularly with other professionals and agencies to support children and their families.
- plans for effective participation by volunteers, student interns, Foster Grandparents, etc.

C-3: The resource/specialty area teacher demonstrates leadership and provides professional development.

The preschool teacher

- provides information/materials to school/teachers as needed or requested.
- determines staff development needs.
- maintains a professional literature file for dissemination as needed.
- provides in-service/training for school/teachers as needed or requested.
- delivers an organized, appropriate, and informative presentation tailored to the needs of the audience.
- provides leadership for activities related to early childhood education.

Professionalism

P-1: The resource/specialty area teacher demonstrates a professional demeanor and practices ethical standards appropriate to the profession.

The preschool teacher

- maintains a professional appearance and demeanor.
- interacts with colleagues in an ethical and professional manner.
- carries out duties in accordance with established policies, practices, and regulations.
- selects appropriate channels for resolving concerns and problems, and maintains confidentiality.
- completes all classroom and school assignments and responsibilities in a timely and effective manner.

P-2: The resource/specialty area teacher participates in a meaningful and continuous process of professional development.

The preschool teacher

- participates in professional growth activities including conferences, workshops, course work, and committees, or membership in professional organizations.
- explores, disseminates, and applies knowledge and information about new or improved methods of instruction and related issues.
- evaluates and identifies areas of personal strength and weakness and seeks improvement of skills and professional performance.

P-3: The resource/specialty area teacher contributes to and supports the profession, the school division, and the effectiveness of the school.

The preschool teacher

- builds professional relationships with colleagues to share teaching insights and to co-ordinate learning activities for students.
- serves on school committees and supports school activities.
- contributes to the development of the profession by serving as a mentor or peer coach/teacher and by supervising student teachers and interns.
- contributes to the overall school climate by supporting school goals and initiatives.

Reading Recovery® Teachers

Reading Recovery® Teachers
Performance Indicators

Program Management

M-1: The resource/specialty area teacher effectively plans, coordinates, and implements a program consistent with established guidelines, policies, and procedures.

The Reading Recovery® teacher

- knows and follows applicable local, state, and federal policies and regulations.
- knows and follows proper school system, department, and/or site procedures.
- knows and follows Reading Recovery® program guidelines.
- keeps abreast of changes in policies, procedures, and regulations.
- demonstrates effective time management and flexibility to allow for student assessment, direct classroom instruction, administrative duties, and consultative services with students, families, and staff.
- implements applicable curriculum objectives.
- plans and implements the Reading Recovery® instruction.

M-2: The resource/specialty area teacher manages program resources effectively.

The Reading Recovery® teacher

- maintains collection of Reading Recovery® leveled books for individual and group use by the Reading Recovery® students.
- is accountable for materials and supplies.
- maintains instructional materials/equipment in good repair.

M-3: The resource/specialty area teacher maintains accurate student/program records.

The Reading Recovery® teacher

- uses an efficient data collection/record keeping system.
- maintains an accurate and up-to-date eligibility list for the Reading Recovery® program.
- maintains individual records for each Reading Recovery® student.
- completes/submits reports in a timely manner.
- provides end-of-year program data to principal.

Assessment

A-1: The resource/specialty area teacher assesses and documents attainment of program objective(s).

The Reading Recovery® teacher

- organizes and implements a data collection system.
- observes and records student assessments in a systematic manner.
- maintains accurate records of test administration and results.
- reviews data to reflect on program objective(s) completion.
- uses a variety of formal and informal methods for evaluating students.
- collects and uses a variety of data to determine program effectiveness.

A-2: The resource/specialty area teacher demonstrates proficiency in administering, scoring/evaluating, and interpreting data from instruments or records.

The Reading Recovery® teacher

♦ selects and administers assessment measures in compliance with established procedures.

♦ analyzes and interprets assessment data correctly.

A-3: The resource/specialty area teacher uses assessment information for decision making.

The Reading Recovery® teacher

♦ interprets data for formal identification or placement purposes.

♦ uses assessment data to evaluate program effectiveness.

♦ uses assessment data to plan instruction.

A-4: The resource/specialty area teacher uses evaluation to improve the delivery of services.

The Reading Recovery® teacher

♦ uses a variety of evaluation strategies and data sources to measure student performance and/or program effectiveness.

♦ uses a variety of formal and informal methods appropriate for evaluating reading.

♦ collects/uses a variety of data to determine the effectiveness of services provided.

♦ selects and administers individual and group assessments.

♦ collects and uses teacher data and student assessments in student selection and evaluation.

♦ integrates data from a variety of assessment techniques and sources.

Direct Services/Instruction

D-1: The resource/specialty area teacher demonstrates current, accurate, and comprehensive knowledge consistent with the profession.

The Reading Recovery® teacher

♦ serves as a resource for schools.

♦ exhibits an understanding of the reading and writing process.

♦ uses professional literature and current resources.

♦ models strategies grounded in current research on reading and writing.

♦ communicates an understanding of the role of reading within the educational system.

D-2: The resource/specialty area teacher provides intervention/instruction that promotes student learning.

The Reading Recovery® teacher

♦ serves as an advocate for students.

♦ observes students in regular classrooms as needed.

♦ works with students to determine individual strengths and needs.

♦ demonstrates student growth in reading/writing ability.

D-3: The resource/specialty area teacher seeks, selects, and uses resources compatible with student/program needs.

The Reading Recovery® teacher

♦ selects resources that are consistent with standard practice and program needs.

- uses/integrates technology in reading instruction when appropriate.
- provides books and materials that are appropriate, yet challenging to students.
- selects materials and resources to meet the needs of individual students.

D-4: The resource/specialty area teacher maintains effective communication and rapport with students.

The Reading Recovery® teacher

- seeks and maintains a satisfactory working relationship with students in a variety of school settings.
- demonstrates concern for students' emotional and physical well-being.
- promotes/models respect for individual and cultural differences.
- communicates personal enthusiasm about language arts.
- seeks information about student's interests and opinions in language arts.

D-5: The resource/specialty area teacher fosters an organized environment.

The Reading Recovery® teacher

- demonstrates understanding of the influence of the physical setting, schedule, routines, and transitions on students.
- uses schedule, routines, and transitions to promote learning.
- has instructional materials readily available during lessons.
- enforces rules of conduct/standards for acceptable behavior.

Collaboration

C-1: The resource/specialty area teacher consults/collaborates with school personnel.

The Reading Recovery® teacher

- collaborates with school staff and other service providers to reach educational decisions in the best interest of the child and to develop/implement appropriate strategies.
- establishes/maintains collaborative relationships with other service providers to facilitate program integration.
- serves on school-based committees when requested.

C-2: The resource/specialty area teacher consults/collaborates with parents and community representatives/agencies.

The Reading Recovery® teacher

- initiates communication with parents concerning student placement, progress, and/or problems.
- serves as a resource for parents regarding the reading needs of children.
- responds promptly to parental concerns.
- coordinates/attends parent conferences as needed/requested.
- makes appropriate student referrals to specialists/community agencies.
- shares professional literature with parents.
- promotes parental involvement in the school.

C-3: The resource/specialty area teacher demonstrates leadership and provides professional development.

The Reading Recovery® teacher

- provides information/materials to school/teachers as needed or requested.
- determines staff development needs.
- provides in-service/training for school/teachers as needed or requested.
- delivers an organized, appropriate, and informative presentation tailored to the needs of the audience.
- maintains a professional literature file for dissemination as needed.
- provides leadership for activities related to reading instruction.

Professionalism

P-1: The resource/specialty area teacher demonstrates a professional demeanor and practices ethical standards appropriate to the profession.

The Reading Recovery® teacher

- maintains a professional appearance.
- relates to co-workers, customers/clients, and others in an ethical and professional manner.
- demonstrates good character and integrity.
- respects confidentiality.
- assumes responsibility for personal actions.
- represents the department/office favorably in the school division/community.
- uses acceptable written and oral language.
- selects appropriate channels for resolving concerns and problems.

P-2: The resource/specialty area teacher participates in a meaningful and continuous process of professional development.

The Reading Recovery® teacher

- uses self-evaluation to identify personal strengths and weaknesses.
- sets/meets goals to improve job performance.
- participates in professional development opportunities appropriate for the work assignment.
- explores and applies knowledge about new or improved techniques and strategies.
- maintains proper licensure and certification.
- has competency in instructional technology.

P-3: The resource/specialty area teacher contributes to and supports the profession, the school division, and the effectiveness of the school.

The Reading Recovery® teacher

- is punctual and has good attendance.
- demonstrates appropriate use of employee leave.
- is flexible and open to change.
- supports/assists co-workers/work team.

- is loyal to the organization and advances the mission/goals.
- makes a positive contribution to the overall climate in the workplace.
- supports school/office activities.
- contributes to the development of the profession by serving as a mentor or peer coach/teacher and/or by supervising student teachers and interns when requested.
- participates in professional organizations.

Reading Specialist Teachers

Reading Specialist Teachers
Performance Indicators

Program Management

M-1: The resource/specialty area teacher effectively plans, coordinates, and implements a program consistent with established guidelines, policies, and procedures.

The reading specialist teacher

- develops a flexible schedule to effectively allow for classroom instruction.
- manages professional and instructional resources efficiently.
- manages scheduling of services effectively.
- promotes a wide variety of print and/or non-print materials throughout the curriculum.
- facilitates the implementation of state and local curriculum standards and objectives.
- adapts programs and suggests strategies for use with specific students and/or groups.
- understands and uses instructional technologies.
- works with teachers and administrators to group students for instruction.
- participates in ongoing curriculum development and program assessment.

M-2: The resource/specialty area teacher manages program resources effectively.

The reading specialist teacher

- is accountable for materials and supplies.
- organizes and makes resources available to appropriate users.
- provides books and materials in sufficient quantity.
- matches/refers materials to best meet the needs of students and teachers.

M-3: The resource/specialty area teacher maintains accurate student/program records.

The reading specialist teacher

- organizes/uses an efficient data collection/record keeping system.
- maintains a record of referrals, consultations, and services provided.
- maintains accurate and up-to-date records of identified students.
- is accountable for student records.
- completes/submits reports in a timely manner.

Assessment

A-1: The resource/specialty area teacher assesses and documents attainment of program objective(s).

The reading specialist teacher

- organizes and implements a data collection system.
- observes and records student assessments in a systematic manner.
- maintains accurate records of test administration and results.
- reviews data to reflect on program objective(s) completion.
- uses a variety of formal and informal methods for evaluating students.

- collects and uses a variety of data to determine program effectiveness.

A-2: The resource/specialty area teacher demonstrates proficiency in administering, scoring/evaluating, and interpreting data from instruments or records.

The reading specialist teacher

- selects/administers appropriate assessment/screening tools that are in compliance with established criteria.
- assesses student performance according to criteria based on instructional objectives.
- administers selected evaluation instruments appropriately.
- analyzes and interprets assessment data correctly.
- seeks an assessment environment conducive to maximizing student response.

A-3: The resource/specialty area teacher uses assessment information for decision making.

The reading specialist teacher

- interprets data for formal identification or placement purposes.
- uses assessment data to evaluate total reading program effectiveness.
- uses assessment information for making instructional and curriculum decisions.
- uses assessment results for the improvement of instruction.

A-4: The resource/specialty area teacher uses evaluation to improve the delivery of services.

The reading specialist teacher

- collects/uses a variety of data to determine the effectiveness of services provided.
- selects and administers individual and group assessments.
- assesses student interests, talents, and strengths through interest surveys and other means.
- uses a variety of measures that are appropriate for students, including student self-assessment.
- uses information from a variety of sources (e.g., interviews, observations, portfolios, journals, and records).
- integrates data from a variety of assessment techniques and sources.

Direct Services/Instruction

D-1: The resource/specialty area teacher demonstrates current, accurate, and comprehensive knowledge consistent with the profession.

The reading specialist teacher

- exhibits an understanding of the instructional process for the position.
- uses professional literature and current resources.
- models strategies grounded in current research of the position.
- understands the multiple causes of academic difficulties.
- serves as a resource for schools regarding concerns, problems, questions, and issues related to educational needs that impact educational performance.
- adapts programs and suggests strategies for use with individual students or groups.
- makes information and activities meaningful and relevant for the ability of the learner.

♦ communicates an understanding of the role of the subject within the educational system.

♦ incorporates enrichment experiences in the classroom.

D-2: The resource/specialty area teacher provides intervention/instruction that promotes student learning.

The reading specialist teacher

♦ serves as an advocate for students.

♦ develops programs and selects strategies appropriate for specific students and situations, including individual and/or group interventions.

♦ differentiates instructions to meet learner needs.

♦ assists students, teachers, families, and other service providers to facilitate behavioral change.

♦ implements a continuum of services based on ability levels of students.

♦ offers consultations and/or suggests strategies to meet student needs and to support student achievement.

♦ plans exploratory experiences, process skills, and product development based on the ability of the learners.

♦ identifies and plans for instructional needs according to the ability of the student.

♦ facilitates students' independent investigations.

♦ assists core teachers with appropriate differentiation of instruction.

♦ provides alternative studies when requested.

D-3: The resource/specialty area teacher seeks, selects, and uses resources compatible with student/program needs.

The reading specialist teacher

♦ selects books/materials/equipment that are interesting, motivating, and challenging to the learner.

♦ plans for and uses appropriate materials, delivery methods, and resources to enhance instructional activities and meet the needs of individual students.

♦ selects resources that are consistent with standard practice and program needs.

♦ uses/integrates technology in instruction.

D-4: The resource/specialty area teacher maintains effective communication and rapport with students.

The reading specialist teacher

♦ seeks and maintains a satisfactory working relationship with students.

♦ demonstrates concern for students' emotional and physical well-being.

♦ promotes/models respect for individual and cultural differences.

♦ communicates personal enthusiasm to engage students.

♦ participates in school and school district advisory committees.

♦ facilitates the development of students' talents and interests.

D-5: The resource/specialty area teacher fosters an organized environment.

The reading specialist teacher

♦ ensures a safe environment for working with students.

- maintains an organized/accessible resource room/center.
- maintains an acceptable personal work space.
- enforces rules of conduct/standards for acceptable behavior.
- uses schedules, physical setting, routines, and transitions to promote development/learning.

Collaboration

C-1: The resource/specialty area teacher consults/collaborates with school personnel.

The reading specialist teacher

- works with the district coordinator, the building administrator, and teams to schedule testing.
- meets with individual teachers and teams to assist in planning instructional units which reflect school system curriculum standards and objectives.
- assists teachers in incorporating reading and writing strategies in other subjects.
- works cooperatively with learning and enrichment resource specialists and guidance counselors to ensure that the needs of students are met.
- works with curriculum leaders, teachers, and other staff members to facilitate curriculum integration.

C-2: The resource/specialty area teacher consults/collaborates with parents and community representatives/agencies.

The reading specialist teacher

- shares professional literature with parents.
- involves parents in cooperative efforts and programs to help students with literacy development.
- models techniques and provides suggestions for parents when appropriate.
- communicates division curriculum standards and objectives, policies, and procedures to parents.
- assists in facilitating parent educational/informational sessions.
- makes appropriate student referrals to specialists/community agencies.
- facilitates the production of newsletters for students, parents, teachers, and administrators.
- provides information for school/PTA publications advisory committees.
- recruits volunteers for support of instructional programs.

C-3: The resource/specialty area teacher demonstrates leadership and provides professional development.

The reading specialist teacher

- provides information/materials to school/teachers as needed or requested.
- determines staff development needs.
- maintains a professional literature file for dissemination as needed.
- provides in-service/training for school/teachers as needed or requested.
- delivers an organized, appropriate, and informative presentation tailored to the needs of the audience.

- demonstrates appropriate differentiation strategies for teachers.
- provides information pertaining to current enrichment and extension opportunities to students, parents, and school personnel.
- responds to requests for information and concerns in a timely manner.
- trains teachers to administer the tests.
- works with teachers to create optimum testing conditions.

Professionalism

P-1: The resource/specialty area teacher demonstrates a professional demeanor and practices ethical standards appropriate to the profession.

The reading specialist teacher

- maintains a professional appearance and demeanor.
- interacts with colleagues in an ethical and professional manner.
- carries out duties in accordance with established policies, practices, and regulations.
- selects appropriate channels for resolving concerns and problems, and maintains confidentiality.
- completes all assignments and responsibilities in a timely and effective manner.

P-2: The resource/specialty area teacher participates in a meaningful and continuous process of professional development.

The reading specialist teacher

- participates in professional growth activities including conferences, workshops, course work, and committees, or membership in professional organizations.
- explores, disseminates, and applies knowledge and information about new or improved methods of instruction and related issues.
- evaluates and identifies areas of personal strength and weakness and seeks improvement of skills and professional performance.

P-3: The resource/specialty area teacher contributes to and supports the profession, the school division, and the effectiveness of the school.

The reading specialist teacher

- builds professional relationships with colleagues to share teaching insights and to coordinate learning activities for students.
- serves on school committees and supports school activities.
- contributes to the development of the profession by serving as a mentor or peer coach/teacher and by supervising student teachers and interns.
- contributes to the overall school climate by supporting school goals and initiatives.

Special Education Resource Teachers

Special Education Resource Teachers
Performance Indicators

Program Management

M-1: The resource/specialty area teacher effectively plans, coordinates, and implements a program consistent with established guidelines, policies, and procedures.

The special education resource teacher

- ◆ knows and follows applicable local, state, and federal regulations, policies, guidelines, and procedures.
- ◆ demonstrates effective time management and flexibility to allow for direct instruction to students, consultation with staff, technical support, and administrative duties.
- ◆ uses time to best advantage, manages scheduling effectively, and follows tasks to completion.
- ◆ is consistently on time for meetings/appointments (e.g., eligibility, IEP) for caseload students.

M-2: The resource/specialty area teacher manages program resources effectively.

The special education resource teacher

- ◆ manages professional and instructional resources efficiently.
- ◆ is accountable for materials and supplies.

M-3: The resource/specialty area teacher maintains accurate student/program records.

The special education resource teacher

- ◆ organizes/uses an efficient data collection/record keeping system.
- ◆ maintains accurate and up-to-date special education information.
- ◆ completes/submits reports in a timely manner.
- ◆ is accountable for student records.
- ◆ documents critical situations and interventions.

Assessment

A-1: The resource/specialty area teacher assesses and documents attainment of program objective(s).

The special education resource teacher

- ◆ organizes and implements a data collection system.
- ◆ observes and records student assessments in a systematic manner.
- ◆ maintains accurate records of test administration and results.
- ◆ reviews data to reflect on program objective(s) completion.
- ◆ uses a variety of formal and informal methods for evaluating students.
- ◆ collects and uses a variety of data to determine program effectiveness.

A-2: The resource/specialty area teacher demonstrates proficiency in administering, scoring/evaluating, and interpreting data from instruments or records.

The special education resource teacher

- selects/administers assessment/screening tools that are appropriate for the disability area and in compliance with established criteria.
- assesses student performance according to criteria based on instructional objectives.
- administers selected evaluation instruments appropriately.
- analyzes and interprets assessment data correctly.
- uses assessment data to assist in documenting student progress.

A-3: The resource/specialty area teacher uses assessment information for decision making.

The special education resource teacher

- uses data to modify assessment and instructional strategies/interventions.
- uses assessment results to identify individual and/or group learning needs.
- recommends instructional accommodations for students taking standardized tests.

A-4: The resource/specialty area teacher uses evaluation to improve the delivery of services.

The special education resource teacher

- uses a variety of evaluation strategies and data sources to measure student performance and/or program effectiveness.
- uses a variety of formal and informal methods appropriate for evaluating special education students.
- integrates data from a variety of assessment techniques and sources.
- collects/uses a variety of data to determine the effectiveness of services provided.

Direct Services/Instruction

D-1: The resource/specialty area teacher demonstrates current, accurate, and comprehensive knowledge consistent with the profession.

The special education resource teacher

- is knowledgeable about assigned disability(ies) and applies relevant techniques.
- uses the adopted curriculum as a basis for planning and implementing instruction.
- adapts programs and suggests strategies for use with individual students or groups.

D-2: The resource/specialty area teacher provides intervention/instruction that promotes student learning.

The special education resource teacher

- develops lesson plans that are clear, logical, and sequential.
- plans instruction appropriate to the developmental levels and needs of students.
- plans a variety of activities/strategies to encourage maximum student involvement and provide for individual differences.
- communicates clear, consistent work expectations to students.
- manages students learning/behavior and adjusts teaching accordingly.
- uses a variety of instructional strategies effectively.
- serves as an advocate for special education students.

D-3: The resource/specialty area teacher seeks, selects, and uses resources compatible with student/program needs.

The special education resource teacher

♦ plans for and uses appropriate materials, delivery methods, and resources to enhance instructional activities.

♦ implements a continuum of services based on ability of students.

♦ uses/integrates technology in special education services (as appropriate).

♦ selects materials and resources that meet the learning styles and needs of individual students.

D-4: The resource/specialty area teacher maintains effective communication and rapport with students.

The special education resource teacher

♦ seeks and maintains a satisfactory working relationship with students in a variety of school settings.

♦ models caring, fairness, humor, courtesy, respect, and active listening.

♦ demonstrates concern for students' emotional and physical well-being.

♦ promotes/models respect for individual and cultural differences.

D-5: The resource/specialty area teacher fosters an organized environment.

The special education resource teacher

♦ takes responsibility for ensuring that assessments and other direct services are conducted and implemented in appropriate settings that are consistent with the IEP.

♦ promotes awareness and acceptance of students.

♦ maintains an acceptable personal work space.

♦ enforces rules of conduct/standards of acceptable behavior.

Collaboration

C-1: The resource/specialty area teacher consults/collaborates with school personnel.

The special education resource teacher

♦ communicates/collaborates with colleagues in order to improve student performance.

♦ collaborates with related school personnel regarding student's academic program.

♦ provides assistance to teachers/teams in planning educational strategies for special needs students.

C-2: The resource/specialty area teacher consults/collaborates with parents and community representatives/agencies.

The special education resource teacher

♦ initiates communication with parents concerning student progress/problems.

♦ responds promptly to parental concerns.

♦ coordinates/attends parent conferences as needed/requested.

♦ initiates communication with other service providers/community agencies.

♦ promotes parental involvement in the school.

C-3: The resource/specialty area teacher demonstrates leadership and provides professional development.

The special education resource teacher

- provides information/materials to schools as needed or requested.
- recommends staff development needs in the area of special education.
- provides in-service/training for schools as needed or requested.
- delivers an organized, appropriate, and informative presentation tailored to the needs of the audience.

Professionalism

P-1: The resource/specialty area teacher demonstrates a professional demeanor and practices ethical standards appropriate to the profession.

The special education resource teacher

- maintains a professional appearance.
- relates to co-workers, customers/clients, and others in an ethical and professional manner.
- demonstrates good character and integrity.
- respects confidentiality.
- assumes responsibility for personal actions.
- represents the department favorably in the school district/community.
- uses acceptable written and oral language.
- selects appropriate channels for resolving concerns and problems.

P-2: The resource/specialty area teacher participates in a meaningful and continuous process of professional development.

The special education resource teacher

- uses self-evaluation to identify personal strengths and weaknesses.
- sets/meets goals to improve job performance.
- participates in professional development opportunities appropriate for the work assignment.
- explores and applies knowledge about new or improved techniques and strategies.
- maintains proper licensure and certification.
- has competency in instructional technology.

P-3: The resource/specialty area teacher contributes to and supports the profession, the school division, and the effectiveness of the school.

The special education resource teacher

- is punctual and has good attendance.
- demonstrates appropriate use of employee leave.
- is flexible and open to change.
- supports/assists co-workers/team members.
- is loyal to the organization and advances the mission/goals.
- makes a positive contribution to the overall climate in the workplace.

- supports school activities.
- contributes to the development of the profession by serving as a mentor or peer coach/teacher and/or by supervising student teachers and interns when requested.
- participates in professional organizations.

Part III

Tools
You Can Use

Overview of Part III: Tools You Can Use

Tools You Can Use contains a variety of forms that can be customized to meet a school or school system's needs. In Part II, eight sets of roles and responsibilities were presented. The associated forms appear in this section. In some cases the same form works regardless of the professional assignment. In other cases, two forms are presented, one for classroom teachers and the other for resource/specialty area teachers. The table below shows the various forms provided within this section as well as those that have been modified for classroom teacher-5 domains, classroom teacher-4 domains, and resource/specialty area teacher. In some cases multiple versions of the form have been created for professionals to select the format they prefer or the applicable target audience. A few forms work regardless of the teacher's position.

Form	Modified by Position				
	One Form for All Positions	Multiple Formats	Classroom Teacher 5-Domains	Classroom Teacher 4-Domains	Resources/Specialty Area Teacher
Performance Assessment Rubric			•	•	•
Teacher Goal Setting for Improving Student Achievement		•			
Teacher Evaluation Records					
◆ Informal Teacher Observation Form			•	•	•
◆ Formal Observation Form			•	•	•
◆ Teacher Performance Review			•	•	•
◆ Portfolio Feedback			•	•	•
Portfolio Guidelines			•	•	•
Client Survey		•			
Teacher Summative Evaluation Forms			•	•	•
Improvement Assistance Plan	•				
Teacher Performance Evaluation Feedback Form	•				

Performance Assessment Rubric

Description of Performance Assessment Rubric

The Performance Assessment Rubric (PAR) assists the teacher and the evaluator in job performance based on the domains and performance standards. For the teacher, the PAR offers a means to reflect on current performance compared to either past or desired performance levels to indicate growth or to inform decision making on how to reach the next level. An evaluator would use the rubric to acknowledge levels of performance. Ratings are applied to individual standards, but not to domains or to performance indicators. The four-level rating scale offers two levels to indicate effective performance (i.e., "exceeds expectations" and "meets expectations") and two levels of feedback for teachers not meeting expectations (i.e., "needs improvement" and "unsatisfactory").

Classroom Teacher— 5 Domains Performance Appraisal Rubric

Classroom Teacher—5 Domains: Instruction

	Exceeds Expectations	*Meets Expectations	Needs Improvement	Unsatisfactory
I-1	The teacher seeks and exhibits high level of knowledge of the subject(s) taught and continually updates curriculum materials.	**The teacher demonstrates current and accurate knowledge of subject matter covered in the curriculum.**	The teacher lacks comprehensive knowledge of the subject(s) taught or does not stay updated with changes in the subject area.	The teacher lacks knowledge of the subject area and does not stay current or follow the curriculum.
I-2	The teacher capitalizes on student interests and needs to achieve the desired student performance on current district curriculum.	**The teacher plans instruction to achieve desired student learning objectives that reflect current district curriculum.**	The teacher inconsistently plans instruction to support students being successful on the current district curriculum.	The teacher fails to plan instruction that reflects the current curriculum.
I-3	The teacher demonstrates awareness, sensitivity, and knowledge in responding to different student needs (e.g., instructional, developmental, and physical).	**The teacher recognizes and plans for individual learning differences and differentiates instruction to meet student needs.**	The teacher inconsistently makes accommodations for student needs.	The teacher does not differentiate instruction and/or does not make appropriate accommodations for students.
I-4	The teacher identifies, modifies, and creates instructional materials that support student learning and the district curriculum.	**The teacher uses materials, technology, and resources compatible with students' needs and abilities that support the current district curriculum.**	The teacher minimally integrates technology and/or inconsistently selects appropriate materials and resources to support student learning.	The teacher does not differentiate materials, technology, and resources to support students accessing and succeeding in learning the district curriculum.
I-5	The teacher actively involves the students in making connections with prior knowledge, experiences, and other subject areas.	**The teacher links present content/skills with past and future learning experiences, other subject areas, and real world experiences/applications.**	The teacher makes superficial connections to prior student knowledge and experiences.	The teacher instructs students on the subject(s) taught in isolation of other experiences, subjects, and knowledge.
I-6	The teacher facilitates student learning through effective use of questioning, organization, performance expectations, and instructional strategies.	**The teacher uses a variety of instructional strategies that promote student learning.**	The teacher lacks variety in the instructional approaches used.	The teacher rarely deviates from a single instructional strategy (e.g., lecture).

* The performance standard is the expectation for satisfactory performance.

Classroom Teacher—5 Domains: Assessment

	Exceeds Expectations	*Meets Expectations	Needs Improvement	Unsatisfactory
A-1	The teacher consistently provides informal and formal assessments to measure student performance.	**The teacher provides a variety of ongoing and culminating assessments to measure student performance.**	The teacher relies primarily on a limited number of assessment formats to measure student performance.	The teacher irregularly assesses student performance and/or uses inappropriate assessment measures.
A-2	The teacher offers prompt feedback, opportunity for remediation, and suggestions for students to continue to excel.	**The teacher provides ongoing and timely feedback to encourage student progress.**	The teacher inconsistently provides feedback on student performance and/or it is not timely or in a usable form.	The teacher offers little to no feedback on student performance and/or feedback is not in a timely fashion such that the student has an opportunity to improve.
A-3	The teacher pre-assesses students and adjusts plans based on the data and uses additional assessment data to inform decisions about instructional content and pacing.	**The teacher uses assessment results to make both daily and long-range instructional decisions.**	The teacher minimally or inconsistently uses assessment data to inform and modify content and approaches.	The teacher does not show evidence of using assessment data to inform instructional decision making.

* The performance standard is the expectation for satisfactory performance.

Classroom Teacher—5 Domains: Learning Environment

	Exceeds Expectations	*Meets Expectations	Needs Improvement	Unsatisfactory
L-1	The teacher communicates and maintains expectations in a constructive and equitable manner.	The teacher communicates and maintains clear expectations about behavior, classroom procedures, and academic achievement.	The teacher inconsistently communicates and reinforces expectations about behavior, classroom procedures, and academic achievement.	The teacher does not communicate expectations in a clear and effective manner to students.
L-2	The teacher utilizes routines and organizational strategies to make smooth transitions and maximize student learning time.	The teacher maximizes the use of instructional time and resources to increase student learning.	The teacher inconsistently uses instructional time and resources.	The teacher loses time in transitions and/or does not have the materials needed for instruction ready.
L-3	The teacher conveys a personal level of respect, fairness, and courtesy towards all students and other individuals encountered.	The teacher demonstrates and models respect toward students and others.	The teacher inconsistently demonstrates high levels of respect towards students/individuals.	The teacher displays a preference for some students/individuals.
L-4	The teacher organizes the learning environment to optimize a safe and orderly classroom through the establishment of procedures and the arrangement of furniture and materials.	The teacher organizes the classroom to ensure a safe academic and physical learning environment.	The teacher inconsistently considers how the classroom layout may impact the safety of the learning environment.	The teacher fails to recognize and/or address safety concerns in the classroom.

* The performance standard is the expectation for satisfactory performance.

Classroom Teacher—5 Domains: Communication/Community Relations

	Exceeds Expectations	*Meets Expectations	Needs Improvement	Unsatisfactory
C-1	The teacher responds appropriately to a variety of communication styles while maintaining precise and logical language usage.	**The teacher communicates effectively with students and models standard English.**	The teacher inconsistently uses correct grammar and pronunciation.	The teacher lacks proper grammar and pronunciation in oral communication and lacks proper diction in written communication.
C-2	The teacher develops and maintains partnerships that benefit the diverse needs of the student population.	**The teacher works collaboratively with families and community resources to support the success of a diverse student population.**	The teacher inconsistently works with families and/or community members to promote student success.	The teacher does not work with families and/or the community to support the success of a diverse student population.
C-3	The teacher establishes and maintains an open communication channel with stakeholders (e.g., parents and support personnel) who work to support student success.	**The teacher initiates and maintains timely communication with parents/guardians, colleagues, and administrators concerning student progress or problems.**	The teacher inconsistently responds or initiates communication with parents/guardians, colleagues, and administrators concerning student progress or problems.	The teacher rarely communicates with others about student progress or concerns, or the teacher communicates in an inappropriate manner.

* The performance standard is the expectation for satisfactory performance.

Classroom Teacher—5 Domains: Professionalism

	Exceeds Expectations	*Meets Expectations	Needs Improvement	Unsatisfactory
P-1	The teacher exhibits a high level of ethical and professional behavior through demeanor, appearance, and execution of responsibilities.	The teacher demonstrates ethical and professional behavior.	The teacher inconsistently demonstrates professional and/or ethical behavior.	The teacher is unprofessional and/or unethical in word and/or action.
P-2	The teacher applies, reflects, and shares with others strategies learned from professional development.	The teacher applies strategies learned from professional development.	The teacher inconsistently uses strategies presented in professional development offerings.	The teacher rarely uses strategies presented in professional development.
P-3	The teacher actively participates in improving the overall school climate through sharing with others, service to the profession, and building professional relationships.	The teacher contributes to the overall school climate by supporting school goals.	The teacher inconsistently supports the growth of a positive school climate.	The teacher does not contribute to fostering a positive school climate.

* The performance standard is the expectation for satisfactory performance.

Classroom Teacher—4 Domains Performance Appraisal Rubric

Classroom Teacher—4 Domains: Instructional Skills

	Exceeds Expectations	*Meets Expectations	Needs Improvement	Unsatisfactory
I-1	The teacher seeks and exhibits high level of knowledge of the subject(s) taught and continually updates curriculum materials.	**The teacher demonstrates current and accurate knowledge of subject matter covered in the curriculum.**	The teacher lacks comprehensive knowledge of the subject(s) taught or does not stay updated with changes in the subject area.	The teacher lacks knowledge of the subject area and does not stay current or follow the curriculum.
I-2	The teacher capitalizes on student interests and needs to achieve the desired student performance on the current district curriculum.	**The teacher plans instruction to achieve desired student learning objectives that reflect the current district curriculum.**	The teacher inconsistently plans instruction to support students being successful on the current district curriculum.	The teacher fails to plan instruction that reflects the current curriculum.
I-3	The teacher identifies, modifies, and creates instructional materials that support student learning and the district curriculum.	**The teacher uses materials, technology, and resources compatible with students' needs and abilities that support the current district curriculum.**	The teacher minimally integrates technology and/or inconsistently selects appropriate materials and resources to support student learning.	The teacher does not differentiate materials, technology, and resources to support students accessing and succeeding in learning the district curriculum.
I-4	The teacher actively involves the students in making connections with prior knowledge, experiences, and other subject areas.	**The teacher links present content/skills with past and future learning experiences, other subject areas, and real world experiences/applications.**	The teacher makes superficial connections to prior student knowledge and experiences.	The teacher instructs students on the subject(s) taught in isolation of other experiences, subjects, and knowledge.
I-5	The teacher responds appropriately to a variety of communication styles while maintaining precise and logical language usage.	**The teacher communicates effectively with students.**	The teacher inconsistently uses correct grammar and pronunciation.	The teacher lacks proper grammar and pronunciation in oral communication and lacks proper diction in written communication.
I-6	The teacher facilitates student learning through effective use of questioning, organization, performance expectations, and instructional strategies.	**The teacher uses instructional strategies that promote student learning.**	The teacher lacks variety in the instructional approaches used.	The teacher rarely deviates from a single instructional strategy (e.g., lecture).
I-7	The teacher demonstrates awareness, sensitivity, and knowledge in responding to different student needs (e.g., instructional, developmental, and physical).	**The teacher provides learning opportunities for individual differences.**	The teacher inconsistently makes accommodations for student needs.	The teacher does not differentiate instruction and/or does not make appropriate accommodations for students.

* The performance standard is the expectation for satisfactory performance.

Classroom Teacher—4 Domains: Assessment Skills

	Exceeds Expectations	*Meets Expectations	Needs Improvement	Unsatisfactory
A-1	The teacher consistently provides informal and formal assessments to measure student performance.	**The teacher provides a variety of ongoing and culminating assessments to measure student performance.**	The teacher relies primarily on a limited number of assessment formats to measure student performance.	The teacher irregularly assesses student performance and/or uses inappropriate assessment measures.
A-2	The teacher offers prompt feedback, opportunity for remediation, and suggestions for students to continue to excel.	**The teacher provides ongoing and timely feedback to encourage student progress.**	The teacher inconsistently provides feedback on student performance and/or it is not timely or in a usable form.	The teacher offers little to no feedback on student performance and/or feedback is not in a timely fashion such that the student has an opportunity to improve.
A-3	The teacher pre-assesses students and adjusts plans based on the data and uses additional assessment data to inform decisions about instructional content and pacing.	**The teacher uses assessment results to make both daily and long-range instructional decisions.**	The teacher minimally or inconsistently uses assessment data to inform and modify content and approaches.	The teacher does not show evidence of using assessment data to inform instructional decision making.

* The performance standard is the expectation for satisfactory performance.

Classroom Teacher—4 Domains: Learning Environment

	Exceeds Expectations	*Meets Expectations	Needs Improvement	Unsatisfactory
E-1	The teacher utilizes routines and organizational strategies to make smooth transitions and maximize student learning time.	**The teacher maximizes the use of instructional time and resources to increase student learning.**	The teacher inconsistently uses instructional time and resources.	The teacher loses time in transitions and/or does not have the materials needed for instruction ready.
E-2	The teacher conveys a personal level of respect, fairness, and courtesy towards all students and other individuals encountered.	**The teacher demonstrates and models respect toward students and others.**	The teacher inconsistently demonstrates high levels of respect towards students/individuals.	The teacher displays a preference for some students/individuals.
E-3	The teacher organizes the learning environment to optimize a safe and orderly classroom through the establishment of procedures and the arrangement of furniture and materials.	**The teacher organizes the classroom to ensure a safe academic and physical learning environment.**	The teacher inconsistently considers how the classroom layout may impact the safety of the learning environment.	The teacher fails to recognize and/or address safety concerns in the classroom.
E-4	The teacher communicates and maintains expectations in a constructive and equitable manner.	**The teacher communicates and maintains clear expectations about behavior, classroom procedures, and academic achievement.**	The teacher inconsistently communicates and reinforces expectations about behavior, classroom procedures, and academic achievement.	The teacher does not communicate expectations in a clear and effective manner to students.

* The performance standard is the expectation for satisfactory performance.

Classroom Teacher—4 Domains: Professionalism

	Exceeds Expectations	*Meets Expectations	Needs Improvement	Unsatisfactory
P-1	The teacher exhibits a high level of ethical and professional behavior through demeanor, appearance, and execution of responsibilities.	**The teacher demonstrates ethical and professional behavior.**	The teacher inconsistently demonstrates professional and/or ethical behavior.	The teacher is unprofessional and/or unethical in word and/or action.
P-2	The teacher applies, reflects, and shares with others strategies learned from professional development.	**The teacher participates in an ongoing process of professional development.**	The teacher inconsistently uses strategies presented in professional development offerings.	The teacher rarely uses strategies presented in professional development.
P-3	The teacher actively participates in improving the overall school climate through sharing with others, service to the profession, and building professional relationships.	**The teacher contributes to the overall school climate by supporting school goals.**	The teacher inconsistently supports the growth of a positive school climate.	The teacher does not contribute to fostering a positive school climate.
P-4	The teacher establishes and maintains an open communication channel with stakeholders (e.g., parents and support personnel) who work to support student success.	**The teacher initiates and maintains timely communication with parents/guardians and administrators concerning student progress or problems.**	The teacher inconsistently responds or initiates communication with parents/guardians, colleagues, and administrators concerning student progress or problems.	The teacher rarely communicates with others about student progress or concerns, or the teacher communicates in an inappropriate manner.

* The performance standard is the expectation for satisfactory performance.

Resource/Specialty Area Teacher Performance Appraisal Rubric

Resource/Specialty Area Teachers—Domain: Program Management

	Exceeds Expectations	*Meets Expectations	Needs Improvement	Unsatisfactory
M-1	The teacher takes a leadership role in identifying, implementing, and evaluating interventions, programs, and/or other services for students.	**The resource/specialty area teacher effectively plans, coordinates, and implements a program consistent with established guidelines, policies, and procedures.**	The teacher participates when approached in planning, developing, implementing, and/or following-up on interventions, programs, and/or services to students.	The resource/specialty area teacher does not participate in the full cycle of program/intervention/service delivery.
M-2	The teacher expertly manages resources (e.g., fiscal, human, material) and provides leadership to others in developing their skills (e.g., mentor, peer coach).	**The resource/specialty area teacher manages program resources effectively.**	The resource/specialty area teacher requires and responds to guidance on management of resources.	The teacher demonstrates questionable practices in managing resources.
M-3	The teacher shares expertise in managing records and submitting reports in accordance with law, policies, and guidelines with others (e.g., provides model reports and peer support).	**The resource/specialty area teacher maintains accurate student/program records.**	The teacher's records and reports are not polished. Additionally, there may be issues with timeliness, accuracy, and/or thoroughness.	The resource/specialty area teacher fails to complete records and reports in a timely and accurate manner.

* The performance standard is the expectation for satisfactory performance.

Resource/Specialty Area Teachers—Domain: Assessment

	Exceeds Expectations	*Meets Expectations	Needs Improvement	Unsatisfactory
A-1	The teacher provides both statistical and anecdotal evidence of successful objective completion.	**The resource/specialty area teacher assesses and documents attainment of program objective(s).**	The resource/specialty area teacher maintains a record of program objective completion, but has weak or incomplete documentation.	The teacher does not complete necessary documentation of program objectives.
A-2	The resource/specialty area teacher is adept at selecting, using, and interpreting data from instruments or records and serves as a resource to others to improve their skills.	**The resource/specialty area teacher demonstrates proficiency in administering, scoring/evaluating, and interpreting data from instruments or records.**	The resource/specialty area teacher knows when and where to seek assistance with instruments or data interpretation and accesses assistance when needed.	The resource/specialty area teacher does not appropriately administer or accurately interpret data from instruments or records.
A-3	The teacher pre-assesses students, seeks additional information, and makes informed decisions regarding the intervention or evaluation of the intervention/program.	**The resource/specialty area teacher uses assessment information for decision making.**	The resource/specialty area teacher makes decisions based heavily on perception with little consideration of other assessment information.	The resource/specialty area teacher's decision making does not show evidence of the use of assessment data.
A-4	The resource/specialty area teacher is a reflective practitioner who continually improves the delivery of services through evaluating multiple sources of feedback and data.	**The resource/specialty area teacher uses evaluation to improve the delivery of services.**	The teacher inconsistently uses evaluation information to improve the delivery of services.	The teacher does not use evaluation to improve performance.

* The performance standard is the expectation for satisfactory performance.

Resource/Specialty Area Teachers—Domain: Direct Services/Intervention

	Exceeds Expectations	*Meets Expectations	Needs Improvement	Unsatisfactory
D-1	The teacher seeks and exhibits high level of professionally related knowledge and continually seeks to relate it to the population served.	**The resource/specialty area teacher demonstrates current, accurate, and comprehensive knowledge consistent with the profession.**	The teacher continues to develop the ability to demonstrate professional knowledge consistently in practice.	The resource/specialty area teacher's professional knowledge is out-of-date.
D-2	The teacher facilitates students' success through using a variety of strategies or approaches to support students meeting their needs.	**The resource/specialty area teacher provides intervention/instruction that promotes student learning.**	The resource/specialty area teacher uses a limited number of strategies or approaches to meet the needs of students.	The teacher does not differentiate strategies or approaches based on student needs.
D-3	The resource/specialty area teacher seeks, selects, and if necessary develops resources compatible with student/program needs.	**The resource/specialty area teacher seeks, selects, and uses resources compatible with student/program needs.**	The teacher inconsistently identifies, selects, and uses resources compatible with student/program needs.	The teacher continually uses the same resources regardless of compatibility with student/program needs.
D-4	The teacher cultivates a positive relationship with students built on trust.	**The resource/specialty area teacher maintains effective communication and rapport with students.**	The teacher makes an effort to communicate with students, but is ineffective.	The teacher addresses students in a cool and impersonal manner.
D-5	The teacher creates a climate in which student learning is highly productive due to learning time being gained from effective use of procedures and routines.	**The resource/specialty area teacher fosters an organized environment.**	The teacher inconsistently organizes the learning environment.	The teacher does not present evidence of using effective routines or strategies to organize the learning environment.

* The performance standard is the expectation for satisfactory performance.

Resource/Specialty Area Teachers—Domain: Collaboration

	Exceeds Expectations	*Meets Expectations	Needs Improvement	Unsatisfactory
C-1	The resource/specialty area teacher systematically seeks input and feedback about program effectiveness from school personnel as a means to enhance services to students.	The resource/specialty area teacher consults/collaborates with school personnel.	The resource/specialty area teacher inconsistently seeks input or feedback regarding program functioning or outcomes.	The school teacher operates the program in isolation from other school personnel.
C-2	The teacher develops and maintains collaborative relationships that assist in meeting the needs of students.	The resource/specialty area teacher consults/collaborates with parents and community representatives/agencies.	The teacher inconsistently works with families and school staff to support the needs of students.	The teacher does not work with others in supporting student success.
C-3	The teacher is a transformational leader who facilitates the program's success.	The resource/specialty area teacher demonstrates leadership and provides professional development.	The resource/specialty area teacher inconsistently provides effective leadership of the program.	The resource/specialty area teacher is an ineffective leader of the program.

* The performance standard is the expectation for satisfactory performance.

Resource/Specialty Area Teachers—Domain: Professionalism

	Exceeds Expectations	*Meets Expectations	Needs Improvement	Unsatisfactory
P-1	The teacher exhibits a high level of ethical and professional behavior through demeanor, appearance, and execution of responsibilities.	**The teacher demonstrates a professional demeanor and practices ethical standards appropriate to the profession.**	The teacher inconsistently demonstrates professional and/or ethical behavior.	The teacher is unprofessional and/or unethical in word and/or action.
P-2	The teacher applies, reflects, and shares with others strategies learned from professional development.	**The teacher participates in a meaningful and continuous process of professional development.**	The teacher inconsistently uses strategies presented in professional development offerings.	The teacher rarely uses strategies presented in professional development.
P-3	The teacher actively participates in improving the overall school climate through sharing with others, service to the profession, and building professional relationships.	**The teacher contributes to and supports the profession, the school district, and the effectiveness of the school.**	The teacher inconsistently contributes to and supports the professional community and its endeavors.	The teacher does not contribute and/or support the profession, school district, and school.

* The performance standard is the expectation for satisfactory performance.

Teacher Goal Setting for Improving Student Achievement

Teacher Goal Setting for Improving Student Achievement Form

Student Performance Measures

Student performance measures are an important information data source for assessing teacher performance. Teachers set annual goals for student performance and collect appropriate measures to document student learning gains. This information can be used as evidence of meeting specific standards. Appropriate measures of student learning gains differ substantially based on the grade level, content area, and ability level of students. For this reason, grade level or department teams can develop guidelines and standards for recommended practice in the use of meaningful measurement tools.

Sample Data Sources for Student Achievement

Pre- /Post-Testing

♦ Edutest
♦ Tests for Highter Standards

Criterion and Norm Referenced Tests

♦ Stanford 9 scores
♦ State-mandated test scores for appropriate grades and end-of-course tests
♦ SAT, PSAT
♦ Advanced Placement Tests
♦ Daberon for Kindergarten screening
♦ Gates-McGinitie reading tests

Cumulative Folders/Previous Academic Records

Teacher Assessment

♦ Quizzes
♦ Tests
♦ Skills Connection
♦ Authentic Assessments/Portfolios/Writing Samples
♦ Marks analysis by marking period/Interim reports
♦ End-of-course examinations, grades 8–12

Benchmark Tests

♦ District designed and administered tests
♦ President's Physical Fitness Test

In addition, school administrators may conduct schoolwide reviews of test data to identify patterns in the instructional program. Such reports are useful in documenting student gains and making comparisons.

Annual Goals for Student Achievement

Teachers (both continuing contract and probationary) should set annual goals for improving student achievement. Each goal should be linked to one or more of the teacher standards. Goals should include specific information to help the evaluator assess appropriateness for a particular teacher and to help determine the teacher's success in goal accomplishment. Information should include the following:

- demographic information about the teacher (e.g., school, subject, grade level).
- baseline information about students (e.g., special designations such as gifted or at-risk, pre-test scores, attendance records, relevant standardized test scores).
- goal statement describing the teacher's desired results.
- strategies the teacher will implement to accomplish the goal.
- progress report at mid-year or other appropriate intervals.
- summary of end-of-year accomplishments.

The *Teacher Annual Goals for Improving Student Achievement Form* follows. Additionally, an alternate format of this form is provided. Teachers may use *either* format for developing annual goals.

Teacher Annual Goals for Improving Student Achievement
Form A

Teacher_____   School _____

Grade/Subject _____   Evaluator _____

School Year _____

Setting: [Describe the population and special learning circumstances.]

_____

_____

Content Area [The area/topic I will address (e.g., reading instruction, long division, problem solving).]

_____

_____

Baseline Data [Where I am now (i.e., status at beginning of year).]

_____

_____

Goal Statement [What I want to accomplish this year (i.e., my desired results).]

_____

_____

Strategies for Improvement [Activities I will use to accomplish my goal.]

_____

_____

_____   _____
Evaluator's Signature/Date   Teacher's Signature/Date

End-of-Year Data/Results [Accomplishments by year end.]

_____

_____

_____   _____
Evaluator's Signature/Date   Teacher's Signature/Date

Teacher Annual Goals for Improving Student Achievement
Form B

Teacher _____ School _____

Grade/Subject _____ Evaluator _____

School Year _____

Directions

- **Setting:** Describe the population and special circumstances of the goal setting.
- **Identify content area** (i.e., the area you will address [e.g., a specific objective, one of the performance standards, a specific curriculum area, etc.]).
- **Provide baseline data** (i.e., list data describing status at the beginning of the year).
- **Write goal statement** (i.e., describe what you want to accomplish or your desired results).
- **List strategies for improvement** (i.e., describe what you will use to accomplish your goal).
- **Provide mid-point review** (i.e., accomplishment at the end of first semester).
- **Describe final results** (i.e., accomplishments at the end-of-year)

1. Setting

2. Content Area

3. Baseline Data

4. Goal Statement

5. Strategies for Improvement

7. End-of-Year Results

6. Mid-Point Review

_____ _____
Evaluator's Signature/Date   Teacher's Signature/Date

Teacher Observation/ Performace Records

Five forms are offered to assist administrators in documenting teacher job performance.

♦ The Informal Teacher Observation form may be used by administrators to document observed performance standards.

♦ The Teacher Performance Review is used to maintain a running record of evidence documented from a variety of sources from portfolios to client surveys and observations.

♦ The Formal Observation Record is used by an evaluator during an observation. The form is intended to help administrators capture a picture of what the teacher is doing without having to continually write. Common performance indicators are provided in a checklist format to facilitate this process. The indicators are not an exhaustive list, merely examples. Not all performance standards will be observed in a single observation.

♦ The Portfolio Feedback Form is adapted from a more extensive form created by the authors in their book, *Handbook on Teacher Portfolios for Evaluation and Professional Development* written with Christopher Gareis and published by Eye on Education in 2002. This form offers evaluators a means to record comments and perceptions of the evidence presented by the teacher in the portfolio.

♦ Summative Evaluation Form is used to offer teachers an appraisal of their performance. Multiple data sources (e.g., observations, portfolio, and survey) are considered by the evaluator when assigning a performance rating.

♦ Improvement Assistance Form is used to record the objectives and strategies that the evaluator and teacher have identified as means to enhance performance to an acceptable level.

Informal Teacher Observation Form

Teacher _____   **School/Time** _____

Date _____

Instruction

_____

_____

_____

Assessment

_____

_____

_____

Learning Environment

_____

_____

_____

Communications/Community Relations

_____

_____

_____

Professionalism

_____

_____

_____

Additional Comments

_____

_____

Evaluator's Signature/Date

Yourtown Public Schools

Classroom Teacher Performance Review
5 Domains

Teacher _____   Evaluator _____

Grade/Subject _____   School Year(s) _____

School _____   Teacher is   ☐ Probationary/Non-Tenured

☐ Continuing Contract/Tenured

Directions: Evaluators use this form to maintain a *running record* of evidence documented for each teacher performance standard. Evidence can be drawn from formal observations, informal observations, portfolio review, and other appropriate sources. This form should be maintained by the evaluator during the course of the evaluation cycle (yearly for probationary teachers; and a three-year cycle for continuing contract teachers).

A copy of this form should be given to a teacher at any time during the evaluation cycle upon request. The teacher should be given a copy of the form at the end of each evaluation cycle.

Domain: Instruction

I-1 The teacher demonstrates current and accurate knowledge of subject matter covered in the curriculum.		*Evidence of Standard*
Date	**Comments**	

I-2 The teacher plans instruction to achieve desired student learning objectives that reflect the current district curriculum.		*Evidence of Standard*
Date	**Comments**	

* If the teacher is probationary, then a new form is generated each year. For continuing contract teachers, the form is cumulative over the three-year period.

I-3

The teacher recognizes and plans for individual learning differences and differentiates instruction to meet student needs.

Date	Comments	Evidence of Standard

I-4

The teacher uses materials, technology, and resources compatible with students' needs and abilities that support the current district curriculum.

Date	Comments	Evidence of Standard

I-5

The teacher links present content/skills with past and future learning experiences, other subject areas, and real world experiences/applications.

Date	Comments	Evidence of Standard

I-6

The teacher uses a variety of instructional strategies that promote student learning.

Date	Comments	Evidence of Standard

Domain: Assessment

A-1		Evidence of Standard
The teacher provides a variety of ongoing and culminating assessments to measure student performance.		
Date	*Comments*	

A-2		Evidence of Standard
The teacher provides ongoing and timely feedback to encourage student progress.		
Date	*Comments*	

A-3		Evidence of Standard
The teacher uses assessment results to make both daily and long-range instructional decisions.		
Date	*Comments*	

Domain: Learning Environment

L-1		Evidence of Standard
The teacher communicates and maintains clear expectations about behavior, classroom procedures, and academic achievement.		
Date	*Comments*	

L-2

The teacher maximizes the use of instructional time and resources to increase student learning.

Date	Comments	*Evidence of Standard*

L-3

The teacher demonstrates and models respect toward students and others.

Date	Comments	*Evidence of Standard*

L-4

The teacher organizes the classroom to ensure a safe academic and physical learning environment.

Date	Comments	*Evidence of Standard*

Domain: Communication/Community Relations

C-1

The teacher communicates effectively with students and models standard English.

Date	Comments	*Evidence of Standard*

C-2

The teacher works collaboratively with families and community resources to support the success of a diverse student population.

Date	Comments	*Evidence of Standard*

C-3

The teacher initiates and maintains timely communication with parents/guardians, colleagues, and administrators concerning student progress or problems.

Date	Comments	*Evidence of Standard*

Domain: Professionalism

P-1

The teacher demonstrates ethical and professional behavior.

Date	Comments	*Evidence of Standard*

P-2

The teacher applies strategies learned from professional development.

Date	Comments	*Evidence of Standard*

P-3		Evidence of Standard
The teacher contributes to the overall school climate by supporting school goals.		
Date	**Comments**	

Additional Notes

_____

_____

_____

_____

_____

_____

_____

_____

_____

_____

_____

_____

_____

_____

_____

_____

_____

_____

_____

_____

_____

_____

Yourtown Public Schools

Classroom Teacher Performance Review
4 Domains

Teacher _____   **Evaluator** _____

Grade/Subject _____   **School Year(s)** _____

School _____   **Teacher is**   ☐ **Probationary/Non-Tenured**

☐ **Continuing Contract/Tenured**

Directions: Evaluators use this form to maintain a *running record* of evidence documented for each teacher performance standard. Evidence can be drawn from formal observations, informal observations, portfolio review, and other appropriate sources. This form should be maintained by the evaluator during the course of the evaluation cycle (yearly for probationary teachers; and a three-year cycle for continuing contract teachers).

A copy of this form should be given to a teacher at any time during the evaluation cycle upon request. The teacher should be given a copy of the form at the end of each evaluation cycle.

Domain: Instruction

I-1 The teacher demonstrates current and accurate knowledge of subject matter covered in the curriculum.		*Evidence of Standard*
Date	*Comments*	

I-2 The teacher plans instruction to achieve desired student learning objectives that reflect the current district curriculum.		*Evidence of Standard*
Date	*Comments*	

* If the teacher is probationary, then a new form is generated each year. For continuing contract teachers, the form is cumulative over the three-year period.

I-3

The teacher uses materials, technology, and resources compatible with students' needs and abilities that support the current district curriculum.

Date	Comments	Evidence of Standard

I-4

The teacher links present content/skills with past and future learning experiences, other subject areas, and real world experiences/applications.

Date	Comments	Evidence of Standard

I-5

The teacher communicates effectively with students.

Date	Comments	Evidence of Standard

I-6

The teacher uses a variety of instructional strategies that promote student learning.

Date	Comments	Evidence of Standard

I-7

The teacher provides learning opportunities for individual differences.

Date	Comments	*Evidence of Standard*

Domain: Assessment

A-1

The teacher provides a variety of ongoing and culminating assessments to measure student performance.

Date	Comments	*Evidence of Standard*

A-2

The teacher provides ongoing and timely feedback to encourage student progress.

Date	Comments	*Evidence of Standard*

A-3

The teacher uses assessment results to make both daily and long-range instructional decisions.

Date	Comments	*Evidence of Standard*

Domain: Learning Environment

E-1

The teacher maximizes the use of instructional time and resources to increase student learning.

Date	Comments	Evidence of Standard

E-2

The teacher demonstrates and models respect toward students and others.

Date	Comments	Evidence of Standard

E-3

The teacher organizes the classroom to ensure a safe academic and physical learning environment.

Date	Comments	Evidence of Standard

E-4

The teacher communicates and maintains clear expectations about behavior, classroom procedures, and academic achievement.

Date	Comments	Evidence of Standard

Domain: Professionalism

P-1		Evidence of Standard
The teacher demonstrates ethical and professional behavior.		
Date	*Comments*	

P-2		Evidence of Standard
The teacher participates in an ongoing process of professional development.		
Date	*Comments*	

P-3		Evidence of Standard
The teacher contributes to the overall school climate by supporting school goals.		
Date	*Comments*	

P-4		Evidence of Standard
The teacher initiates and maintains timely communication with parents/guardians and administrators concerning student progress or problems.		
Date	*Comments*	

Additional Notes

_____

_____

Performance Review
Resource/Specialty Area Teacher

Teacher _____   Evaluator _____

Grade/Subject _____   School Year(s) _____

School _____   Teacher is ☐ Probationary/Non-Tenured

                                                                        ☐ Continuing Contract/Tenured

Directions: Evaluators use this form to maintain a *running record* of evidence documented for each teacher performance standard. Evidence can be drawn from formal observations, informal observations, portfolio review, and other appropriate sources. This form should be maintained by the evaluator during the course of the evaluation cycle (yearly for probationary teachers; and a three-year cycle for continuing contract teachers).

A copy of this form should be given to a teacher at any time during the evaluation cycle upon request. The teacher should be given a copy of the form at the end of each evaluation cycle.

Domain: Program Management

M-1

The resource/specialty area teacher effectively plans, coordinates, and implements a program consistent with established guidelines, policies, and procedures.

Date	Comments	Evidence of Standard

M-2

The resource/specialty area teacher manages program resources effectively.

Date	Comments	Evidence of Standard

* If the teacher is probationary, then a new form is generated each year. For continuing contract teachers, the form is cumulative over the three-year period.

M-3

The resource/specialty area teacher maintains accurate student/program records.

Date	Comments	Evidence of Standard

Domain: Assessment

A-1

The resource/specialty area teacher assesses and documents attainment of program objective(s).

Date	Comments	Evidence of Standard

A-2

The resource/specialty area teacher demonstrates proficiency in administering, scoring/evaluating, and interpreting data from instruments or records.

Date	Comments	Evidence of Standard

A-3

The resource/specialty area teacher uses assessment information for decision making.

Date	Comments	Evidence of Standard

A-4		Evidence of Standard
The resource/specialty area teacher uses evaluation to improve the delivery of services.		
Date	**Comments**	

Domain: Direct Services/Instruction

D-1		Evidence of Standard
The resource/specialty area teacher demonstrates current, accurate, and comprehensive knowledge consistent with the profession.		
Date	**Comments**	

D-2		Evidence of Standard
The resource/specialty area teacher provides intervention/instruction that promotes student learning.		
Date	**Comments**	

D-3		Evidence of Standard
The resource/specialty area teacher seeks, selects, and uses resources compatible with student/program needs.		
Date	**Comments**	

D-4

The resource/specialty area teacher maintains effective communication and rapport with students.

Date	Comments	*Evidence of Standard*

D-5

The resource/specialty area teacher fosters an organized environment.

Date	Comments	*Evidence of Standard*

Domain: Collaboration

C-1

The resource/specialty area teacher consults/collaborates with school personnel.

Date	Comments	*Evidence of Standard*

C-2

The resource/specialty area teacher consults/collaborates with parents and community representatives/agencies.

Date	Comments	*Evidence of Standard*

C-3 The resource/specialty area teacher demonstrates leadership and provides professional development.		Evidence of Standard
Date	**Comments**	

Domain: Professionalism

P-1 The resource/specialty area teacher demonstrates a professional demeanor and practices ethical standards appropriate to the profession.		Evidence of Standard
Date	**Comments**	

P-2 The resource/specialty area teacher participates in a meaningful and continuous process of professional development.		Evidence of Standard
Date	**Comments**	

P-3 The resource/specialty area teacher contributes to and supports the profession, the school district, and the effectiveness of the school.		Evidence of Standard
Date	**Comments**	

Additional Notes

Yourtown Public Schools

Classroom Teacher 5 Domains
Formal Observation Record

Teacher _____   Evaluator _____

Grade/Subject _____   School Year(s) _____

School _____   Teacher is   ☐ Probationary/Non-Tenured

                                                     ☐ Continuing Contract/Tenured

Directions: This form is to be used at the discretion of the evaluator for documenting ongoing performance. The completed form should be retained in the principal's file and a copy distributed to the teacher. *Please note: All performance standards may NOT be observed or documented during a single visit.*

Domain: Instruction

I-1: The teacher demonstrates current and accurate knowledge of subject matter covered in the curriculum.

- exhibits an understanding of the subject area(s) taught
- demonstrates skills relevant to the subject area
- demonstrates an ability to make topics and activities meaningful and relevant to each other
- exhibits/demonstrates an understanding of technology skills appropriate for the grade level/subject matter
- bases instruction on goals that reflect high expectations, understanding of the subject, and importance of learning

Comments _____

I-2: The teacher plans instruction to achieve desired student learning objectives that reflect the current district curriculum.

- selects student objectives for lessons consistent with district guidelines and curriculum
- selects learning activities for lessons consistent with district curriculum and student needs
- develops lesson plans that are clear, logical, and sequential
- plans purposeful assignments for teacher assistants, substitute teachers, student teachers, and others
- assists students in planning, organizing, and preparing for assignments, long-range projects, and tests

Comments _____

I-3: The teacher recognizes and plans for individual learning differences and differentiates instruction to meet student needs.

- demonstrates sensitivity, respect, and responsiveness for individual, cultural, religious, and racial differences within the classroom
- works with resource/monitoring teachers to implement IEPs and Section 504 plans for identified students
- identifies and plans for the instructional and developmental needs of all students
- selects material and media that match learning styles of individual students
- demonstrates an ability to evaluate and refine existing materials and to create new materials when necessary

Comments _____

I-4: The teacher uses materials, technology, and resources compatible with students' needs and abilities that support the current district curriculum.

- selects a variety of materials and media that support the curriculum
- integrates available technology

- selects resources including outside personnel that offer added dimensions to the curriculum

Comments _____

I-5: The teacher links present content/skills with past and future learning experiences, other subject areas, and real world experiences/applications.

- solicits comments, questions, examples, demonstrations, and other contributions from students throughout the lesson
- matches content/skills taught with the overall scope and sequence of the lesson
- links current objectives with prior student learning

Comments _____

I-6: The teacher uses a variety of instructional strategies that promote student learning.

- The teacher communicates clear performance expectations for student learning.
- The teacher uses a variety of teaching strategies (e.g., cooperative learning, inquiry, lecture, discussion, problem-based learning).
- The teacher uses questioning strategies effectively.
- The teacher checks for understanding and modifies instruction accordingly.
- The teacher summarizes and reviews major concepts from the lessons.

Comments _____

Domain: Assessment

A-1: The teacher provides a variety of ongoing and culminating assessments to measure student performance.

- assesses student performance based on instructional objectives
- continuously monitors student progress before, during, and after instruction
- demonstrates competence in the use of acceptable grading, ranking, and scoring practices in recording student achievement
- uses multiple assessment strategies including teacher-made, criterion-referenced, and standardized tests
- uses oral, non-verbal, and written forms of assessment to measure student performance
- includes information on student participation, performance, and/or products in assessment

Comments _____

A-2: The teacher provides appropriate and timely feedback to encourage student progress.

- provides prompt feedback to help students monitor and improve their performance
- provides prompt feedback to help students monitor and improve their performance
- provides meaningful and timely feedback to students and parents
- communicates and collaborates with colleagues in order to improve student performance
- collects sufficient assessment data to support accurate reporting of student progress
- gives performance feedback to students before, during, and after instruction

Comments _____

A-3: The teacher uses assessment results to make both daily and long-range instructional decisions.

- uses pre-assessment data to develop expectations for students and for documenting learning.
- uses results of a variety of formal and informal assessments to plan, monitor, and modify instruction as needed
- uses a variety of assessments to monitor and modify instructional content and strategies
- uses student assessment data to identify individual and group learning needs
- uses informal assessments to adjust instruction while teaching

Comments _____

Domain: Learning Environment

L-1: The teacher communicates and maintains clear expectations about behavior, classroom procedures, and academic achievement.

- communicates academic and behavioral expectations to students and parents in a clear, concise, and reasonable manner
- manages student behavior and provides feedback in a constructive and equitable manner to students and parents
- responds in a timely manner to concerns regarding students
- relays information about school activities and function

Comments _____

L-2: The teacher maximizes the use of instructional time and resources to increase student learning.

- establishes and utilizes effective routines and procedures
- prepares materials in advance
- structures transitions in an efficient and constructive manner
- utilizes a variety of available resources to develop engaging instruction

Comments _____

L-3: The teacher demonstrates and models respect toward students and others.

- models fairness, courtesy, respect, and active listening towards students and others
- respects students, families, colleagues, and others
- models concern for students' emotional and physical well-being

Comments _____

L-4: The teacher organizes the classroom to ensure a safe academic and physical learning environment.

- creates a physical setting that promotes learning and minimizes disruption
- creates a learning environment that encourages student participation, inquiry, and risk-taking
- manages emergency situation appropriately
- arranges and adapts the classroom setting to accommodate individual and group learning needs

Comments _____

Domain: Communication/Community Relations

C-1: The teacher communicates effectively with students and models standard English.

- uses standard English grammar when communicating with students
- uses precise language, acceptable oral expression, and written communication
- explains concepts and lesson content to students in a logical and sequential appropriate manner
- gives clear and appropriate directions
- models various effective communication strategies for conveying ideas and information for a variety of learning styles
- emphasizes major points of concern by using techniques e.g., repetition and verbal or non-verbal cues
- actively listens and responds constructively

Comments _____

C-2: The teacher works collaboratively with families and community resources to support the success of a diverse student population.

- shares major instructional goals and classroom expectations with parents
- establishes and maintains multiple modes of communication between school and home
- initiates communication and responds in a timely manner
- forges partnership and offers strategies for families to assist in their children's education
- uses community resources to enhance student learning and works with the community members in planning and conducting school and community functions

Comments _____

C-3: The teacher initiates and maintains timely communication with parents/guardians, colleagues, and administrators concerning student progress or problems.

- communicates in a positive and congenial manner
- works with school staff and other service providers to reach educational decisions that enhance student learning
- adheres to school district policies regarding communication of student information
- communicates concerns and problems in a constructive manner maintaining confidentiality as appropriate

Comments _____

Domain: Professionalism

P-1: The teacher demonstrates ethical and professional behavior.

- maintains a professional demeanor and appearance
- serves as a positive role model
- carries out responsibilities in accordance with established policies, practices, and regulations in a timely manner
- adheres to ethical and professional standards

Comments _____

P-2: The teacher applies strategies learned from professional development.

- participates in appropriate professional growth activities (e.g., committees, course work, workshops, conferences) consistent with personal growth and district identified needs
- uses self-assessment and evaluation feedback to improve performance
- explores and applies knowledge and information about effective methods

Comments _____

P-3: The teacher contributes to the overall school climate by supporting school goals.

- builds professional relationships with colleagues that foster increased student learning
- shares teaching methods, materials, research, and insights with colleagues
- serves on school and/or district committees and supports school activities
- supports the vision, mission, and goals of the school and district and supports community initiatives if appropriate
- contributes to the development of the profession by serving as a mentor, peer coach, and/or supervisor to pre-service teachers or interns

Comments _____

Additional Notes

_____

_____

_____

_____

_____

_____

_____

_____

_____

_____

_____

Yourtown Public Schools

Classroom Teacher 4 Domains
Formal Observation Record

Teacher _____   Evaluator _____

Grade/Subject _____   School Year(s) _____

School _____   Teacher is   ☐ Probationary/Non-Tenured

☐ Continuing Contract/Tenured

Directions: This form is to be used at the discretion of the evaluator for documenting ongoing performance. The completed form should be retained in the principal's file and a copy distributed to the teacher. *Please note: All performance standards may NOT be observed or documented during a single visit.*

Domain: Instructional Skills

I-1: The teacher demonstrates current and accurate knowledge of subject matter covered in the curriculum.

- exhibits an understanding of the subject area(s) taught
- demonstrates skills relevant to the subject area
- demonstrates an ability to make topics and activities meaningful and relevant to each other
- exhibits/demonstrates an understanding of technology skills appropriate for the grade level/subject matter
- bases instruction on goals that reflect high expectations, understanding of the subject, and importance of learning

Comments _____

I-2: The teacher plans instruction to achieve desired student learning objectives that reflect the current district curriculum.

- selects student objectives for lessons consistent with district guidelines and curriculum
- selects learning activities for lessons consistent with district curriculum and student needs
- develops lesson plans that are clear, logical, and sequential
- plans purposeful assignments for teacher assistants, substitute teachers, student teachers, and others
- assists students in planning, organizing, and preparing for assignments, long-range projects, and tests

Comments _____

I-3: The teacher uses materials, technology, and resources compatible with students' needs and abilities that support the current district curriculum.

- selects a variety of materials and media that support the curriculum
- integrates available technology
- selects resources including outside personnel that offer added dimensions to the curriculum

Comments _____

I-4: The teacher links present content/skills with past and future learning experiences, other subject areas, and real world experiences/applications.

- solicits comments, questions, examples, demonstrations, and other contributions from students throughout the lesson
- matches content/skills taught with the overall scope and sequence of the lesson
- links current objectives with prior student learning

Comments _____

I-5: The teacher communicates effectively with students.

- uses standard English grammar when communicating with students
- uses precise language, acceptable oral expression, and written communication
- explains concepts and lesson content to students in a logical and sequential manner
- emphasizes major points of concerns by using techniques such as repetition and verbal or non-verbal clues
- listens actively and responds in a constructive manner

Comments _____

I-6: The teacher uses instructional strategies that promote student learning.

- communicates clear performance expectations for student learning
- uses a variety of teaching strategies (e.g., cooperative learning, inquiry, lecture, discussion, problem-based learning) use questioning strategies effectively
- checks for understanding and modifies instruction accordingly
- summarizes and reviews major concepts from the lessons

Comments _____

I-7: The teacher provides learning opportunities for individual differences.

- identifies and plans for the instructional needs of all students and provides remedial and enrichment activities as necessary
- explains content and demonstrates skills in a variety of ways to meet the needs of each student
- gives each student an equal opportunity for involvement in learning
- holds each student individually responsible for learning

Comments _____

Domain: Assessment Skills

A-1: The teacher provides a variety of ongoing and culminating assessments to measure student performance.

- assesses student performance based on instructional objectives
- continuously monitors student progress before, during, and after instruction
- demonstrates competence in the use of acceptable grading, ranking, and scoring practices in recording student achievement
- uses multiple assessment strategies including teacher-made, criterion-referenced, and standardized tests
- uses oral, non-verbal, and written forms of assessment to measure student performance
- includes information on student participation, performance, and/or products in assessment

Comments _____

A-2: The teacher provides appropriate and timely feedback to encourage student progress.

- provides prompt feedback to help students monitor and improve their performance
- provides meaningful and timely feedback to students and parents
- communicates and collaborates with colleagues in order to improve student performance
- collects sufficient assessment data to support accurate reporting of student progress
- gives performance feedback to students before, during, and after instruction

Comments _____

A-3: The teacher uses assessment results to make both daily and long-range instructional decisions.

- uses pre-assessment data to develop expectations for students and for documenting learning
- uses results of a variety of formal and informal assessments to plan, monitor, and modify instruction as needed
- uses a variety of assessments to monitor and modify instructional content and strategies

- uses student assessment data to identify individual and group learning needs
- uses informal assessments to adjust instruction while teaching

Comments _____

Domain: Learning Environment

L-1: The teacher maximizes the use of instructional time and resources to increase student learning.

- establishes and utilizes effective routines and procedures
- prepares materials in advance
- structures transitions in an efficient and constructive manner
- utilizes a variety of available resources to develop engaging instruction

Comments _____

L-2: The teacher demonstrates and models respect toward students and others.

- models fairness, courtesy, respect, and active listening towards students and others
- respects students, families, colleagues, and others
- models concern for students' emotional and physical well-being

Comments _____

L-3: The teacher organizes the classroom to ensure a safe academic and physical learning environment.

- creates a physical setting that promotes learning and minimizes disruption
- creates a learning environment that encourages student participation, inquiry, and risk-taking
- manages emergency situation appropriately
- arranges and adapts the classroom setting to accommodate individual and group learning needs

Comments _____

L-4: The teacher communicates and maintains clear expectations about behavior, classroom procedures, and academic achievement.

- communicates academic and behavioral expectations to students and parents in a clear, concise, and reasonable manner
- manages student behavior and provides feedback in a constructive and equitable manner to students and parents
- responds in a timely manner to concerns regarding students
- relays information about school activities and function

Comments _____

Domain: Professionalism

P-1: The teacher demonstrates ethical and professional behavior.

- maintains a professional demeanor and appearance
- serves as a positive role model
- carries out responsibilities in accordance with established policies, practices, and regulations in a timely manner
- adheres to ethical and professional standards

Comments _____

P-2: The teacher participates in an ongoing process of professional development.

- participates in appropriate professional growth activities (e.g., committees, course work, workshops, conferences) consistent with personal growth and district identified needs
- uses self-assessment and evaluation feedback to improve performance
- explores and applies knowledge and information about effective methods

Comments _____

P-3: The teacher contributes to the overall school climate by supporting school goals.

- builds professional relationships with colleagues that foster increased student learning
- shares teaching methods, materials, research, and insights with colleagues
- serves on school and/or district committees and supports school activities
- supports the vision, mission, and goals of the school and district and supports community initiatives if appropriate
- contributes to the development of the profession by serving as a mentor, peer coach, and/or supervisor to pre-service teachers or interns

Comments _____

P-4: The teacher initiates and maintains timely communication with parents/guardians, colleagues, and administrators concerning student progress or problems.

- communicates in a positive and congenial manner
- works with school staff and other service providers to reach educational decisions that enhance student learning
- adheres to school district policies regarding communication of student information
- communicates concerns and problems in a constructive manner maintaining confidentiality as appropriate

Comments _____

Additional Notes

_____

_____

_____

_____

_____

_____

_____

_____

_____

_____

_____

_____

_____

_____

_____

_____

_____

_____

_____

_____

Formal Observation Record General Form
Research/Specialty Area Teacher

Teacher _____   Evaluator _____

Grade/Subject _____   School Year(s) _____

School _____   Teacher is ☐ Probationary/Non-Tenured

                                                      ☐ Continuing Contract/Tenured

Directions: This form is to be used at the discretion of the evaluator for documenting ongoing performance. The completed form should be retained in the principal's file and a copy distributed to the teacher. *Please note: All performance standards may NOT be observed or documented during a single visit.*

Program Management

M-1: The resource/specialty area teacher effectively plans, coordinates, and implements a program consistent with established guidelines, policies, and procedures.

- develops a flexible schedule to effectively allow for classroom instruction
- manages professional and instructional resources efficiently
- manages scheduling of services effectively
- facilitates the implementation of state and local curriculum standards and objectives
- adapts programs and suggests strategies for use with specific students and/or groups
- understands and uses instructional technologies
- works with teachers and administrators to group students for instruction
- participates in ongoing curriculum development and program assessment

Comments _____

M-2: The resource/specialty area teacher manages program resources effectively.

- is accountable for materials and supplies
- organizes and makes resources available to appropriate users
- provides materials in sufficient quantity
- matches/refers materials to best meet the needs of students and teachers

Comments _____

M-3: The resource/specialty area teacher maintains accurate student/program records.

The reading specialist teacher
- organizes/uses an efficient data collection/record keeping system
- maintains a record of referrals, consultations, and services provided
- maintains accurate and up-to-date records of identified students
- is accountable for student records
- completes/submits reports in a timely manner

Comments _____

Assessment

A-1: The resource/specialty area teacher assesses and documents attainment of program objective(s).

- organizes and implements a data collection system
- observes and records student assessments in a systematic manner
- maintains accurate records of test administration and results
- reviews data to reflect on program objective(s) completion
- uses a variety of formal and informal methods for evaluating students
- collects and uses a variety of data to determine program effectiveness

Comments _____

A-2: The resource/specialty area teacher demonstrates proficiency in administering, scoring/evaluating, and interpreting data from instruments or records.

- selects/administers appropriate assessment/screening tools that are in compliance with established criteria
- assesses student performance according to criteria based on instructional objectives
- administers selected evaluation instruments appropriately
- analyzes and interprets assessment data correctly
- seeks an assessment environment conducive to maximizing student response

Comments _____

A-3: The resource/specialty area teacher uses assessment information for decision making.

- interprets data for formal identification or placement purposes
- uses assessment data to evaluate total program effectiveness
- uses assessment information for making instructional and curriculum decisions
- uses assessment results for the improvement of instruction

Comments _____

A-4: The resource/specialty area teacher uses evaluation to improve the delivery of services.

- collects/uses a variety of data to determine the effectiveness of services provided
- selects and administers individual and group assessments
- assesses student interests, talents, and strengths through interest surveys and other means
- uses a variety of measures that are appropriate for students, including student self-assessment
- uses information from a variety of sources (e.g., interviews, observations, portfolios, journals, and records)
- integrates data from a variety of assessment techniques and sources

Comments _____

Direct Services/ Instruction

D-1: The resource/specialty area teacher demonstrates current, accurate, and comprehensive knowledge consistent with the profession.

- exhibits an understanding of the instructional process for the position
- uses professional literature and current resources
- models strategies grounded in current research of the position
- understands the multiple causes of academic difficulties
- serves as a resource for schools regarding concerns, problems, questions, and issues related to educational needs that impact educational performance
- adapts programs and suggests strategies for use with individual students or groups
- makes information and activities meaningful and relevant for the ability of the learner
- communicates an understanding of the role of the subject within the educational system
- incorporates enrichment experiences in the classroom

Comments _____

D-2: The resource/specialty area teacher provides intervention/instruction that promotes student learning.

- serves as an advocate for students.
- identifies and plans for instructional needs according to the ability of the student
- differentiates instructions to meet learner needs
- assists core teachers with appropriate differentiation of instruction
- implements a continuum of services based on ability levels of students
- offers consultations and/or suggests strategies to meet student needs and to support student achievement
- plans exploratory experiences, process skills, and product development based on the ability of the learners
- provides alternative studies when requested

Comments _____

D-3: The resource/specialty area teacher seeks, selects, and uses resources compatible with student/program needs.

- selects books/materials/equipment that are interesting, motivating, and challenging to the learner
- uses/integrates technology in instruction
- plans for and uses appropriate materials, delivery methods, and resources to enhance instructional activities and meet the needs of individual students
- selects resources that are consistent with standard practice and program needs

Comments _____

D-4: The resource/specialty area teacher maintains effective communication and rapport with students.

- seeks and maintains a satisfactory working relationship with students
- demonstrates concern for students' emotional and physical well-being
- promotes/models respect for individual and cultural differences
- communicates personal enthusiasm to engage students
- participates in school and division advisory committees
- facilitates the development of student talents and interests

Comments _____

D-5: The resource/specialty area teacher fosters an organized environment.

- ensures a safe environment for working with students
- maintains an organized/accessible resource room/center
- maintains an acceptable personal work space
- enforces rules of conduct/standards for acceptable behavior
- uses schedules, physical setting, routines, and transitions to promote development/learning

Comments _____

Collaboration

C-1: The resource/specialty area teacher consults/collaborates with school personnel.

- works with the district coordinator, the building administrator, and teams to schedule testing
- meets with individual teachers and teams to assist in planning instructional units that reflect school system curriculum standards and objectives
- assists teachers in incorporating reading and writing strategies in other subjects
- works cooperatively with learning and enrichment resource specialists and guidance counselors to ensure that the needs of students are met
- works with curriculum leaders, teachers, and other staff members to facilitate curriculum integration

Comments _____

C-2: The resource/specialty area teacher consults/collaborates with parents and community representatives/agencies.

- shares professional literature with parents
- involves parents in cooperative efforts and programs to support student learning
- models techniques and provides suggestions for parents when appropriate
- communicates district curriculum standards and objectives, policies, and procedures to parents
- assists in facilitating parent educational/informational sessions
- makes appropriate student referrals to specialists/community agencies
- facilitates the production of newsletters for students, parents, teachers, and administrators
- provides information for school/PTA publications advisory committees
- recruits volunteers for support of instructional programs

Comments _____

C-3: The resource/specialty area teacher demonstrates leadership and provides professional development.

- provides information/materials to school/teachers as needed or requested.
- determines staff development needs
- maintains a professional literature file for dissemination as needed
- provides in-service/training for school/teachers as needed or requested
- delivers an organized, appropriate, and informative presentation tailored to the needs of the audience
- demonstrates appropriate differentiation strategies for teachers
- provides information pertaining to current enrichment and extension opportunities to students, parents, and school personnel
- responds to requests for information and concerns in a timely manner

Comments _____

Professionalism

P-1: The resource/specialty area teacher demonstrates a professional demeanor and practices ethical standards appropriate to the profession.

- maintains a professional appearance and demeanor
- interacts with colleagues in an ethical and professional manner
- carries out duties in accordance with established policies, practices, and regulations
- selects appropriate channels for resolving concerns and problems, and maintains confidentiality
- completes all assignments and responsibilities in a timely and effective manner

Comments _____

P-2: The resource/specialty area teacher participates in a meaningful and continuous process of professional development.

- participates in professional growth activities including conferences, workshops, course work, and committees, or membership in professional organizations
- explores, disseminates, and applies knowledge and information about new or improved methods of instruction and related issues
- evaluates and identifies areas of personal strength and weakness and seeks improvement of skills and professional performance

Comments _____

P-3: The resource/specialty area teacher contributes to and supports the profession, the school division, and the effectiveness of the school.

- builds professional relationships with colleagues to share teaching insights and to coordinate learning activities for students
- serves on school committees and supports school activities
- contributes to the development of the profession by serving as a mentor or peer coach/teacher and by supervising student teachers and interns
- contributes to the overall school climate by supporting school goals and initiatives

Comments _____

Additional Notes

_____

_____

_____

_____

_____

_____

_____

_____

_____

_____

_____

_____

_____

_____

_____

_____

_____

_____

_____

_____

_____

_____

_____

_____

_____

_____

_____

Yourtown Public Schools

Portfolio Feedback Form
Classroom Teacher 5 Domains

Teacher _____   Evaluator _____

Grade/Subject _____   School Year(s) _____

School _____   Teacher is   ☐ Probationary/Non-Tenured

                                                        ☐ Continuing Contract/Tenured

Part I Directions: Please read the following statements carefully and then respond to the statements by checking the most appropriate descriptor based on your review of the teacher's portfolio. In the event that a performance standard is not applicable to a teacher, please mark "NA." Space is provided to note what type of evidence was presented for each standard along with comments.

	Evidence				
	Clear	*Some*	*None*	NA	*Evidence/Comments*
Domain: Instruction					
I-1 The teacher demonstrates current and accurate knowledge of subject matter covered in the curriculum.					
I-2 The teacher plans instruction to achieve desired student learning objectives that reflect the current district curriculum.					
I-3 The teacher recognizes and plans for individual learning differences and differentiates instruction to meet student needs.					
I-4 The teacher uses materials, technology, and resources compatible with students' needs and abilities that support the current district curriculum.					
I-5 The teacher links present content/skills with past and future learning experiences, other subject areas, and real world experiences/applications.					
I-6 The teacher uses a variety of instructional strategies that promote student learning.					
Domain: Assessment					
A-1 The teacher provides a variety of ongoing and culminating assessments to measure student performance.					

	Evidence				
	Clear	*Some*	*None*	*NA*	*Evidence/Comments*
A-2 The teacher provides ongoing and timely feedback to encourage student progress.					
A-3 The teacher uses assessment results to make both daily and long-range instructional decisions.					
Domain: Learning Environment					
L-1 The teacher communicates and maintains clear expectations about behavior, classroom procedures, and academic achievement.					
L-2 The teacher maximizes the use of instructional time and resources to increase student learning.					
L-3 The teacher demonstrates and models respect toward students and others.					
L-4 The teacher organizes the classroom to ensure a safe academic and physical learning environment.					
Domain: Communication/Community Relations					
C-1 The teacher communicates effectively with students and models standard English.					
C-2 The teacher works collaboratively with families and community resources to support the success of a diverse student population.					
C-3 The teacher initiates and maintains timely communication with parents/guardians, colleagues, and administrators concerning student progress or problems.					
Domain: Professionalism					
P-1 The teacher demonstrates ethical and professional behavior.					
P-2 The teacher applies strategies learned from professional development.					
P-3 The teacher contributes to the overall school climate by supporting school goals.					

Part II Directions: Based on the activities noted on this form, the following comments are provided.

Commendations:

_____

Recommendations:

_____

Portfolio Feedback Form
Classroom Teacher 4 Domains

Teacher _____   Evaluator _____

Grade/Subject _____   School Year(s) _____

School _____   Teacher is ☐ Probationary/Non-Tenured

                                                        ☐ Continuing Contract/Tenured

Part I Directions: Please read the following statements carefully and then respond to the statements by checking the most appropriate descriptor based on your review of the teacher's portfolio. In the event that a performance standard is not applicable to a teacher, please mark "NA." Space is provided to note what type of evidence was presented for each standard along with comments.

	Evidence				
	Clear	*Some*	*None*	NA	*Evidence/Comments*
Domain: Instructional Skills					
I-1 The teacher demonstrates current and accurate knowledge of subject matter covered in the curriculum.					
I-2 The teacher plans instruction to achieve desired student learning objectives that reflect the current district curriculum.					
I-3 The teacher uses materials, technology, and resources compatible with students' needs and abilities that support the current district curriculum.					
I-4 The teacher links present content/skills with past and future learning experiences, other subject areas, and real world experiences/ applications.					
I-5 The teacher communicates effectively with students.					
I-6 The teacher uses instructional strategies that promote student learning.					
I-7 The teacher provides learning opportunities for individual differences.					
Domain: Assessment Skills					
A-1 The teacher provides a variety of ongoing and culminating assessments to measure student performance.					

	Evidence				
	Clear	*Some*	*None*	*NA*	*Evidence/Comments*
A-2 The teacher provides ongoing and timely feedback to encourage student progress.					
A-3 The teacher uses assessment results to make both daily and long-range instructional decisions.					
Domain: Learning Environment					
E-1 The teacher maximizes the use of instructional time and resources to increase student learning.					
E-2 The teacher demonstrates and models respect toward students and others.					
E-3 The teacher organizes the classroom to ensure a safe academic and physical learning environment.					
E-4 The teacher communicates and maintains clear expectations about behavior, classroom procedures, and academic achievement.					
Domain: Professionalism					
P-1 The teacher demonstrates ethical and professional behavior.					
P-2 The teacher participates in an ongoing process of professional development.					
P-3 The teacher contributes to the overall school climate by supporting school goals.					
P-4 The teacher initiates and maintains timely communication with parents/guardians and administrators concerning student progress or problems.					

Part II Directions: Based on the activities noted on this form, the following comments are provided.

Commendations:

_____

_____

Recommendations:

_____

_____

Portfolio

Portfolio Guidelines

The professional portfolio is an organized collection of work that demonstrates the educator's skills, talents, and accomplishments. The portfolio is an opportunity to demonstrate professional competence with regard to meeting the performance standards for instruction, management, assessment, communication, community relations and collaboration, and professionalism.

Purpose

The purpose of the portfolio is to document teaching excellence. The portfolio provides the teacher with an opportunity for self-reflection, demonstration of quality work, and a basis for two-way communication with an evaluator. The emphasis is on the quality of work, not the quantity of materials presented.

The Professional Portfolio

Your portfolio . . .

♦ is a 1.5 inch, three-ring binder with a cover and dividers provided by the school district.

♦ belongs to you (even if you change schools or leave the school district).

♦ is one component of a multi-source evaluation.

♦ includes a brief description or explanation for each entry. See the Portfolio Table of Contents at the end of this section for a format to use.

♦ contains appropriate documentation.

♦ contains the items you wish to present to your evaluator. You have full responsibility for contents, pacing, and development.

♦ is limited to items that will fit within the binder. Larger items can be photographed or photocopied for inclusion. Artifacts that do not fit in the binder (e.g., video or audio tapes) may be submitted, if agreed to by the evaluator in advance.

♦ is a work in progress and is to be maintained throughout the term of your evaluation period.

♦ remains in your possession except when reviewed by your evaluator.

♦ should have an emphasis on summary information and analysis whenever possible.

♦ contains the contents collected over the three-year period of evaluation (probationary teachers will maintain the same portfolio for all three years).

Recommendations

♦ Think of the portfolio as a natural harvesting of what you do.

♦ Work on your portfolio over time.

♦ Obtain a file folder to store potential items until you are ready to put them in the portfolio.

♦ Begin working on the ASSESSMENT and PROFESSIONALISM sections first because the standards in these domains cannot be observed as readily as can standards in other domains.

♦ Make your portfolio user friendly (i.e., neat, organized) so that your documentation is concise, clear, and easily located.

♦ Have your portfolio available every time you meet with your evaluator.

♦ While not required, if you have a current résumé, it could be placed in the front of your portfolio.

Examples of Items that May be Included in the Portfolio

The items listed below are not intended to be prescriptive nor do they represent an exhaustive list. They are provided merely as examples of what a teacher may choose to include to document performance. As many materials will address more than one performance standard, they are organized by domain. A table begins each listing of examples with suggestions of which domain in the items would fit depending on whether the teacher was being evaluated using the Classroom Teacher: 5 Domains, Classroom Teacher: 4 Domains, or Resource/Specialty Area Teacher performance standards.

Sample for	Classroom Teacher: 5 Domains	Classroom Teacher: 4 Domains	Resource/Specialty Area Teacher
Domain is called	Instruction	Instructional Skills	Direct Services/ Instruction

- Copy of an interdisciplinary unit taught
- Outline of a lesson with differentiation
- Annotated photographs of teacher-made displays used in instruction
- Summary of consultation notes with appropriate teachers and student support personnel to enhance a student's unique needs
- List of writing activities integrated into core content areas
- Copies of student work demonstrating a teacher's feedback—remove or blank out students' names and other identifying information
- Sample of technology integration
- Lesson plan with goals, objectives, activities, materials, and evaluation
- Copies of materials made to differentiate for student needs
- Copy of long-range plans
- Copy of the current lesson plan book
- Notations of meetings for team planning of interdisciplinary units

Sample for	Classroom Teacher: 5 Domains	Classroom Teacher: 4 Domains	Resource/Specialty Area Teacher
Domain is called	Assessment	Assessment Skills	Assessment

- Copies of grading rubrics
- Notations made on a unit of how it was modified based on informal and formal feedback
- Copies of teacher-made tests
- Schedules of tests given
- Summary of grading procedures

- Samples of educational reports, progress reports, or summary test data
- Explanation of the teacher's record-keeping system

Sample for	Classroom Teacher: 5 Domains	Classroom Teacher: 4 Domains	Resource/Specialty Area Teacher
Domain is called	Learning Environment	Learning Environment Skills	Program Management

- List of classroom rules
- Explanation of the interventions used when students do not follow the classroom rules
- Diagram of the room arrangement(s) used
- Schedule of daily events
- Explanation of routines or classroom procedures used to maximize time

Sample for	Classroom Teacher: 5 Domains	Classroom Teacher: 4 Domains	Resource/Specialty Area Teacher
Domain is called	Communication/ Community Relations	*this domain is incorporated into all the others	Collaboration

- Copies of letters sent to parents/guardians
- Copies of class newsletters
- Phone log of parents/guardian, community member, and professional contacts
- Agenda of "back to school" events
- Copies of programs from class events (e.g., drama play, band concert, science fair)
- Copies of letters thanking community members and/or volunteers for contributions
- Log of collaborations

Sample for	Classroom Teacher: 5 Domains	Classroom Teacher: 4 Domains	Resource/Specialty Area Teacher
Domain is called	Professionalism	Professionalism	Professionalism

- Post-graduate transcript
- Certificates (e.g., Attendance, Participation, Certification, Appreciation)
- Letters (e.g., announcing a grant award, thanking the teacher for presenting)
- PowerPoint handouts from presentations given by the teacher
- Copies of articles published

Review

♦ Your evaluator (principal, associate principal, or other direct supervisor) will NOT grade your portfolio. Rather, the evaluator will review the portfolio as part of the overall assessment of your work quality. The Teacher Portfolio Feedback form is provided in the Teacher Evaluation Records section to facilitate this process and provide feedback.

♦ Your portfolio provides documentation that complements the observation component of the multiple data evaluation system.

♦ Your evaluator will look for evidence in the portfolio and through observation to determine that you meet the standards and expectations stated in your teacher evaluation system.

♦ Your evaluator and you will review and discuss the contents of the portfolio during periodic review conferences.

Additional Resource

For additional and more detailed information about teacher portfolios, refer to the *Handbook on Teacher Portfolios for Evaluation and Professional Development* by Pamela D. Tucker, James H. Stronge, and Christopher R. Gareis published in 2002 by Eye on Education.

Portfolio Feedback Form
Resource/Specialty Area Teacher

Teacher _____   Evaluator _____

Grade/Subject _____   School Year(s) _____

School _____   Teacher is ☐ Probationary/Non-Tenured

☐ Continuing Contract/Tenured

Part I Directions: Please read the following statements carefully and then respond to the statements by checking the most appropriate descriptor based on your review of the teacher's portfolio. In the event that a performance standard is not applicable to a teacher, please mark "NA." Space is provided to note what type of evidence was presented for each standard along with comments.

| | Evidence | | | | |
	Clear	*Some*	*None*	*NA*	*Evidence/Comments*
Domain: Program Management					
M-1 The resource/specialty area teacher effectively plans, coordinates, and implements a program consistent with established guidelines, policies, and procedures.					
M-2 The resource/specialty area teacher manages program resources effectively.					
M-3 The resource/specialty area teacher maintains accurate student/program records.					
Domain: Assessment					
A-2 The resource/specialty area teacher demonstrates proficiency in administering, scoring/evaluating, and interpreting data from instruments or records.					
A-2 The resource/specialty area teacher demonstrates proficiency in administering, scoring/evaluating, and interpreting data from instruments or records.					
A-3 The resource/specialty area teacher uses assessment information for decision making.					
A-4 The resource/specialty area teacher uses evaluation to improve the delivery of services.					

	Evidence				
	Clear	*Some*	*None*	*NA*	*Evidence/Comments*
Domain: Direct Services/Instruction					
D-1 The resource/specialty area teacher demonstrates current, accurate, and comprehensive knowledge consistent with the profession.					
D-2 The resource/specialty area teacher provides intervention/instruction that promotes student learning.					
D-3 The resource/specialty area teacher seeks, selects, and uses resources compatible with student/program needs.					
D-4 The resource/specialty area teacher maintains effective communication and rapport with students.					
D-5 The resource/specialty area teacher fosters an organized environment.					
Domain: Collaboration					
C-1 The resource/specialty area teacher consults/collaborates with school personnel.					
C-2 The resource/specialty area teacher consults/collaborates with parents and community representatives/agencies.					
C-3 The resource/specialty area teacher demonstrates leadership and provides professional development.					
Domain: Professionalism					
P-1 The resource/specialty area teacher demonstrates a professional demeanor and practices ethical standards appropriate to the profession.					
P-2 The resource/specialty area teacher participates in a meaningful and continuous process of professional development.					
P-3 The resource/specialty area teacher contributes to and supports the profession, the school district, and the effectiveness of the school.					

Part II Directions: Based on the activities noted on this form, the following comments are provided.

Commendations:

_____

Recommendations:

_____

Portfolio Table of Contents for

Classroom Teacher—5 Domains
Classroom Teacher—4 Domains
Resource/Specialty Area Teacher

Table of Contents: Instruction

The teacher should complete a table of contents for each domain in the portfolio and place it immediately behind the divider for that section to serve as a guide for the reviewer.

Primary Performance Standard(s) Documented	Activity Name	Teacher Comments (Optional)

Table of Contents: Assessment

The teacher should complete a table of contents for each domain in the portfolio and place it immediately behind the divider for that section to serve as a guide for the reviewer.

Primary Performance Standard(s) Documented	Activity Name	Teacher Comments (Optional)

Table of Contents: Learning Environment

The teacher should complete a table of contents for each domain in the portfolio and place it immediately behind the divider for that section to serve as a guide for the reviewer.

Primary Performance Standard(s) Documented	Activity Name	Teacher Comments (Optional)

Table of Contents:
Communication/Community Relations

The teacher should complete a table of contents for each domain in the portfolio and place it immediately behind the divider for that section to serve as a guide for the reviewer.

Primary Performance Standard(s) Documented	Activity Name	Teacher Comments (Optional)

Table of Contents: Professionalism

The teacher should complete a table of contents for each domain in the portfolio and place it immediately behind the divider for that section to serve as a guide for the reviewer.

Primary Performance Standard(s) Documented	Activity Name	Teacher Comments (Optional)

Table of Contents: Instructional Skills

The teacher should complete a table of contents for each domain in the portfolio and place it immediately behind the divider for that section to serve as a guide for the reviewer.

Primary Performance Standard(s) Documented	Activity Name	Teacher Comments (Optional)

Table of Contents: Assessment Skills

The teacher should complete a table of contents for each domain in the portfolio and place it immediately behind the divider for that section to serve as a guide for the reviewer.

Primary Performance Standard(s) Documented	Activity Name	Teacher Comments (Optional)

Table of Contents: Learning Environment Skills

The teacher should complete a table of contents for each domain in the portfolio and place it immediately behind the divider for that section to serve as a guide for the reviewer.

Primary Performance Standard(s) Documented	Activity Name	Teacher Comments (Optional)

Table of Contents: Professionalism

The teacher should complete a table of contents for each domain in the portfolio and place it immediately behind the divider for that section to serve as a guide for the reviewer.

Primary Performance Standard(s) Documented	Activity Name	Teacher Comments (Optional)

Table of Contents: Program Management

The teacher should complete a table of contents for each domain in the portfolio and place it immediately behind the divider for that section to serve as a guide for the reviewer.

Primary Performance Standard(s) Documented	Activity Name	Teacher Comments (Optional)

Table of Contents: Assessment

The teacher should complete a table of contents for each domain in the portfolio and place it immediately behind the divider for that section to serve as a guide for the reviewer.

Primary Performance Standard(s) Documented	Activity Name	Teacher Comments (Optional)

Table of Contents: Direct Services/Instruction

The teacher should complete a table of contents for each domain in the portfolio and place it immediately behind the divider for that section to serve as a guide for the reviewer.

Primary Performance Standard(s) Documented	Activity Name	Teacher Comments (Optional)

Table of Contents: Collaboration

The teacher should complete a table of contents for each domain in the portfolio and place it immediately behind the divider for that section to serve as a guide for the reviewer.

Primary Performance Standard(s) Documented	Activity Name	Teacher Comments (Optional)

Table of Contents: Professionalism

The teacher should complete a table of contents for each domain in the portfolio and place it immediately behind the divider for that section to serve as a guide for the reviewer.

Primary Performance Standard(s) Documented	Activity Name	Teacher Comments (Optional)

Client Surveys

Client surveys are another facet of a multi-source teacher evaluation system. The teacher uses the feedback from the surveys for professional growth and development. The surveys are not shared with the teacher's evaluator. However, the teacher is encouraged to include a summary of the surveys in the portfolio. There are two types of surveys, one for parents and the other for students.

Due to the developmental levels of students, there are three versions of the survey for students. Questions are posed to students to give feedback on areas of performance that they are best qualified to answer. Each elementary school teacher should administer the survey to the group of students seen most frequently. Depending on the reading level of the group, lower elementary teachers may wish to read the statements aloud. In middle and high school, teachers often have multiple classes; those teachers should select two classes that represent the student population taught and give the surveys to them. Surveys should be administered about mid-year and results should be used to enhance professional growth.

Client Survey Summary

Grade _____   **Date the survey was administered** _____

Summary

1. Who is your survey population (e.g., homeroom class made up of 15 girls and 14 boys, 1 male student was absent and did not participate)?

    _____

    _____

    _____

    _____

2. How did you distribute your questionnaires?

    ☐ U.S. Mail   ☐ Directly to students   ☐ Other (please state) _____

3. Where did students complete the survey?

    ☐ In class   ☐ At home   ☐ Other (please state) _____

4. How did you collect your questionnaires?

    ☐ U.S. Mail   ☐ Directly to students   ☐ Other (please state) _____

5. How many questionnaires did you distribute? _____

6. How many completed questionnaires were returned? _____

7. What is the percentage of completed questionnaires you received (#6 divided by #5) _____

Attach a blank copy of your questionnaire after this page

Client Survey Analysis

Note that the first page and the blank questionnaire are appropriate for inclusion of the portfolio. The Client Survey Analysis is to be used to guide your reflections.

Consider that rarely will 100% agreement be reached. Look at items where approximately 20% (or more) of the clients agree and then ask yourself if the information is accurate and are you satisfied with the perception. If the information is inaccurate, consider why the students/parents have that particular perception and what changes you may need to make to alter or improve the clients' perceptions. If the clients' feedback is justified, consider setting a personal or instructional goal.

Describe your survey population(s) in terms of demographics.

_____

_____

_____

List factors that might have influenced the results (e.g., the survey was administered at the end of the day prior to bus dismissal).

_____

_____

_____

Analyze survey responses and answer the following questions:

_____

_____

_____

What did the respondents perceive as your major strengths (list 2–5 key strengths)?

_____

_____

_____

What information did the respondents provide that will help you select goals for continuous improvement (list 1 or 2 potential goal areas suggested by the survey data)?

_____

_____

_____

Additional thoughts / reflections raised from the survey results.

_____

_____

_____

Client Survey

Parents

Teacher's Name _____   Class _____

School _____   School Year _____

The purpose of this survey is to give you an opportunity to give the teacher feedback on his or her work with parents and students.

Directions: *DO NOT put your name on the survey.* Please read the following statements carefully. Then circle your response to each statement in the center column. If the statement does not apply to the teacher, circle "NA." If you wish to explain your responses, write your comments in the space provided after each item.

The teacher generally:	*Check One*	*Comments*
1. makes me feel comfortable in contacting her/him.	☐ Yes ☐ Sometimes ☐ No ☐ NA	
2. communicates in an understandable way.	☐ Yes ☐ Sometimes ☐ No ☐ NA	
3. provides helpful information during conferences.	☐ Yes ☐ Sometimes ☐ No ☐ NA	
4. addresses my concerns.	☐ Yes ☐ Sometimes ☐ No ☐ NA	
5. communicates with me concerning my child's progress in a timely manner.	☐ Yes ☐ Sometimes ☐ No ☐ NA	
6. helps my student learn.	☐ Yes ☐ Sometimes ☐ No ☐ NA	

The teacher generally:	Check One	Comments
7. assigns an appropriate amount of homework/projects.	☐ Yes ☐ Sometimes ☐ No ☐ NA	
8. assigns homework/projects that my child can complete independently.	☐ Yes ☐ Sometimes ☐ No ☐ NA	
9. clearly defines projects and long-term assignments.	☐ Yes ☐ Sometimes ☐ No ☐ NA	
10. provides adequate time to complete projects and long-term assignments.	☐ Yes ☐ Sometimes ☐ No ☐ NA	
11. offers additional help when necessary.	☐ Yes ☐ Sometimes ☐ No ☐ NA	
12. sets high expectations.	☐ Yes ☐ Sometimes ☐ No ☐ NA	
13. provides reasonable opportunities for the completion of make-up work.	☐ Yes ☐ Sometimes ☐ No ☐ NA	

Please use this space to comment on the outstanding strengths and/or weaknesses of the teacher and the course. Thank you for your assistance.

_____

_____

_____

_____

_____

_____

Yourtown Public Schools

Students: Grades K–3

Teacher_____   School Year _____

Directions: The teacher is asked to read the following statements carefully, then request that the children respond to the statements by circling or coloring the face that shows whether they agree with that sentence. The face with a smile means "yes," the face with a straight mouth means "sometimes," and the face with an upside-down mouth means "no."

	Yes	*Sometimes*	*No*
Example: I ride a school bus.	☺	😐	☹
1. My teacher listens to me.	☺	😐	☹
2. My teacher gives me help when I need it.	☺	😐	☹
3. My teacher shows us how to do new things.	☺	😐	☹
4. I know what I am supposed to do in class.	☺	😐	☹
5. I am able to do the work in class.	☺	😐	☹
6. I learn new things in my class.	☺	😐	☹

Comments:

_____

_____

_____

_____

_____

_____

Yourtown Public Schools

Client Survey

Students: Grades 4–5

Teacher _____   School Year _____

Directions: Read the following statements carefully, then respond to the statements by placing an **X** beneath the response—"YES," "SOMETIMES," or "NO"—that best describes whether you agree with that statement.

	Yes	*Sometimes*	*No*
EXAMPLE: I like listening to music.			
1. My teacher listens to me.			
2. My teacher gives me help when I need it.			
3. My teacher shows us how to do new things.			
4. I know what I am supposed to do in class.			
5. I am able to do the work in class.			
6. I learn new things in my class.			
7. I feel safe in this class.			
8. My teacher uses many ways to teach.			
9. My teacher explains how my learning can be used outside school.			
10. My teacher manages the class with few disruptions.			
11. My teacher makes sure class time is used for teaching and learning.			
12. My teacher explains why I get things wrong on my work.			
13. My teacher shows respect to all students.			
14. My teacher enforces disciplinary rules fairly.			

Comments:

_____

_____

_____

_____

_____

Yourtown Public Schools

Students: Grades 6–12

Teacher's Name _____ **Class Period** _____

School Year _____

Directions: *Do not put your name on this survey.* Write your class period in the space provided. Listed below are several statements about this class. Circle your response to each statement in the center column. If you wish to comment, please write your comments in the space after the item.

In this class, my teacher...	*Check One*	*Comments/Examples*
1. gives clear instructions.	☐ Yes ☐ Sometimes ☐ No ☐ NA	
2. treats everyone fairly.	☐ Yes ☐ Sometimes ☐ No ☐ NA	
3. is available for help outside of class time.	☐ Yes ☐ Sometimes ☐ No ☐ NA	
4. clearly states the objectives for the lesson.	☐ Yes ☐ Sometimes ☐ No ☐ NA	
5. returns my work in a reasonable time.	☐ Yes ☐ Sometimes ☐ No ☐ NA	
6. relates lesson to other subjects or the real world.	☐ Yes ☐ Sometimes ☐ No ☐ NA	

In this class, my teacher...	Check One	Comments/Examples
7. respects different opinions.	☐ Yes ☐ Sometimes ☐ No ☐ NA	
8. encourages all students to learn.	☐ Yes ☐ Sometimes ☐ No ☐ NA	
9. uses a variety of activities in class.	☐ Yes ☐ Sometimes ☐ No ☐ NA	
10. communicates in a way I can understand.	☐ Yes ☐ Sometimes ☐ No ☐ NA	
11. manages the classroom with a minimum of disruptions.	☐ Yes ☐ Sometimes ☐ No ☐ NA	
12. shows respect to all students.	☐ Yes ☐ Sometimes ☐ No ☐ NA	
13. enforces disciplinary rules fairly.	☐ Yes ☐ Sometimes ☐ No ☐ NA	
14. makes sure class time is used for learning.	☐ Yes ☐ Sometimes ☐ No ☐ NA	

Comments:

_____

_____

_____

_____

Yourtown Public Schools

Summative Evaluation Form
Classroom Teacher 5 Domains

Teacher's Name _____   **Date** _____

School _____

Personnel Status   *Performance Review Dates*

☐ 1st year teacher (Probationary)   1st _____

☐ 2nd year teacher   2nd _____

☐ 3rd year teacher   3rd _____

☐ Continuing Contract   _____

☐ Other _____   _____

Strengths

_____

_____

_____

Areas for Continuous Improvement

_____

_____

_____

Recommendation

☐ Continued Employment   ☐ Non-renewal of contract*   ☐ Improvement Assistance Plan*

Signatures

_____   _____
Evaluator/Date   Teacher/Date

Employee signature acknowledges receipt of form, not necessarily concurrence.

Written comments may be attached. If comments are attached, initial and date here.

_____

_____

* Attach explanation if necessary.

Instruction	Standard Ratings			
Comments	*Exceeds Expectations*	*Meets Expectations*	*Needs Improvement*	*Unsatisfactory*
I-1 The teacher demonstrates current and accurate knowledge of subject matter covered in the curriculum.				
I-2 The teacher plans instruction to achieve desired student learning objectives that reflect the current district curriculum.				
I-3 The teacher recognizes and plans for individual learning differences and differentiates instruction to meet student needs.				
I-4 The teacher uses materials, technology, and resources compatible with students' needs and abilities that support the current district curriculum.				
I-5 The teacher links present content/skills with past and future learning experiences, other subject areas, and real world experiences/applications.				
I-6 The teacher uses a variety of instructional strategies that promote student learning.				

Assessment	Standard Ratings			
Comments	*Exceeds Expectations*	*Meets Expectations*	*Needs Improvement*	*Unsatisfactory*
A-1 The teacher provides a variety of ongoing and culminating assessments to measure student performance.				
A-2 The teacher provides ongoing and timely feedback to encourage student progress.				
A-3 The teacher uses assessment results to make both daily and long-range instructional decisions.				

Learning Environment	Standard Ratings			
Comments	Exceeds Expectations	Meets Expectations	Needs Improvement	Unsatisfactory
L-1 The teacher communicates and maintains clear expectations about behavior, classroom procedures, and academic achievement.				
L-2 The teacher maximizes the use of instructional time and resources to increase student learning.				
L-3 The teacher demonstrates and models respect toward students and others.				
L-4 The teacher organizes the classroom to ensure a safe academic and physical learning environment.				

Communication/Community Relations	Standard Ratings			
Comments	Exceeds Expectations	Meets Expectations	Needs Improvement	Unsatisfactory
C-1 The teacher communicates effectively with students and models standard English.				
C-2 The teacher works collaboratively with families and community resources to support the success of a diverse student population.				
C-3 The teacher initiates and maintains timely communication with parents/guardians, colleagues, and administrators concerning student progress or problems.				

Professionalism	Standard Ratings			
Comments	Exceeds Expectations	Meets Expectations	Needs Improvement	Unsatisfactory
P-1 The teacher demonstrates ethical and professional behavior.				
P-2 The teacher applies strategies learned from professional development.				
P-3 The teacher contributes to the overall school climate by supporting school goals.				

Summative Evaluation Form
Classroom Teacher 4 Domains

Teacher's Name _____   **Date** _____

School _____

Personnel Status

☐ 1st year teacher (Probationary/Non-tenured)
☐ 2nd year teacher
☐ 3rd year teacher/Tenured
☐ Continuing Contract
☐ Other _____

Performance Review Dates

1st _____
2nd _____
3rd _____
_____
_____

Strengths

_____
_____
_____

Areas for Continuous Improvement

_____
_____
_____

Recommendation

☐ Continued Employment   ☐ Non-renewal of contract*   ☐ Improvement Assistance Plan*

Signatures

_____   _____
Evaluator/Date   Teacher/Date

Employee signature acknowledges receipt of form, not necessarily concurrence.

Written comments may be attached. If comments are attached, initial and date here.

_____

_____

* Attach explanation if necessary.

Instructional Skills	Standard Ratings			
Comments	*Exceeds Expectations*	*Meets Expectations*	*Needs Improvement*	*Unsatisfactory*
I-1 The teacher demonstrates current and accurate knowledge of subject matter covered in the curriculum.				
I-2 The teacher plans instruction to achieve desired student learning objectives that reflect the current district curriculum.				
I-3 The teacher uses materials, technology, and resources compatible with students' needs and abilities that support the current district curriculum.				
I-4 The teacher links present content/skills with past and future learning experiences, other subject areas, and real world experiences/applications.				
I-5 The teacher communicates effectively with students.				
I-6 The teacher uses instructional strategies that promote student learning.				
I-7 The teacher provides learning opportunities for individual differences.				

Assessment Skills	Standard Ratings			
Comments	*Exceeds Expectations*	*Meets Expectations*	*Needs Improvement*	*Unsatisfactory*
A-1 The teacher provides a variety of ongoing and culminating assessments to measure student performance.				
A-2 The teacher provides ongoing and timely feedback to encourage student progress.				
A-3 The teacher uses assessment results to make both daily and long-range instructional decisions.				

Learning Environment Skills	Standard Ratings			
Comments	Exceeds Expectations	Meets Expectations	Needs Improvement	Unsatisfactory
E-1 The teacher maximizes the use of instructional time and resources to increase student learning.				
E-2 The teacher demonstrates and models respect toward students and others.				
E-3 The teacher organizes the classroom to ensure a safe academic and physical learning environment.				
E-4 The teacher communicates and maintains clear expectations about behavior, classroom procedures, and academic achievement.				

Professionalism	Standard Ratings			
Comments	Exceeds Expectations	Meets Expectations	Needs Improvement	Unsatisfactory
P-1 The teacher demonstrates ethical and professional behavior.				
P-2 The teacher participates in an ongoing process of professional development.				
P-3 The teacher contributes to the overall school climate by supporting school goals.				
P-4 The teacher initiates and maintains timely communication with parents/guardians and administrators concerning student progress or problems.				

Yourtown Public Schools

Summative Evaluation Form
Resource/Specialty Area Teacher

Teacher's Name _____   Date _____

School _____

Personnel Status

☐ 1st year teacher (Probationary/Non-tenured)
☐ 2nd year teacher
☐ 3rd year teacher
☐ Continuing Contract/Tenured
☐ Other _____

Performance Review Dates

1st _____
2nd _____
3rd _____
_____
_____

Strengths

_____

_____

_____

Areas for Continuous Improvement

_____

_____

_____

Recommendation

☐ Continued Employment   ☐ Non-renewal of contract*   ☐ Improvement Assistance Plan*

Signatures

_____   _____
Evaluator/Date   Teacher/Date

Employee signature acknowledges receipt of form, not necessarily concurrence.

Written comments may be attached. If comments are attached, initial and date here.

_____

_____

* Attach explanation if necessary.

Program Management	Standard Ratings			
Comments	Exceeds Expectations	Meets Expectations	Needs Improvement	Unsatisfactory
M-1 The resource/specialty area teacher effectively plans, coordinates, and implements a program consistent with established guidelines, policies, and procedures.				
M-2 The resource/specialty area teacher manages program resources effectively.				
M-3 The resource/specialty area teacher maintains accurate student/program records.				

Assessment	Standard Ratings			
Comments	Exceeds Expectations	Meets Expectations	Needs Improvement	Unsatisfactory
A-1 The resource/specialty area teacher assesses and documents attainment of program objective(s).				
A-2 The resource/specialty area teacher demonstrates proficiency in administering, scoring/evaluating, and interpreting data from instruments or records.				
A-3 The resource/specialty area teacher uses assessment information for decision making.				
A-4 The resource/specialty area teacher uses evaluation to improve the delivery of services.				

Direct Services/Instruction	Standard Ratings			
Comments	Exceeds Expectations	Meets Expectations	Needs Improvement	Unsatisfactory
D-1 The resource/specialty area teacher demonstrates current, accurate, and comprehensive knowledge consistent with the profession.				
D-2 The resource/specialty area teacher provides intervention/instruction that promotes student learning.				
D-3 The resource/specialty area teacher seeks, selects, and uses resources compatible with student/program needs.				
D-4 The resource/specialty area teacher maintains effective communication and rapport with students.				
D-5 The resource/specialty area teacher fosters an organized environment.				

Collaboration	Standard Ratings			
Comments	Exceeds Expectations	Meets Expectations	Needs Improvement	Unsatisfactory
C-1 The resource/specialty area teacher consults/collaborates with school personnel.				
C-2 The resource/specialty area teacher consults/collaborates with parents and community representatives/agencies.				
C-3 The resource/specialty area teacher demonstrates leadership and provides professional development.				

Professionalism	Standard Ratings			
Comments	Exceeds Expectations	Meets Expectations	Needs Improvement	Unsatisfactory
P-1 The resource/specialty area teacher demonstrates a professional demeanor and practices ethical standards appropriate to the profession.				
P-2 The resource/specialty area teacher participates in a meaningful and continuous process of professional development.				
P-3 The resource/specialty area teacher contributes to and supports the profession, the school district, and the effectiveness of the school.				

Improvement Assistance Plan

Teacher _____   **School Year** _____

Evaluator _____   **Date Initiated** _____

School _____

Domain(s) and standards requiring improvement:

_____

_____

_____

Objectives and strategies for improvement:[1]

Performance Objective	Procedures/Resources	Target Dates

Results of improvement plan:[1]

Performance Objective	Comments	Review Dates[2]

Recommendation based on outcome of improvement plan:

☐ Sufficient improvement has been achieved: The teacher is no longer on an improvement plan.

☐ Some improvement has been achieved, but more improvement is needed: The teacher remains on an improvement plan.

☐ Little or no improvement has been achieved: The teacher is recommended for non-renewal or dismissal.

_____   _____
Evaluator/Date Completed   Teacher/Date Completed

_____

[1] These sections should be completed collaboratively by the evaluator and teacher. Additional pages may be added, if needed.

[2] Review dates should be prior to target dates for each improvement objective. Each review is intended to document support and assistance provided to the employee.

Teacher Performance Evaluation System Feedback Form

This form may be used by the teacher to provide feedback on the evaluation system including its components and implementation. Just as targeted feedback enhances employee performance, so can comments offered by those using the system be instrumental in tailoring the evaluation process to meet a school or school district's needs. Often times forms or wording are improved once several people start using and customizing them.

Yourtown Public Schools

Teacher Performance Evaluation System Feedback

Please assist us in improving your performance evaluation system by sharing what is working and suggestions for improvement. If you need additional room, please use the reverse of this sheet or add additional pages. Send the form to the building principal on or before _____.

Indicate the setting where you currently teach:

☐ Elementary   ☐ Middle   ☐ High School

Indicate your teacher designation:

☐ Classroom   ☐ Resource/Specialty Area

Performance Evaluation Component	*What worked well?*	*What suggestions do you have for improving the program?*
The Teacher Performance Standards		
Portfolio		
Academic Goal Setting		
Forms • Observation Feedback • Summative Evaluation		
Client Surveys		
Other components of the program		

DATE DUE

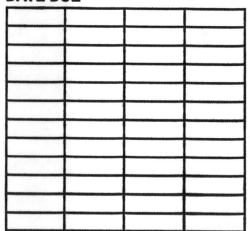